CE

STUDIES IN EARLY ENGLISH HISTORY

Edited by H. P. R. Finberg

V

THE EARLY CHARTERS OF EASTERN ENGLAND

STUDIES IN EARLY ENGLISH HISTORY

Other volumes are in preparation.

THE
EARLY CHARTERS
OF EASTERN ENGLAND

by

C. R. HART

M.A., M.B., F.R.HIST.S.

LEICESTER UNIVERSITY PRESS

1966

PRINTED IN GREAT BRITAIN
BY THE BROADWATER PRESS LTD
WELWYN GARDEN CITY, HERTFORDSHIRE

© C. R. Hart 1966

TO
MONICA

CONTENTS

8 CONTENTS

INTRODUCTION

IN THE first part of this book an attempt is made to list all the 'charters' known from surviving evidence to have been drawn up as records of land transactions in eastern England before the Norman Conquest. The region covered is the whole of the eastern seaboard between the rivers Thames and Humber, comprising the modern counties of Essex,[1] Suffolk, Norfolk, Cambridgeshire, Huntingdonshire, the Soke of Peterborough, Rutland, and Lincolnshire.

The conventions employed in summarizing this mass of material, and the criteria adopted for its inclusion in the hand-list, have been established already in the course of surveys of other areas, to which readers are referred for a general account of the principles which have guided the production of the series.[2] The term 'charter' in this context embraces all forms of contemporary written records of land transactions, but only in a few cases does the original document itself survive; for the most part we have to be content with a post-Conquest copy, very often defective and occasionally incorporating spurious material. A code of symbols has been devised to give some indication as to the authenticity of surviving texts, but this study is still in its infancy, and until a fresh edition of the whole *corpus* of the charters is produced, it will often be impossible to reach a final judgement on the validity of a particular document.

In addition to the many records surviving in charter form, details are often preserved in various post-Conquest memoranda of early land transactions for which the charters themselves are now lost; sometimes it is doubtful if there ever was a contemporary written record of the transaction, for instance in the case of nuncupative wills, or small land transfers made before the hundred or shire court. Here, too, our information of such dealings usually reaches us in the form of post-Conquest compilations by monastic houses which preserved accounts of their benefactors. All known cases have been embodied in Part III of

---

[1] Essex was dealt with in a previous publication, which is brought up to date on pp. 250–2.

[2] Essex, Devon, Cornwall, West Midlands, and Wessex: see Bibliography.

9

A*

the hand-list, for the historian is more concerned with the trans-action itself than with the form in which it is recorded.

In addition to two hitherto unpublished texts which are edited in the appropriate sections of Part I of the hand-list,[1] in Part II appears an edition of all the known pre-Conquest charters of the abbeys of Barking and Thorney. This is believed to be the first full-scale edition of a group of Latin charters of the Anglo-Saxon period to appear in the present century, and it is much to be hoped that it will not long enjoy this isolation, for the neglect of such work hampers greatly our ability to come to grips with some of the fundamental problems of early English history.

Our dependence upon monastic records as sources of written information for the pre-Conquest period is all but absolute. The only literate sections of the population were to be found in the ranks of the Church (particularly the tonsured members) and the higher nobility, and it follows almost as a corollary that virtually the only repositories for archives were the cathedral, monastic, and collegiate churches, apart from such records as were pre-served with the king's *haligdom* or sacred relics, which accom-panied him upon his perambulations.[2]

In view of this, it is not surprising that the pattern of survival of early charters and other records of land transactions followed a very different course for eastern England than for Wessex and Mercia, which largely escaped depredation at the hands of the Vikings in the closing years of the ninth century. Against the many hundreds of charters of the seventh, eighth, and ninth centuries extant for southern and western England and the Midlands, we can set only the few brief records that have somehow survived for eastern England at Peterborough, Barking, and St Paul's.

After these there is a long gap, and even the reconquest of the eastern Danelaw by Edward the Elder did not break it. A few records appear for the fifth and sixth decades of the tenth cen-tury, but it is not until the Benedictine revival got under way

---

[1] See pp. 73 and 86.

[2] Towards the end of the Old English period, however, it is probable that some title-deeds and primitive manorial records were kept by reeves and clerics in the service of the larger lay landowners, and possibly legal and fiscal memoranda were preserved by officials of the shire courts. None of this material has survived.

in the seventh decade, under the leadership of Bishops Oswald and Æthelwold, that muniments survive in any quantity.

Then quite suddenly we are presented with a mass of material, the quality and richness of which is still not appreciated to the full by historians of the period. Thanks largely to the reforming activities of Æthelwold, we have remarkably detailed knowledge of the affairs of four of the five great fenland monasteries from the time of their second foundation. Valuable records survive from the Peterborough and Thorney archives, and in the case of Ramsey and particularly Ely the wealth of information is so great that we can reconstruct with some degree of completeness the whole process of their endowment.[1] Only for Crowland, the most poorly endowed of the five, do the records fail us, a disastrous fire having wiped out the whole of its muniments in 1091.[2]

For a later period we are also impoverished by the loss of the Barking cartularies, but this is more than compensated for by the remarkable state of preservation of the muniments of Cnut's foundation at Bury St Edmunds. This house is indeed the chief single source of our knowledge of Old English land records written in the vernacular. More writs for Bury survive than for any house other than Westminster; nearly half the wills in Professor Whitelock's book come from Bury, and its series of late Old English charters and other memoranda (in which the newly discovered text here edited must take its place[3]) is unsurpassed elsewhere.

---

[1] In a paper entitled 'Charter Scholarship in England' published in the *University of Birmingham Historical Journal*, VIII, 1961, H. A. Cronne gave an unfortunate account of the activities of the Ramsey chronicler, to which I do not subscribe. No one would wish to defend the authenticity of the royal charters entered in the Ramsey Chronicle, but setting these on one side, there is every reason to believe that the large amount of invaluable information recorded by the chronicler for the hundred years preceding the Norman Conquest is indeed derived from reliable Latin translations of Old English muniments of unimpeachable authority.

[2] In an attempt to make good this loss, the writer of the pseudo-Ingulf composed a most outrageous series of forgeries which continue on occasion to mislead historians. These 'charters' have no place in the present volume: the curious may consult them in CS 135, 140, 268, 325, 409, 461, 521, 872, 1178, and 1179.

[3] No. 133.

All this means that in direct contrast to the barrenness of material for earlier periods, we have more knowledge of land transactions in eastern England during the last century of the Anglo-Saxon state than for any other part of the country. It is from this fact, as yet barely recognized, that any value which may lie in this present attempt to digest and classify the information is derived.

ACKNOWLEDGEMENTS

IT WOULD be wearisome to tabulate the long succession of scholars who have sent courteous and generous replies to my persistent and often exasperating enquiries, but my indebtedness to four in particular must be placed on record. Chapters I and IX, in their original form, were part of a thesis for which I was awarded the first M.A. of the University of Leicester, and to my external examiner, Dr F. E. Harmer, I owe the elimination of many inaccuracies and the inclusion of much useful material. It would have been impossible to deal adequately with the contents of the *Liber Eliensis* had not its editor, Dr E. O. Blake, most kindly placed a set of advance proofs at my disposal. Mr P. H. Sawyer made two special visits in order to collate my material with his own hand-list of Anglo-Saxon Charters shortly to be published by the Royal Historical Society, and in the process immeasurably enriched my knowledge of the sources. Finally, I gladly acknowledge the inspiration of Professor H. P. R. Finberg, the general editor of this series, without whose detailed direction and wise guidance over the past ten years I could never have hoped to bring this work to completion. The publication of the book has been assisted by a grant from the Marc Fitch Fund.

BIBLIOGRAPHY AND ABBREVIATIONS

Abingdon   =Stenton, F. M., *The Early History of the Abbey of Abingdon*. Reading, 1913.

ASC   =Anglo-Saxon Chronicle.

Asser   =*Asser's Life of King Alfred*, ed. W. H. Stevenson. Oxford, 1904.

Barlow   =Barlow, F., *The English Church 1000–1066*. London, 1963.

BBL   =Lists of Benefactors to Bury St Edmunds Abbey; see p. 248.

BM   =British Museum.

BM Facs   =*Facsimiles of Ancient Charters in the British Museum*. 4 parts. London, 1873–8.

Cart Rams   =*Cartularium Monasterii de Rameseia*, ed. W. H. Hart and P. A. Lyons. 3 vols. Rolls Series, 79. 1884–93.

CAS   =Cambridge Antiquarian Society (*Proceedings*).

Chron Rams   =*Chronicon Abbatiæ Rameseiensis*, ed. W. Dunn Macray. Rolls Series, 83. 1886.

Clemoes   =Clemoes, P. (ed.), *The Anglo-Saxons*. London, 1959.

Collect Topogr   ='Saxon Charters to Thorney Abbey, in Cambridgeshire', in *Collectanea Topographica et Genealogica*, IV, 1837, pp. 54–9.

Crawf   =*The Crawford Collection of Early Charters and Documents*, ed. A. S. Napier and W. H. Stevenson. Oxford, 1895.

CS   =*Cartularium Saxonicum*, ed. W. de G. Birch. 3 vols. London, 1885–93.

CUL   =Cambridge University Library.

Davis   =Davis, G. R. C., *Medieval Cartularies of Great Britain*. London, 1958.

DB   =Domesday Book.

Dugdale   =Dugdale, W., *Monasticon Anglicanum*, ed. J. Caley, H. Ellis, and B. Bandinel. 6 vols in 8. London, 1817–30.

ECBA   =Hart, C., *The Early Charters of Barking Abbey*. Colchester, 1953.

ECDC	=Finberg, H. P. R., *The Early Charters of Devon and Cornwall* (2nd ed.). Leicester University Press, 1963.
ECEss	=Hart, C., *The Early Charters of Essex*. Parts I and II. Leicester University Press, 1957.
ECW	=Finberg, H. P. R., *The Early Charters of Wessex*. Leicester University Press, 1964.
ECWM	=Finberg, H. P. R., *The Early Charters of the West Midlands*. Leicester University Press, 1961.
EHD	=*English Historical Documents*, ed. D. C. Douglas. London (Vol. I, ed. D. Whitelock, 1955; Vol. II, ed. D. C. Douglas and G. W. Greenaway, 1959).
EHR	=*English Historical Review*.
Ekwall	=Ekwall, E., *The Oxford Dictionary of English Place-Names* (3rd ed.). Oxford, 1947.
FE	=Round, J. H., *Feudal England*. London, 1895.
Feud Docs	=Douglas, D. C. (ed.), *Feudal Documents from the abbey of Bury St Edmunds*. British Academy, 8. London, 1932.
Fo	=Forsberg, R., *A Contribution to a Dictionary of English Place-Names*. Uppsala, 1950.
Freeman, NC	=Freeman, E. A., *History of the Norman Conquest*. 5 vols. and index. Oxford, 1867–79.
H	=Harmer, F. E. (ed.), *Anglo-Saxon Writs*. Manchester, 1952.
HC	=Mellows, W. T. (ed.), *The Chronicle of Hugh Candidus*. Oxford, 1949.
HE	=Bede's *Historia Ecclesiastica*, in *Venerabilis Baedae Opera Historica*, ed. C. Plummer. Oxford, 1896.
ICC	=Hamilton, N. E. S. A. (ed.), *Inquisitio Comitatus Cantabrigiensis*. Royal Society of Literature. London, 1876.
IE	=*Inquisitio Eliensis*, in ICC.
K	=Kemble, J. M. (ed.), *Codex Diplomaticus Aevi Saxonici*. 6 vols. London, 1839–48.
Ker	=Ker, N. R., *Catalogue of Manuscripts containing Anglo-Saxon*. Oxford, 1957.
LC	=Stenton, F. M., *The Latin Charters of the Anglo-Saxon Period*. Oxford, 1955.

LE = Blake, E. O. (ed.), *Liber Eliensis*. Royal Historical Society, Camden 3rd series, Vol. 92. London, 1962.

Levison = Levison, W., *England and the Continent in the Eighth Century*. Oxford, 1946.

Lincs DB = *The Lincolnshire Domesday*, ed. C. W. Foster and T. Longley. Lincoln Record Society, 1924.

Lobel = Lobel, M. D., *The Abbey of Bury St Edmunds*. Oxford, 1925.

LT = John, E., *Land Tenure in Early England*. Leicester University Press, 1960.

LVTh = Whitelock, D., 'Scandinavian Personal Names in the Liber Vitae of Thorney Abbey', in *Saga-Book of the Viking Society*, XII, 1937–45, pp. 127–53.

Memorials = Arnold T. (ed.), *Memorials of St Edmund's Abbey*. Rolls Series, 96. 3 vols. 1890–6.

Miller = Miller, E., *The Abbey and Bishopric of Ely*. Cambridge, 1951.

OE = Old English.

Oleson = Oleson, T. J., *The Witenagemot in the Reign of Edward the Confessor*. Oxford, 1955.

ON = Old Norse.

OS = Ordnance Survey.

OS Facs = *Facsimiles of Anglo-Saxon Manuscripts*, ed. W. B. Sanders. 3 parts. Southampton, 1878–84.

PN = (followed by the name of a county) the publications of the English Place-Name Society.

PN Elements = Smith, A. H., *English Place-Name Elements*. 2 parts. English Place-Name Society, xxv–xxvi. Cambridge, 1956.

PRO = Public Record Office.

R = Robertson, A. J. (ed.), *Anglo-Saxon Charters* (2nd ed.). Cambridge, 1956.

RE = Lennard, R., *Rural England 1086–1135*. Oxford, 1959.

Riley = Riley, H. T. (trans.), *Ingulph's Chronicle of the Abbey of Croyland*. London (Bohn), 1893.

Robinson = Robinson, J. A., *The Times of St Dunstan*. Oxford, 1923.

Searle   =Searle, W. G., *Ingulf and the Historia Croylandensis.*
                 CAS, 1894.

Stenton   =Stenton, F. M., *Anglo-Saxon England* (2nd ed.). Ox-
                 ford, 1946.

Stenton,   =Stenton, F. M., 'Medeshamstede and its Colonies',
Medeshamstede   in *Historical Essays in Honour of James Tait*. Man-
                 chester, 1933.

Stenton, *Types* =Stenton, F. M., *Types of Manorial Structure in the
                 Northern Danelaw*. Oxford, 1910.

Thorpe   =Thorpe, B. (ed.), *Diplomatarium Anglicum*. London,
                 1865.

TRE   =in the time of King Edward the Confessor.

VCH   =(followed by the name of a county) Victoria County
                 History.

W   =Whitelock, D. (ed.), *Anglo-Saxon Wills*. Cambridge,
                 1930.

Widmore,   =Widmore, R., *Enquiry into the Time of the first Founda-
Westminster   tion of Westminster Abbey*. 1743.

CODE OF SYMBOLS

† Original charter, authenticity not in doubt.

* Charter available only in later copy or copies, authenticity not in doubt. This classification includes otherwise reliable charters which lack short portions of the original text, such as names in the witness list, and boundary clauses.

** Charter available only in later copy or copies, thought to embody the substance of the original, but having some material, spurious or genuine, substituted or interpolated; or having late forms of personal or place-names.

*** Charter thought to be fundamentally a fabrication, but which may embody some authentic material or record a genuine transaction.

**** Charter thought to be a complete fabrication.

♦ English translation.

PART I

CHAPTER I

THE EARLY CHARTERS OF HUNTINGDONSHIRE

1. 664 ****WULFHERE, king of the Mercians and Middle and Southern Angles, to the monastery at *Medeshamstede* (Peterborough). Foundation charter. Lands granted include *Fletton* (Fletton), *Overton* (Orton Waterville), *Alewalton* (Alwalton), and "all the meres and fens in *Huntedunensis prouincia* (the shire of Huntingdon), with *Scælfremere* (Chalderbeach Farm in Holme) and *Witlesmere* (Whittlesey Mere), with all the lands and houses lying on the south side of *Scælfremere*." Lands in Kent, Leics., Lincs., Notts., Rutland, Salop, Soke of Peterborough, and Yorks. CS 22, 22a.

ASC (E) *s.a.* 656. The description of the land gifts appears also in HC pp. 10–13, and part of the charter is recited in Cart Rams, I, pp. 160, 165, an account of the foundation of the abbey of Sawtry. No genuine charter of Wulfhere has been preserved (cf. EHR xxxiii, 1918, p. 434), and the various versions of this charter show signs of having been fabricated after the Norman Conquest. See also pp. 97, 107, and 110.

2. 670–1 ***WIGHARD to the abbess Beorngyth and her minster [at Bath]. 40 "manentes" at *Slæpi* (? St Ives). CS 28.

The grant claims to have been made with the consent of King Wulfhere of Mercia, in the fourteenth year of his reign, i.e. in 670–1. But the formula used, and the indiction, together with the list of witnesses, are taken from CS 57, another charter entered on the following page of the same register, which may represent an authentic text of the year 681. A possible explanation is that *Slæpi* was given by Wighard in 670–1, that this was recorded in the abbey's list of benefactors, and that subsequently, when charter evidence for the abbey's possession of the estate was called for, this information was written into charter form, using diplomatic and witness list borrowed from the original (or an early copy of the original) of CS 57. Cf. EHD I, pp. 343, 444.

The identification of the *Slæpi* of this charter with St Ives is not certain, for there are several place-names, such as the two Islips in Oxfordshire and Northants., in which OE *slæp* is compounded with other elements, either as prefixes or suffixes (cf. Ekwall, pp. 405–6). The early forms for St Ives, however, are all uncompounded, as is the form in Wighard's charter. Other points in favour of this identification are that St Ives was certainly under Mercian overlordship in 670–1, and that its DB hidage of 30 suggests a large and primitive holding.

3. (674) ***WULFHERE, king of the Mercian people, to Berferðe his kinsman, for 30 mancuses of gold. 5 "manentes" at *Dilingtun* (Dillington in Great Staughton), free of all but the three common dues.   CS 32.

> Contemporary endorsement: *dillingtun*. A small, poorly preserved charter in a minuscule hand, probably post-Conquest. Its condition has deteriorated badly since it was reproduced in facsimile in 1878 (BM Facs IV, pl. 1), and even with the aid of ultra-violet light it is not now possible to distinguish as much of the text as appears in the facsimile edition. The date is given as DC XXIIII, but there is space for an "L" and this may have been present originally, which gives DCLXXIIII, a possible date for King Wulfhere. Two of the episcopal witnesses and two lay witnesses belong to the second quarter of the eighth century (CS 157). The diplomatic of the rest of the text, together with the boundary clause (now, unfortunately, almost illegible), dates from the mid-tenth century. The hidage is the same as that of Dillington in DB, cf. EHR XXXIII, 1921, p. 434 n. 6.

4. 937 *King ATHELSTAN to Sigulf. 5 "manentes" at *Niwantun* (Water Newton), free of all but the three common dues.
                                                                                CS 712.

> Edited on p. 150.

5. 948 *EADRED, king of the English and ruler of the other peoples round about, to his thegn Frytheric. 4 "mansae" at *Ofærtune* (Orton), free of all but the three common dues.
                                                                                CS 875.

This grant has not previously been ascribed to one of the Huntingdonshire Ortons. The new identification rests on the discovery that the River Nene was formerly called the *Use* (p. 153); a river called *Wusan* forms part of the bounds of *Ofærtune*. The estate is therefore almost certainly the 3½ hides at Orton (identified as part of Orton Waterville) which was held in 1066 by Godwine, and was given to Peterborough Abbey in the time of the Conqueror (VCH *Hunts.*, I, p. 346*b*; III, p. 191). It is not yet possible, in the absence of a detailed study of the minor place-names of the county, to identify all the places mentioned in the bounds of CS 875, but *Wusan* is undoubtedly the River Nene, and *ða stræt* is the road from Peterborough to Oundle. The district abounds in small tributaries of the Nene, and it is noteworthy that *ða riðe*, *ðone broc*, *ða dic*, and *ða ea* all occur in the bounds of this estate.

6. 951 *EADRED, king of the English, to the thegn Ælfsige. 5 hides at *Haddedune* (Haddon), free of all but the three common dues. CS 893.

Edited on p. 155.

7. 955 *EADRED, king and emperor of all Britain, to the thegn Ælfsige Hunlafing. 5 hides at *Æthelwoldingtune* (Alwalton), free of all but the three common dues, church-scot, burial fees, and tithes. ♦R xxx.

The bounds, which can easily be followed, embrace the whole of Alwalton; they include *Earninga stræte* (Ermine Street), and the common boundaries with *Ceastertuninga* and *ofertuninga* (the people of Chesterton and Orton). Cf. VCH *Hunts.*, I, p. 330 n. 4.

8. 956 **EADWIG, king of the English and ruler of the whole land of Britain, to his thegn Ælfwine. 10 "mansae" *æt Geakeslea* (Yaxley), and 5 *æt Fearresheafde* (Farcet). CS 940.

Edited on p. 159.

9. 957 †EADWIG, king of the English and ruler of the other peoples round about, to his thegn Wulfstan. 9 "mansae" at *Cunictune* (Conington), free of all but the three common dues. CS 1003.

OS Facs II, pl. 2. The original charter is still preserved at Winchester Cathedral. It seems likely, therefore, that this is the Wulfstan Uccea who had dealings with Bishop Æthelwold of Winchester (No. 12). Conington at this date probably included within its bounds the area of the post-Domesday vill of Holme. Owing to the early eleventh-century redistribution of the south-western parts of Whittlesey Mere between Conington and the adjacent vills (p. 237), it is not possible in our present state of knowledge to locate with precision all the boundary points in this charter, but *Earninga stræte* in the bounds is Ermine Street, now the Great North Road; *glædtuninga wege* is the eastern end of the road from Glatton to Conington, of which the stretch lying to the west of Ermine Street is still called Glatton Ways; *eneda wylle* was a small stream which ran through Duckpit Fen until the drainage of Whittlesey Mere a century ago; it is still a dyke. *Gyruwan fen* in the bounds preserves the name of the Gyrwe, a local people mentioned in the Tribal Hidage, and earlier in Bede, and is important evidence for the western limit of their territory. The *Liber Vitae* of Hyde Abbey refers to Crowland as being sited *on middan Gyrwan fenne*, so that the name must have applied originally to a very large extent of fenland stretching southwards from the Nene, of which Ermine Street formed the western boundary.

10.   958   *EDGAR, king of the English and ruler of the other peoples round about, to his thegn Ælfheah. 5 "cassati" *æt Ofertune* (Orton Waterville), free of all but the three common dues.   CS 1043.

VCH *Hunts.*, I, p. 330 n. 4. Edgar's title in this charter is noteworthy. When King Eadred died in 956, he was succeeded by his nephew Eadwig, who could not have been much older than 14. In 957 Mercia and Northumbria revolted and chose Edgar, Eadwig's younger brother, for their king (Edgar was born in 943). Eadwig continued to rule Wessex, and died on 1 October 959, whereupon Edgar succeeded to the whole kingdom. This charter, however, together with a companion piece discussed below, shows that Edgar was claiming to rule the whole of England as early as 958. It may be that his claim had some justification, for the only charters said to have been issued by Eadwig in 959 are of doubtful authenticity (CS 1045, 1046, 1047).

The formulae, dating clause, and witness list of his grant of Orton agree closely with those of CS 1044, a charter of Edgar to Archbishop Oscytel of York, and there can be little doubt that the originals of these two charters were based on a common exemplar, and witnessed on the same occasion. It is worth recalling Professor Whitelock's suggestion that Archbishop Oscytel may have retained the see of Dorchester (in which Orton then lay) after his accession to York (cf. Clemoes, pp. 73–5).

11.   N.D.   (963 × 973)   HENRIC of *Waneting* (Wantage, Berks.) to Æthelwold, bishop of Winchester, for 200 mancuses of gold. *Grantedene* (Great and Little Gransden, in Hunts. and Cambs. respectively).   *Lost.*

LE II, c. 46. The transaction is witnessed by King Edgar, the three ealdormen Ælfhere of Mercia, Æthelwine of East Anglia, and Brihtnoth of Essex; Ælfric Cild (who succeeded Ælfhere of Mercia in 983); Ringulf, Thurferth, and others. On the dates, see No. 16, where Æthelwold's holding in *Grantedene* is described as "15 hides of fertile land." From the DB hidage it is clear that this must have comprised the bulk of both Great and Little Gransden.

12. N.D. (963 × 975) *WULFSTAN UCCEA to Æthelwold, bishop [of Winchester], in exchange for Washington, Sussex. *Jaceslea* (Yaxley) and Ailsworth, Northants.

♦R XXXVII.

Cf. W pp. 129–30. The account goes on to say that Bishop Æthelwold granted the Yaxley estate to Thorney Abbey. Another version of this transaction is given in the Thorney foundation charter, see p. 179.

13. N.D. (963 × 984) *Record of the gifts of ÆTHELWOLD, bishop of Winchester, to Peterborough Abbey, at its restoration. *Inter alia*, *Geaceslea* (Yaxley), *Farresheafde* (Farcet), *Witlesmere* (Whittlesey Mere), and "the two hundreds which owe suit to *Normannes cros*" (Norman Cross). Lands in the Soke of Peterborough and Northants. ♦R XXXIX.

See also p. 111.

14. N.D. (969 × 974) WINSIGE to Ramsey Abbey, to make amends for an injury formerly done to the abbey. ½ hide in *Stivecle* (Little Stukeley); witnessed by Ealdorman Æthelwine, his wife, and sons. *Lost.*

Chron Rams pp. 51–2. The chronicle goes on to say that subsequently Winsige's son sold a further hide in Stukeley to the abbey. For Wynsige, see No. 256, and Chron Rams p. 50.

15. (972) ***EDGAR, king of Great Britain [!], to Peterborough Abbey. Charter of refoundation. Lands given by the king, on the petition of Bishop Æthelwold, include "two thirds of *Witlesmere* (Whittlesey Mere), with its waters, weirs, and fens, of which the boundaries are: to the north, *Merelade* and the River Nene; to the east, King's Delph; to the south, Aldwine's barrow, which lies in the

middle of *Ubbemerelade* (Ugg Mere lode in Ramsey); to the west, the water (called) *Deopbece*." The charter continues: "And I desire that the right of toll over the following area shall be given (to Peterborough): first from Whittlesey Mere all the way to the king's toll of the hundreds of Norman Cross, and then back in the opposite direction from Whittlesey Mere through *Merelade* straight on to the Nene, and so as the water runs to Wansford, and from Wansford to Stamford, and from Stamford along the water course to Crowland, and from Crowland to the Muscat (the river boundary between Cambs. and Northants.), and from the Muscat to King's Delph and to Whittlesey Mere." Lands in Northants., the Soke of Peterborough, and Lincs.

CS 1258, 1280 (Latin), 1281 (OE).

The most reliable version appears in the Chronicle of Hugh Candidus, printed in HC pp. 32–7, where several inferior texts are collated, including that used by Kemble (K 575). Another text appears in the pseudo-Ingulf (Searle pp. 176–8; Riley pp. 91–5). The abbreviated version in ASC(E) *s.a.* 963 is important because it preserves the reference to the *hundreds* (plural) of Norman Cross (see p. 25). Like the foundation charter of Thorney (No. 16), this spurious Peterborough pancharta derives its witness-list from CS 1270, the charter by which King Edgar granted Barrow-on-Humber to Bishop Æthelwold for the endowment of Peterborough (No. 150). The two passages quoted above are clearly derived from No. 32, which supplies the correct reading *aqua Deopbece*, "deep river," for the erroneous *aqua de Opebece* which appears in K 575, CS 1258, and HC p. 35, and was further mutilated to "the river Opebethe" by Riley (p. 93). See also pp. 101 and 112.

16. (973) **King EDGAR to Thorney Abbey. Foundation charter.   CS 1297.

Edited on p. 165.

17. N.D. (973 × 975) Will of WULFSTAN of DALHAM (Cambs.). 6 hides in *Winningetune al. Winniggetune* (Wennington in Abbots Ripton), and 30 hides in *Hemmingeford* (parts of Hemingford Abbots and Hemingford Grey) to Ely.
Lost.

LE pp. 79–80; 126–7. For Wulfstan, see Chron Rams p. 79;

Miller p. 30; R pp. 366–7; and Robinson p. 121. The charter quoted by Miss Robertson shows that he was still alive in 973, but he predeceased King Edgar (LE p. 107). The 30 hides at Hemingford, like the 6 at Wennington, descended from Ely to Ramsey via Ealdorman Æthelwine (Nos. 26, 311). At a later date, Ramsey acquired 11 hides at Hemingford Grey from King Hathacnut (Nos. 34, 38). These 11 hides may be identified with one of the DB estates called Hemingford (VCH *Hunts.*, I, pp. 352b, 354a). The remaining DB estates at Hemingford and "the other" Hemingford (i.e. Hemingford Abbots and Hemingford Grey) add up to 29 hides (*ibid.*, pp. 350a, 353a, 344a–b). It is probable that these represent the 30 hides at Hemingford in the will of Wulfstan of Dalham.

18. (28 Dec 974)   ***King EDGAR to Ramsey Abbey. Foundation charter, confirming the gifts of lands by various donors. *Inter alia*, Upwood, with its berewick of Raveley, Hemingford (Abbots), Sawtry (Moynes), (Little) Stukeley, Brington, and Old Weston, all given by Ealdorman Æthelwine the founder; Warboys, given by Archbishop Dunstan; Wistow, with its berewicks of Raveley and Bury, given by Archbishop Oswald; *Slepe* (St Ives) given by Æthelstan Mannessune; Houghton, Wyton, (Abbots) Ripton, Ellington, and Bythorn, all given by Alfwold, brother of Ealdorman Æthelwine; (Great) Staughton, Dillington (in Great Staughton), and Yelling, given by the widow *Livith* (Leofgifu). Lands in Cambs., Norfolk, and Northants.

CS 1310, 1311.

Chron Rams pp. 181–9; Cart Rams II, pp. 51–9. The only gift omitted is that of Gidding by Ealdorman Æthelwine (see p. 232). It can be shown that several of these estates did not descend to Ramsey until some time after the date claimed for this charter, see Nos. 22, 272, 318, 326, and Dr E. O. Blake in LE p. 419. The charter is the only evidence for the gift by Ealdorman Brihtnoth to Ramsey of Whiston and Isham in Northants. The charter is plainly spurious in its present form, but its diplomatic deserves further investigation. Barlow (*English Church*, p. 102 n. 1) notes that it embodies the electoral rules for an abbot which are to be found in the *Regularis Concordia*. See also pp. 44, 79.

19. N.D.   (975 × 984)   Foundation charter of a monastery at St Neots, in subjection to Ely.   *Lost.*

LE II, c. 29. According to the Ely account, Bishop Æthelwold of Winchester (who died in 984) refounded a monastery which had first been founded by St Neot, but had been destroyed by the Danes, and lay desolate for a long time. The site was given by a certain Leofric (LE p. 104), who was present with his wife Leof-flæd at the dedication of the church, when they requested Bishop Æthelwold and Abbot Brihtnoth of Ely to institute monks there; at the desire of all those present at the ceremony, the monastery was populated by monks from Ely and Thorney. And Bishop Æthelwold and Abbot Brihtnoth ordained that the monks there should observe the religious life; they should always be subject to the abbot of Ely and his successors, and the prior should always be instituted by the church of Ely, unless the monks were able to supply one from among themselves, and obtain the consent of the brothers of Ely to his institution. And 18 hides (*sic*) were assigned for the food, clothing, and other necessary provisioning of the monks, namely 2 in the town of *Henulvesbery* (Eynesbury, St Neots), 6 at *Weresle* (Waresley), and 9 at Gamlingay (Cambs.). A charter in English was drawn up to establish this settlement, and witnessed by Bishop Æscwig (of Dorchester, the see in which St Neots lay, 975 × 1002) who performed the dedication; Eadric Pape; Ælfhelm Polga, and others present. Three copies were made, of which one was kept by the monks of St Neots, one was retained by Bishop Æscwig, and the third was deposited at Ely by Bishop Æthelwold. This third copy was still in the Ely archives in the early twelfth century, when the *Liber Eliensis* was written.

There is some doubt whether St Neot lived before the time of the Danish attacks in the second half of the ninth century (cf. Asser p. 297), but there appears to be no reason to disbelieve the claim that Bishop Æthelwold founded (or refounded) the monastery. The account of the foundation charter in OE certainly sounds convincing. There is an early reference to the monastery at St Neots in Chron Rams p. 96, where it is stated that those present at the dedication of the new church at Ramsey in 991 confirmed the possessions of Crowland and of St Neots, which was at that time under the patronage and custody of Ealdorman Æthelwine. Dr Blake (LE p. 420) has suggested that the priory did not survive the Danish raids in the early years of the following century, when according to the Crowland tradition as preserved by Ordericus Vitalis (*Historia Ecclesiastica*, ed. Le Prevost, II, p. 283), Leofgifu, lady of Eynesbury and sister of Abbot Oscytel of Crowland, handed the relics of St Neot to the monks of Crowland, because it was not possible to maintain the service of the church at St Neots. It may be surmised that Leofgifu had inherited Eynesbury from Leofric and Leofflæd, the donors of the priory site; possibly she was their daughter. In spite of this tradition, however, the body of St Neot rested at Eynesbury according to the OE list of English saints and their burial places compiled about 1020 (F. Liebermann, *Die Heiligen Englands*, Hanover, 1889, p. 13; *Liber Vitae* of Hyde, p. 90).

DB shows that the late tenth-century endowment of the monastery was broken up before the Conquest (LE p. 420). In 1079 a new community was established at St Neots by Rohais, the wife of Richard fitz Gilbert of Clare, in subjection to the Abbey of Bec (cf. LE p. 188 n. 3, and M. Morgan, *The English Lands of the Abbey of Bec*, 1946, p. 11), and it is noteworthy that Hugh Candidus, who translated the OE list of English saints at Peterborough early in the following century with many additions drawn from local knowledge, still left St Neot at Eynesbury (HC p. 63).

Goscelin's *Life of St Ivo* claims Æthelflæd as the foundress of St Neots (cf. Asser p. 298). Presumably the wife of Ealdorman Æthelwine is intended, and this may derive from the Ramsey tradition that Æthelwine was the protector of St Neots; but the claim cannot be sustained in the face of the Ely account of the foundation. Still later tradition is undoubtedly wrong in naming as the founder Earl Leofric of Mercia (VCH *Hunts.*, I, pp. 385–6).

20. 979 × 1016   King Æthelred II to Ramsey. 9 hides at *Broctuna* (Broughton).   *Lost.*

Chron Rams pp. 75–6. The Ramsey account adds: "*literisque suis eandem donationem ad futurae posteritatis notitiam commendavit,*" which suggests that a royal writ was issued in connection with the grant. See further, Nos. 42, 316–17, and 320.

21. N.D.   (986)   *Will of Æthelstan Mannessune. *Haliwella* (Holywell) to his wife for her to dispose of as she pleases; land in *Grantedene* (Great Gransden) to his eldest daughter, just as it had been left for her by her godmother Æthelswyth; land in *Slepe* (St Ives) to his youngest daughter Alfwenna, with reversion to Ramsey after her death. Land in Cambs.   Chron Rams pp. 59–60, 192; LE p. 91.

Fully discussed in CAS LVI–LVII, 1964, pp. 61–7. See also p. 45.

22. N.D.   (14 June 987)   *Agreement between the widow of Æthelstan Mannessune and the brothers of Ramsey, concerning the disposal of Æthelstan's estates. She is to have the estate at Elsworth (Cambs.) during her lifetime,

provided that upon the death of her daughter Alfwenna the estate at *Slepe* (St Ives) is to descend directly to the abbey. This was agreed at *Slepe* on the day when Æthelstan's anniversary was commemorated, by the witness of Æthelsige the son of Ealdorman Æthelstan (of East Anglia), Leofric the son of Ealdorman Æthelwine (of East Anglia), Eadric, Leofric, Leofwine the son of Ætholf, Ælfnoth of *Ailricheseya* (Arlesey, Beds.), Osward the priest, and many others.

Chron Rams pp. 60–1.

Date: presumably a year after Æthelstan's death in 986. His anniversary was celebrated on 14 June (Cart Rams III, p. 166; Dugdale II, p. 566). The same sources give 13 October 987 as the date of the death of Æthelsige, the son of Ealdorman Æthelstan, who witnessed the agreement. For Osward the priest, see No. 23. See also CAS LVI–LVII, 1964, pp. 61–7.

23. N.D.   (c.987)   Record of a transaction concerning 10 hides at *Slepe* (St Ives), 2 hides at *Thirninge* (Thurning, formerly in Hunts., now in Northants.), and land in Northants.   Chron Rams pp. 76–8.

Date: soon after the death of Æthelstan Mannessune (Nos. 21–2). This is a complicated three-cornered transaction, which reads like a Latin abstract of one of the OE law memoranda characteristic of the period. The three parties were the monks of Ramsey (represented by their prior, Eadnoth), Leofwine the son of Ealdorman Æthelwine of East Anglia, and a priest called Osward who was related to Alfwenna, the youngest daughter (wrongly called the *wife* in this account) of Æthelstan Mannessune. By virtue of his relationship with Æthelstan, Osward had acquired 10 hides at St Ives, which ought to have descended to Ramsey (No. 22 above). At the same time, Leofwine had succeeded in a lawsuit against Osward's son, in which he claimed 8 hides at Oakley and 10 at Weekley (both in Northants.), although this issue was still being contested. The monks at Ramsey, for their part, had 18 hides at Barnwell (Northants.), the possession of which had also been in dispute, a shire court held at Northampton in the reign of Edward the Martyr (975–9) having declared that the estate should descend to the king. King Edward, however, had allowed it to stay in the possession of Ramsey. Osward's solution, which was accepted by Eadnoth and agreed to by the king (presumably Æthelred II) ,was as follows: Ramsey should give 2 hides at Thurning to Leofwine, together with the tenancy of its 18 hides at Barnwell; Leofwine should forgo his claim to Oakley and Weekley in favour of Osward's son, and Osward should surrender the 10 hides at St Ives to Ramsey.

24. N.D.   (989)   †Will of ÆLFHELM POLGA. *Stoctune* (? Great Staughton) to Leofsige and his wife, in return for 100 mancuses of gold towards the payment of his heriot; his long-ship to Ramsey, half to the abbot and half to the community, for his soul. Land in Cambs., Essex, Suffolk, Herts., and Beds.   ◆W XIII.

OS Facs III, No. 37; ECEss I, p. 18; LT pp. 33, 122. Professor Whitelock (W p. 136) tentatively identified *Stoctune* with Stockton near Bungay, Norfolk, but pointed out that it was far removed from the remainder of Ælfhelm's estates. The location at Great Staughton was first suggested in PN *Hunts.*, p. 267, and supported in VCH *Hunts.*, II, p. 356. Ælfhelm had close connections with Ramsey Abbey (CAS LVI–LVII, 1964, pp. 61–7), to which Great Staughton eventually descended (No. 326); he also attended the dedication of the abbey church at St Neots (No. 19). Ramsey sources give his death as 31 October 989 (Cart Rams III, p. 166, where his name is misspelt *Alfelinus*; Dugdale II, p. 566, misspelt *Alwen*). The date of his death is of importance, since Ælfhelm left an estate to Westminster Abbey in his will, which is the earliest datable reference to the abbey after its refoundation. See also pp. 45 and 60.

25. N.D.   (991)   Will of BRIHTNOTH, ealdorman of Essex. *Spaldewich* (Spaldwick) and *Sumeresham* (Somersham) to Ely. Land in Cambs., Essex, Norfolk, Suffolk, and Northants.
                                        Lost.

LE II, c. 62; Chron Rams pp. 116–17; ECEss I, p. 18. See also pp. 46, 61, and 80.

26. N.D.   (990 × c.1000)   *Will of ÆLFHILD. Confirmation to Ramsey of lands left *viva voce* in reversion to the abbey by her late husband Alfwold, the brother of Ealdorman Æthelwine: *Riptone*, *Wenintone*, and *Elintone* (Abbots Ripton, Wennington in Abbots Ripton, and Ellington). The land of *Bitherna* (Bythorn) to Ramsey, with the request that the abbey receive her daughter's son Eadnoth as a monk there.   CS 1061.

According to the Ramsey obits (Cart Rams III, p. 166; Dugdale II, p. 566), Alfwold died on 14 April 990. He must have obtained Wennington from his brother Æthelwine (No. 318). In addition to the estates mentioned, Ælfhild was left estates at *Hoctone* and *Wittone* (Houghton and Wyton) by her husband, with reversion to Ramsey (Chron Rams p. 63). She left to her chaplain Ælfmær land at *Cloptuna*, which must have been at Clapton, Northants., near Bythorn.

27. **N.D.** (c.1000 × 1025) †Assignments of property to Thorney Abbey by Ely Abbey. Thorney estates receiving stock include *Niwantune* (Water Newton), *Fearresheafde* (Farcet), *Stangrunde* (Stanground), *Geaceslea* (Yaxley), *Witlesmere* (Whittlesey Mere), and *Huntandune* (Huntingdon). A mill at . . . . *tesham* (? Bluntisham) is also mentioned. Estates in Cambs.   ◆R App II, No. IX.

The total value in money and kind is recorded as 16 pounds less 40 pence. The text does not make it clear whether this was an outright gift by Ely, whether some obligation was incurred, or whether a money transaction took place. Miss Robertson suggests that the property was assigned to Thorney soon after its second foundation in 972. However, the record mentions land at (Little) Thetford, which did not descend to Ely until c.1007 (No. 28). This document cannot, therefore, be assigned to the group of OE records compiled under Bishop Æthelwold's direction. Ker (pp. 126–7) dates the hand of this part of the MS. as the first quarter of the eleventh century. See also p. 47.

28. **N.D.** (c.1007) Will of ÆLFWARU. Land at *Haliwelle* (Holywell) to Ramsey. Lands in Norfolk, Suffolk, Cambs., and Herts.   *Lost.*

Chron Rams pp. 84–5; LE II, c. 61. Ælfwaru was probably the eldest daughter of Æthelstan Mannessune (No. 21, cf. CAS LVI–LVII, 1964, pp. 61–7). See also pp. 48, 62, and 80.

29. **N.D.** (c.1007) *GODRIC to his younger son Eadnoth. Land at *Acleya* (Oakley, a wood in St Ives). Land in Norfolk.
K 928.

Chron Rams pp. 111–12. For the date, see CAS LVI–LVII, 1964, pp. 61–7. The account goes on to say that Eadnoth left this estate to Ramsey upon his death. See also p. 80.

30. 1012 *King ÆTHELRED (II) to Godwine, bishop of Rochester. 15 hides *æt Stantun* (Fen Stanton) and *æt Hiltun* (Hilton). K 719.

♦LC pp. 79–81 (part); *Proc. Soc. Antiq.* 2nd ser., III, 1864–7, pp. 49–50 (bounds). Kemble's text is derived from Thomas Hearne's edition of the *Textus Roffensis*, which is shown by collation with the original entry to be substantially correct. The boundary clause ends with a list of eight (possibly nine, but one name is repeated) fisheries belonging to the manor: *This is se fixnað þe to stantune gebyrað. Þ is æt holanwere. 7 æt deopanwere. 7 æt suðan ea. 7 æt niwanwere. 7 æt dinde. 7 æt biscopes were. 7 æt bradan were. 7 æt niwanwere. 7 æt merbece.* They are mentioned again in later records of the manor (VCH *Hunts.*, II, p. 283), and it is evident that they comprised a series of nets across the River Ouse. They should be compared with the "weirs" at Fordham and Hilgay, see R p. 257. At the time of DB, Fen Stanton and Hilton were still a single estate, assessed at only 13 hides (VCH *Hunts.*, I, p. 352a). They were not then in the possession of Rochester, having been alienated TRE or earlier.

31. N.D. (1017 × 1035) *Will of MANTAT the Anchorite. Twywell (Northants.) and *Cunintun* (Conington) to Thorney. ♦W XXIII.

Edited on p. 204.

32. 1020 × 1021 *Record of the purchase by ÆLFSIGE, abbot of Peterborough, from Thored, the king's thegn, of a quarter of the lake called *Wittlesmere* (Whittlesey Mere), giving for it the land of *Ouertune* (Orton) and an agreed sum of money. K 733.

♦VCH *Hunts.*, III, pp. 251–2 (bounds only). The best edition is by T. Stapleton, *Chronicon Petroburgense*, Camden Series No. XLVII, London, 1849, pp. 182–3. Useful place-name variants are contained in the text entered in Swaffham's Register (D and C Peterborough MS. 1) ff. cxixd–cxx.

33. N.D. (1029 × 1035) *LEOFSIGE, abbot of Ely, with the consent of King Cnut, settles the food rents due to the monastery from its estates in Cambs., Hunts., Essex, Norfolk, and Suffolk. Those from Huntingdonshire comprise: *Spaldewic* (Spaldwick) and *Sumeresham* (Somersham) which

B

each provide two weeks' food farm, *Bluntesham* (Bluntis-ham) and *Colne* (Colne), each providing food for one week.
Lost.

LE II, c. 84. Lennard, RE p. 131 n. 1, points out that the listed farms provide only 51 weeks' food, and suggests that an item must have dropped out of the LE text. The system of farming is discussed by Miller pp. 38–9. Examination of the list shows that it is compiled geographically, commencing with 15 estates in Cambridgeshire, together with two on the Essex side of the border (cf. ECEss I, p. 23); four estates in Huntingdonshire are then listed, followed by seven in Suffolk, and finally seven in Norfolk. If these are plotted on a map it will be seen that the Ely estates in the Norfolk marshland and in the Five and a half Hundreds of Wicklow, Suffolk, were all exempt from the farm, together with outlying estates in Essex, Herts., Suffolk, and Norfolk. No estate in Huntingdonshire or Cambridgeshire escaped, but the whole of the Isle of Ely was exempt, except that it had to make good any losses from the listed estates. No doubt the more distant Ely estates rendered money payments in the place of food farms, as was the custom with the outlying estates of Westminster and Canterbury (RE pp. 131 n. 1, 137 n. 1). See also pp. 49, 65, and 81.

34. N.D. (1040 × 1042) *King HARTHACNUT and his mother Queen Ælfgifu to Bishop Eadnoth, Earl Thuri, Kinric, and all his thegns of Huntingdonshire. Writ declaring that they have given to the church of Ramsey, for their souls and for the soul of King Cnut, the "east" land of *Hemmingeforde* (Hemingford Grey), with sake and soke, as fully as they themselves possessed it.   ♦H 57.

35. N.D. (1042 × 1057) *King EDWARD, king of the English, to Ely Abbey. Confirmation of estates, including *Spaldewich* (Spaldwick) with appendages, *Sumeresham* (Somersham), *Colne* (Colne), and *Bluntesham* (Bluntisham). Estates in Cambs., Suffolk, Norfolk, Essex, and Herts.
K 907.

LE II, c. 92. Date and authenticity: LE pp. 417–18. Cf. ECEss II, p. 27. This charter is often declared to be spurious (e.g. Barlow p. 42), but in LE p. 418 Dr Blake effectively defends its authenticity. Its surviving form lacks date and witness list, but there appears to be no reason to reject outright any portion of the text on diplomatic or historical grounds. The acquisition of Colne by Ely is not recorded elsewhere. See also pp. 50, 67, and 84.

36. N.D. (1042 × 1066) The abbot of Thorney to the burgesses of Huntingdon, in pledge. The church of St Mary of Huntingdon, with the land annexed to it. *Lost.*

> DB fo. 208. VCH *Hunts.*, I, p. 325. C. Hart, 'The Church of St Mary of Huntingdon', in CAS LIX, forthcoming.

37. N.D. (1042 × 1066) Writ of King EDWARD, giving Leuric with all his land into the bishopric of Lincoln, with sake and soke. *Lost.*

> DB fo. 208b; VCH *Hunts.*, I, p. 355b; H p. 544. This DB reference is anachronistic, in that the see of Dorchester (which was probably the recipient of King Edward's gift) was not transferred to Lincoln until 1072. Leuric held 3 hides and 1 virgate at Orton, of the king's soke (DB, fo. 203b). King Edward's writ was exhibited by Bishop Remigius of Lincoln before the Domesday jurors.

38. N.D. (1043 × 1049) *King EDWARD to Bishop Eadnoth, Earl Thuri, Kinric, and all his thegns of Huntingdonshire. Writ declaring that St Benedict of Ramsey is to have the land at *Hemmingfordia* (Hemingford Grey), with everything pertaining thereto, as fully and completely as King Harthacnut and Queen Ælfgifu granted it to that church. ♦H 58.

39. N.D. (1043 × 1065) *EADNOTH and his wife to Ramsey Abbey. The reversion of land at *Acleia* (Oakley, a wood in St Ives). K 919.

> Chron Rams pp. 173–4, 198–9; RE p. 164. The gift was made in the time of Abbot Ælfwine, on the occasion of the admission of Eadnoth's son Æthelric as a novice at the abbey.

40. N.D. (1043 × 1065) Abbot ÆLFWINE of Ramsey to Sexi of Walton, a relative of Earl Leofric. The estate at *Westmilne* (Westmill, Herts.) for his lifetime, with reversion to the abbey, which is also to inherit Sexi's estate of *Waltona* (Woodwalton). *Lost.*

Chron Rams p. 146; RE p. 164 and n. 5. The dates are those of Abbot Ælfwine. Earl Leofric of Mercia died in 1057. The Ramsey account goes on to say that Sexi's estates were confiscated by the Conqueror.

41. **N.D.   (c.1044)**   Abbot ÆLFWINE and the brethren of Ramsey to Wulfwine the son of Ælfwine, for his lifetime, with reversion to the abbey. 5 hides at *Gillinge* (Yelling) and the land in the east of *Hemmingforde* (Hemingford Grey) all of which had been given them by King Harthacnut.

Lost.

Chron Rams pp. 152–3. This grant was made in the chapter house at Ramsey, on the eve of Pentecost (Whit-Sunday), with the proviso that upon Wulfwine's death his own estates of *Uggle* and *Bumstede* (Ugley and Bumpstead, Essex), *Abbintune* (Abington, Cambs.), and *Weldingefeld* (Waldingfield, Suffolk) should descend to the abbey, in alms for his soul.

Abbot Ælfwine was elected late in 1043, and this lease was apparently transacted soon afterwards. For Harthanut's gift of Yelling and Hemingford Grey, see Nos. 17 and 34. The latter was confirmed to Ramsey by King Edward, at Abbot Ælfwine's request (No. 38). Wulfwine, a thegn of King Edward, was a large landholder in Suffolk, Cambs., and Essex. He was possibly the Wulfwine, King Edward's huntsman, who held land in Isleham, Cambs. (DB I fo. 190b). He survived until the Conquest, when Abington, Waldingfield, Ugley, and Bumpstead passed together with the rest of his estates to Aubrey de Vere (DB I, ff. 190a, 195b, 199b; II, 418–19; ECEss No. 60). The lease to him by Ramsey of Yelling and Hemingford Grey must have undergone some modification, the details of which have not survived, for DB records that Ramsey leased these two estates to Aluric, who was killed at the battle of Hastings (DB I, fo. 208a; VCH *Hunts.*, I, pp. 329, 354a and b). The terms of this lease were very similar to those of the one previously granted to Wulfwine, for upon Aluric's death, not only were Yelling and Hemingford Grey to revert to the abbey, but so also was his own estate at Boxted in Essex. As Boxted is not so very far from Waldingfield, it appears probable that there was some connection between Wulfwine and Aluric; possibly they were related to each other, for after the Conquest Aluric's leasehold lands at Yelling and East Hemingford passed to Aubrey de Vere (DB I, fo. 207a; VCH *Hunts.*, I, p. 352), as Wulfwine's had done. Lennard, in RE p. 164 n. 5, offers a rather different interpretation of this transaction.

42. N.D. (1050 × 1052) **King EDWARD to Bishop Ulf, Earl Siward, the sheriff Alric, and all his thegns in Huntingdonshire. Writ declaring that he has given to Ramsey the land at *Broctona* (Broughton) which he himself possessed, with sake and soke. ♦H 59.

DB I, fo. 208 states that this gift, of five hides, was made in return for a service which Abbot Ælfwine rendered King Edward in Saxony. For further details of Ælfwine, see H pp. 551–2.

It is difficult to account for the hidation of Broughton. There is good reason to believe that in common with other territory surrounding Huntingdon, it had been royal property from the time of its reconquest by King Edward the Elder (cf. C. Hart, 'The Church of St Mary, Huntingdon', in CAS LIX, forthcoming). Originally Broughton must have been a 20-hide estate. King Edgar gave one hide to Bishop Æthelwold (No. 16), who gave it to Ramsey (No. 317). King Edward the Martyr gave Ramsey another two hides there (No. 316), and King Æthelred II gave 9 more hides (No. 20). A further 3 hides at Broughton were given to Ramsey by Æthelric, bishop of Dorchester, who was related to the royal family (No. 320). Yet apart from the 5 hides which had been given by King Edward the Confessor (above), the only other DB estate there was of 4 hides, held by Ramsey in demesne (DB I, fo. 204; VCH *Hunts.*, I, pp. 342b, 343a). It is very probable that 10 of the remaining 11 hides are entered in DB under *Slepe* (St Ives), which was rated at that time as a 20-hide estate, and included the berewicks of Woodhurst and Old Hurst (CAS LVI–LVII, 1964, p. 64 n. 1). But in the late tenth century, St Ives appears to have been rated at only 10 hides. It seems likely, therefore, that Old Hurst and Woodhurst were originally reckoned as half of the 20-hide estate of Broughton, and were later separated and attached to St Ives to form part of the endowment of the monastery there, which was founded in 1001–2 (CAS LVI–LVII, 1964, pp. 61–7).

43. N.D. (c. 1055) King EDWARD to Earl Siward (of Northumbria and Huntingdon). Swineshead, with sake and soke, except that the men of the manor are to pay geld in the hundred (court), and go against the enemy with them (i.e. serve in the hundred *fyrd*). *Lost.*

DB I, fo. 208; VCH *Hunts.*, I, pp. 347b, 354b; III, p. 104. For Earl Siward, who died in 1055, see VCH *Hunts.*, II, pp. 4–5.

Swineshead was formerly in Huntingdonshire, but was transferred to Bedfordshire in 1888.

44. N.D.   (c.1055)   **Delineation of the boundary between the lands of the abbeys of Ramsey and Thorney in the marsh of King's Delph.   Cart Rams I, p. 188; III, pp. 38–9.

A second, unpublished, version is in the Red Book of Thorney, CUL Add. MS. 3021, fo. 372. Discussed by Dr Harmer (H pp. 253–6).

45. N.D.   (1055 × 1065)   **King EDWARD to Bishop Wulf-wig, Earl Tostig, the sheriff Northman, and all his thegns in Northamptonshire. Writ declaring that he has confirmed the exchange and the agreement made between Ælfwine, abbot of Ramsey, and Leofric, abbot of Peterborough; and also the boundaries along King Cnut's Delph as Ælfwine, abbot of Ramsey, proved his claim to them against Siward, abbot of Thorney.   ♦H 62.

Dr Harmer edits this writ, and No. 135 below, from an entry in the Charter Rolls. The charter of inspeximus from which this entry is derived is now in the possession of Ramsey Abbey Grammar School. Dr Harmer discusses the relationship between the second half of this writ and No. 44. Each contains the name *Wend(e)lesmere*, which does not appear elsewhere. In the Thorney version of No. 44, this is given as *Witlesmere* (i.e. Whittlesey Mere), which possibly the original form. Perhaps the change was influenced by the existence of Trundle Mere in Yaxley, for which we have the reliable early form *Trendelmere* in 956 (No. VI). It may be, therefore, that in dealing with No. 44, the compiler of the Ramsey Cartulary had before him a text which was already corrupt when he transcribed it. This corrupt text, or a derivative, could have been used by whoever manufactured the spurious writ under discussion.

46. N.D.   (c.1060)   The abbot of Ramsey to Turkil of Har-ringworth (Northants.) for his lifetime. 6 hides at *Cunintune* (Conington) for an annual *caritas* of one mark, with rever-sion to Ramsey, which is also to inherit the 3 hides he owned there himself.   *Lost*.

There are three records of this lease: two in DB (ff. 206b, 208b; VCH *Hunts.*, I, pp. 351a, 355b), and one containing a good deal more detail in the Red Book of Thorney (Dugdale II, p. 604). It cannot be dated precisely.

47. (c. 1062)   ***King EDWARD to Ramsey Abbey. Confirmation of title to lands in Lincs., Cambs., Beds., Norfolk, Suffolk, Northants., and Herts.   K 809.

The witnesses include Leofric, earl of Mercia, who died in 1057 (cf. Oleson p. 153) and Baldwin, abbot of Bury St Edmunds, who was not appointed until 1065. According to Chron Rams p. 177, this charter was obtained by Ælfsige, the deputy of Abbot Ælfwine after the latter's illness, which could not have occurred before 1062. The opening clauses are identical with those of No. 118A. The first part of the list of lands is derived from the same source as the list in the spurious charter of King Edgar (No. 18), for both omit Æthelwine's donation of Gidding. Many later donations are also omitted. The Huntingdonshire estates included, in addition to those appearing in King Edgar's charter, are Elton, Oakley in St Ives, Yelling, and Hemingford Grey. See also pp. 52, 77, 95, and 106.

CHAPTER II

THE EARLY CHARTERS OF
CAMBRIDGESHIRE

48. 895 ****ALFRED, king of the Anglo-Saxons, to Bishop Burric of Rochester. *Yselham* (Isleham), and land in Suffolk.
CS 571.

> Analysed in Asser p. 201 n. 4, where this charter, which exists as a single membrane written in a twelfth-century imitative hand, is shown conclusively to be a late forgery, based partly on a passage in *Asser's Life of King Alfred*. The charter is referred to in the Rochester list of benefactors printed in Dugdale 1, p. 161. See also p. 53.

49. N.D. (942 × 951) *Will of THEODRED, bishop of London. *Dukeswrthe* (Duxford) and *Earningtone* (Arrington) to the king, as part of his heriot. Lands in Norfolk, Suffolk, Essex, Middlesex, and Surrey. ♦W 1.

> ECEss No. 9. See also pp. 53 and 79.

50. N.D. (946 × 951) *Will of ÆLFGAR (ealdorman of Essex). *Dittone* (Fen Ditton) to his daughter Æthelflæd, and then to whatever foundation she chooses, for the souls of their ancestors. Land in Suffolk and Essex. ♦W II.

> ECEss No. 11. On the identification of Ditton, see LE p. 423. See also p. 58.

51. 954 × 955 *EADRED, king of the Anglo-Saxons, emperor of the Northumbrians, ruler of the pagans, defender of the Britons, and Eadgifu, the king's mother, to God and St Peter the Apostle and to St Ætheldreda the virgin and her sacred lineage resting in the church at Ely, for the use of the servants of God therein. The *villa* called *Stapelforda* (Stapleford); and Wulfstan, *sequipedus* of the king, is to have charge of the 15 "cassati" at Stapleford. CS 1346.

> LE II, c. 28. For Dr Blake's comment, see LE p. 416. The

charter survives in an incomplete version, lacking bounds and most of the witness list; the only witnesses whose names are recorded are Oda, archbishop of Canterbury, and the brothers Eadwig and Edgar, king Eadred's nephews and successors. The charter claims to be drawn up in the ninth year of Eadred, i.e. 954–5; the dating clause was evidently partly illegible to the Ely copyist, who recorded the year of grace as 956, the last figure *sexto* being added in the margin in a contemporary hand. The Ely account states that Eadred added to this estate 3 hides at *Berdefeld* (Bardfield in Stapleford), and a mill and pasture at *Derneforde* (Dernford Farm and Mill); it seems probable that this information was contained in the version of the charter which lay before the copyist. Professor Whitelock (LE p. xii) considers that the charter "was originally a grant to Wulfstan, emended later into a direct gift to the abbey," but other interpretations are possible, and a case can be made out for considering the charter to be authentic as it stands. It seems to me that Queen Eadgifu (the widow of King Edward the Elder) owned Ely, where there was a community of some kind, and Wulfstan (who can be identified with Wulfstan of Dalham, see Nos. 54, 208, 241, 257, 272, 278) administered the estate for her. Wulfstan and Eadgifu were associated in other transactions concerning Ely—LE II, c. 31, 43.

52. 9 May 957 †EADWIG, king of all Britain, to Oda, archbishop of Canterbury. 40 "mansae" *æt Helig* (Ely), free of all but the three common dues.   Crawf v.

Dated from *Eðandune* (Edington, Wilts.). Cf. Robinson p. 118, and Miller's *Ely*, p. 15. Presumably Ely came into the hands of Eadwig when Queen Eadgifu's estates were confiscated (No. 51). Eadwig's charter was not effective for long; later that year his brother Edgar took over the kingdom of Mercia, in which Cambridgeshire was then included. Oda died a year later, and in 964 or thereabouts Edgar offered Ely to Oda's nephew, Bishop Oswald of Worcester (Anon, *Vita S. Oswaldi*, in *Historians of the Church of York*, I, p. 427), who refused it. See further, No. 55.

53. 969 King EDGAR to Ramsey Abbey, at the time of its foundation. 5 hides at *Burewelle* (Burwell).   *Lost.*

Chron Rams p. 47, where the entry *scripto suo eidem ecclesiæ perpetuo possidendas confirmavit* suggests that the gift was by charter. This estate is not to be confused with another 5-hide estate there; see No. 327.

B*

54. N.D.   (969 × 990)   *ÆLFWOLD, brother of Ealdorman
Æthelwine, to Ramsey Abbey, in exchange for 2 hides
which the monks had purchased at *Stapelforde* (Stapleford).
Land at *Suafham* (Swaffham) which he had bought from
Æthelwold, a relative of Wulfstan of Dalham.

Chron Rams pp. 78–80.

The Ramsey account, which appears to be drawn from a law
memorandum, goes on to say that after the death of Ælfwold
(which the Ramsey obits give as 14 April 990), one Ælfnoth son
of Goding claimed the land at Swaffham from Ramsey. The claim
was heard before Ealdorman Æthelwine and Eadric the king's
reeve at a place called *Wendlesbiri*. Thirty-six lawmen were
chosen from among the friends of both sides. Eadnoth the prior
and a monk named Ælfwine appeared for Ramsey, and the claim
was decided in their favour after Ealdorman Æthelwine had used
his influence on their behalf. After Æthelwine's death, however,
Ælfnoth succeeded in regaining possession of the land.

W. Dunn Macray, the editor of the Ramsey Chronicle, located
Wendlesbiri at Wellingborough, Northants., an identification accepted by Professor Whitelock, who concludes that Æthelwine's
jurisdiction included Northamptonshire (LE p. xiii). As the plea
concerned a Cambridgeshire estate, however, it is in that county
that the site of the trial should be sought, and a more likely identification is Wandlebury, the Iron-Age fort in the Gogmagog Hills,
the site chosen for the famous plea before nine hundreds held by
Bishop Nigel of Ely in 1133–5, when many Ely holdings were restored to the church (LE p. 287; Miller p. 167). Reference to a
map confirms the identification, for Wandlebury lies halfway
between Stapleford and Swaffham. See, further, No. 73.

55. 970   †EDGAR, king of the island of Albion, and ruler of
the Scots, Cumbrians, and Britons and all the regions thereabout, to the monastery at Ely. Bishop Æthelwold has exchanged the manor of Harting (Sussex) for the monastic
site at Ely, which was in the king's hands; to this the king
has added, for the redemption of his soul and those of his
ancestors, the manors of *Meldeburna* and *Earningaford* (Melbourn, and land in Armingford hundred), and also Northwold (Norfolk); and a gift of 10,000 eels yearly for the
monks, which had accrued to the king in place of military
service within the isle (of Ely) from the people at *Well*
(Outwell and Upwell in Cambs. and Norfolk); and soke

over the fenlands included within the two hundreds (of
Ely), and over the five hundreds at *Wicklawan* in East Anglia
(Suffolk), and over the lands now assigned to the monastery,
and those which will yet come to it, by purchase or grant;
and the fourth penny of all the public penalties paid at
Grantanbricge (Cambridge).

CS 1266 (Latin) and ♦R xlviii (OE).

OS Facs iii, 32. Dated at *Uulfamere* (Woolmer Forest, Hants.).
The OE version of this charter is thought not to have been composed until the early part of the following century, cf. A. Mc-
Intosh, 'Wulfstan's Prose', *Proc. Brit. Acad.*, xxxiv, 1949, and LE
pp. 414–15. The Latin version (CS 1266), which it follows except for minor deviations (cf. R pp. 345–7), supplies the date and
witness list. Its authenticity is established in a forthcoming paper
by Mr Eric John. A subsidiary Latin charter of the same date (CS
1265), which bears some signs of tampering, repeats part of the
donations recited in the main text, and gives a little more detail
concerning the nature of the jurisdiction granted to the abbey.
A summary of Edgar's gift in LE ii, c. 4 also supplies more details
than the surviving forms of the donation charter; it states that
5 hides at Melbourn, 3½ at *Ærningeford*, and 12 at Northwold were
obtained by Bishop Æthelwold from King Edgar in exchange for
40 hides at Harting, Sussex, which had been given to Æthelwold
by King Æthelstan. This summary must be derived from material
compiled before the Conquest, when Norfolk was still hidated.

56. 970   *EDGAR, king of all Britain, to the monastery at Ely.
10 "cassati" at *Lintune* (Linden End in Aldreth), free of all
but the three common dues.   CS 1268.

LE ii, c. 9. Comments: LE pp. 414–15, and Stenton, *Types*,
p. 83. In the place of the usual bounds appears a statement in OE:
"This is the land belonging to *Lintune* which Æþelferð gave his
son Leofric, which lies hide by hide and acre by acre (*hidmælum ꝺ
æcermælum*) in *Wilburhtune*, *Hædenham*, *Hylle*, and *Wichamme* (Wilburton, Haddenham, Hill Row, and West Wickham). He (Leofric) gave it without reserve to King Edgar, just as his ancestors
had bought it; and the king gave it to God and St Ætheldreda for
the redemption of his soul." The transaction underlying the charter is described in LE ii, c. 8, which states that Bishop Æthelwold
bought the twelve (*sic*) hides at Linden End, with its berewicks
at Hill Row, West Wickham, and Wilburton, from Leofric of
Brandon (Suffolk) son of Æthelferth, for 100 mancuses of gold;

in addition Æthelwold returned to Leofric an estate at *Bessingtune* (Bishampton, Worcs., cf. ECWM pp. 115–16) which he had previously bought from Leofric's wife Æthelflæd. This transaction (the statement continues) was made before witnesses at Cambridge. After King Edgar's death, Leofric tried to undo the agreement, but the lawmen (*legales viri*) Eðric *rufus* and Leofric of *Berle* (? Barley, Herts.) and Siferth the Foolish (*vecors*), who enquired into the matter, did not accept Leofric's claim.

57. 974   †EDGAR, king of all Britain, to his faithful thegn Ælfhelm. 2½ "mansae" *æt Wreattinge* (West Wratting), free of all but the three common dues.   CS 1305.

Reproduction by S. J. A. Evans, 'A Saxon Charter', in *Annual Report of the Friends of Ely Cathedral*, I, 1937, p. 24, and plate. The boundary clause includes references to the common boundary with Weston Colville, West Wickham, Yen Hall in West Wickham, and Balsham. Ælfhelm Polga, the recipient, died in 989, leaving the estate to Ely.—LE II, c. 73.

(18) (28 Dec. 974)   ***Foundation Charter of Ramsey Abbey. King EDGAR confirms the gifts of lands by various donors, including Chatteris, the east part of Elsworth, and Graveley. Lands in Hunts., Norfolk, and Northants.

CS 1310, 1311.

Chron Rams pp. 181–9; Cart Rams II, pp. 51–9. See also pp. 27 and 79.

(19) N.D.   (975 × 984)   Foundation Charter of the monastery of St Neots. 9 hides at *Gamingeia* (Gamlingay), and lands in Hunts.   *Lost*.

LE pp. 102–3. It is not stated who gave the estate. See also p. 27.

58. N.D.   (975 × 991)   *Will of ÆTHELFLÆD of Damerham (Wilts.). An estate *æt Dictunæ* (Fen Ditton) to Ely. Lands in Berks., Wilts., Essex, Herts., and Suffolk.   ♦W XIV.

ECEss No. 17; LE II, c. 64. See also p. 59.

59. N.D.   (c.985)   *ÆTHELGIFU to Ramsey Abbey. Land at *Stowe* (Long Stow) and *Brunne* (Bourn) after her death; and the new mill; and one mark of gold, to be divided half

for the needs of the monastery, and half for food for the monks; and 2 silver goblets, weighing 12 marks according to the measure of the husting at London, for the service of the brethren in the refectory. CS 1060

The surviving form of the charter is a Latin translation from OE. Æthelgifu, the second wife of Ealdorman Æthelwine, is said in the Ramsey obits to have died in 985 (Cart Rams III, p. 166). This appears to be the earliest record of the husting at London, cf. Stenton p. 532.

(21) N.D. (986) *Will of ÆTHELSTAN MANNESSUNE. Land at *Chateriz* (Chatteris) to Ramsey, just as his father had held it; land at *Walde* (Wold near Witchford) to Ely; *Gravele* (Graveley) and *Ellesworthe* (Elsworth) to his wife, with reversion to Ramsey; half a fishery at *Welle* (Upwell and Outwell in Cambs. and Norfolk), land at *Owra* (Over), and half of *Cnapwelle* (Knapwell) to his wife; the other half of Knapwell to his relative Leofsige; land at *Coteham* (Cottenham) to his son if he will take the advice of his friends; if not, it is to stay in the hands of Ealdorman Æthelwine; land at *Grantadene* (Gransden) to his eldest daughter, as it had been left for her by her godmother Æthelswyth; 2 hides at *Hettenleiam* (Hatley) to his sister, and the remainder of Hatley to Leofsige. Estates in Beds., Hunts., and Lincs.

Chron Rams pp. 59–60, 192; LE p. 91.
See also pp. 29 and 101.

60. N.D. (986 × 989) *ÆLFHELM and his wife Æffa to Ramsey. Land at *Hattenleia* (Hatley in Cambs. and Beds.), and Potton (Beds.). CS 1062.

W p. 133. Dates: between the wills of Æthelstan Mannessune (No. 21) and Ælfhelm Polga (No. 24). Drawn up at Wheathampstead, Herts., in the presence of Ealdorman Æthelwine.

(24) N.D. (989) †Will of ÆLFHELM POLGA. The estate at *Wrættincge* (West Wratting) to Ely, except the 2 hides which Æthelric has; confirmation of 3 hides at *Heanhealan* (Enhale in West Wickham) to his wife as part of her *morgengifu*; he had also given her 2 hides at *Wilburgeham* (Wilbra-

ham) "when we first came together," and he grants to her *Carletunes* (Carlton); and half the estate at *Cunningtune* (Conington) is to be divided between his wife and daughter, except the 4 hides which he grants to Æthelric and Ælfwold, and the half-hide which he grants to his servant Osmær; the hide at *Icelingtune* (Ickleton) and the property at *Mawyrþe* (unidentified) to Ælfhelm; *Hættanlea* (Hatley, Cambs., and Beds.) to be divided between the brothers Ælfmær and Ælfstan, except what he grants to Osgar. Land in Hunts., Herts., Beds., Essex, and Suffolk.   ♦W XIII.

OS Facs III, 37; CAS LVI–LVII, 1964, pp. 64–5; LT pp. 33, 122. See also pp. 31 and 60.

(25) N.D.   (991)   Will of Ealdorman BRIHTNOTH of Essex. *Trumpintune* (Trumpington), *Hesberie* (unidentified), *Seham* (Soham), *Fuulburne* (Fulbourn), *Theveresham* (Teversham), *Impetune* (Impington), *Pampewrðe* (Pampisford), *Tripelaue* (Triplow), and *Herduuic* (Hardwick) to Ely. Lands in Hunts., Essex, Suffolk, Norfolk, and one hide at *Dodintonam* (Great Doddington, Northants.).   *Lost.*

LE II, c. 62; Chron Rams pp. 116–17. Comments: LE pp. 422–3. See also pp. 31, 61, and 80.

61. N.D.   (992)   GODRIC to Ramsey Abbey. Land at *Grettona* (Girton).   *Lost.*

Chron Rams pp. 65–6. Witnessed by Abbot Brihtnoth of Ely and by Germanus, who acted as abbot of Ramsey for a short period in 992, before moving to Cholsey. Other witnesses included Wulfnoth of *Stowe* (Stowe, Cambs.), Ælfnoth son of Goding, and Leofsige son of Gode, all of whom figure in the *Liber Eliensis*. *Grettona* is wrongly assigned to Gretton, Northants., in the indexes to Chron Rams and LE, but the estate left by Godric is probably the 8½ hides owned by Ramsey at Girton, entered in DB I, fo. 129b.

62. N.D.   (995 × 1001)   Will of Oswi. Estates at *Stevecheswrðe* (Stetchworth), *Merch* (March), *Chertelinge* (Kirtling), *Dullingeham* (Dullingham), and a virgate at *Swafham* (Swaffham) to Ely.   *Lost.*

LE II, c. 67. Oswi, the brother of Ufi (No. 63) and husband of

Leofflæd (No. 68), died at the battle of *Ringmere* in Norfolk in 1010. The terminal dates of his will were established by Dr Blake (LE p. 139 n. 4), and contradict the assignment of the will to the time of Cnut, made elsewhere by Dr Blake (LE p. 423).

63. N.D. (996 × 1001) Will of UFI. The vill of *Wivelinge-ham* (Willingham) and land at *Cotenham* (Cottenham) to Ely.

Lost.

LE II, c. 66, which records that the OE will, which was preserved at Ely, contained the names of Ealdorman Leofsige (of Essex) and Abbot Ælfsige of Ely, whence the outside dates quoted. Ufi was the brother of Oswi (No. 62) and Æðeric (No. 81); possibly he was the Ufi of No. VII (see p. 177).

64. N.D. (1000 × 1002) *Will of ÆLFFLÆD, widow of Ealdorman Brihtnoth. Lands *æt Sægham* (Soham), *æt Dictune* (Fen Ditton), and one hide *æt Ceafle* (Cheveley) to Ely. Lands in Suffolk, Essex, and Herts. ♦W xv.

ECEss No. 34. She was the sister of Æthelflæd of Damerham (No. 58), who left Cheveley to Ælfflæd. See, further, LE II, c. 63. See also p. 61.

(27) N.D. (c.1000 × 1025) †Assignments of property to Thorney Abbey by Ely Abbey. Ely estates mentioned include *Thiutforda* (Thetford), *Middeltune* (Milton), *Lindune* (Linton), *Strætham* (Stretham), *Horningesige* (Hornsey), *Hafucestune* (Hauxton), [*M*]*eldeburnan* (Melbourn), and *Fordham* (Fordham). Estates in Hunts. ♦R App II, No. IX.

Miss Robertson indexes *Thiutforda* as Thetford in Norfolk, but the Cambridgeshire Thetford would seem to be the correct identification, for this estate was Ely property TRE. I take the meaning of the MS. to be that Ely bought 3 plots of ground at Thetford from Thorney for . . . ores and 12 pence. See also p. 32.

65. N.D. (1002 × c.1016) LEOFWINE son of Æthulf to Ely. Land at *Estereia* (Eastrea) and *Cothenham* (Cottenham), the third part of *Withleseya* (Whittlesey), and fisheries at *Upstaue* (Starnea Dyke). Lands in Suffolk, Essex, and London.

Lost.

LE II, c. 60; ECEss No. 35. For Leofwine, see No. 16. His gifts to Ely were by an OE charter witnessed by Archbishop Wulfstan of York (accession 1002) and Abbot Ælfsige of Ely (died c.1016), whence the outside dates for the charter. At Whittlesey Ely held 2 out of a total of 6 hides in 1066 (DB), the remainder being held by Thorney. See also p. 62.

(28) N.D.   (c.1007)   Will of ÆLFWARU. A toft called *Chinnora* (Over Chain), and part of the estate of *Elesworth* (Elsworth), together with the church there, of which she was patron, to Ramsey. Lands in Norfolk, Suffolk, Hunts., and Herts.   *Lost.*

> Chron Rams pp. 84–5; LE II, c. 61. The Ramsey entry reads like a Latin abstract of an OE will. See CAS LVI–LVII, 1964, p. 63, for the identification of *Chinnora*. See also pp. 32, 62, and 80.

66. 1008   *ÆTHELRED, king of all Britain, to Ely. 7 "cassati" at *duo Lintunum* (Great and Little Linton), free of all but the three common dues. Land in Essex.   K 725.

> LE II, c. 77; ECEss No. 41. The surviving version of this charter lacks boundary clause and witness list. Linton did not survive as Ely property.

67. 1015   †Will of the Ætheling ÆTHELSTAN. *Mordune* (Morden) to the Old Minster, Winchester. Estates in East Anglia and many other counties.   ♦W xx.

> OS Facs I, 18; III, 38. Morden is said to have been leased to Æthelstan by his father, King Æthelred. See also p. 63.

68. N.D.   (1017 × 1035)   *Will of LEOFFLÆD. *Belesham* (Balsham) to Ely Abbey, together with the reversion of *Stevechesworðe* (Stetchworth), which her two daughters Ælfwen and Æthelswyth now hold. Land in Suffolk.   LE II, c.88.

> Leofflæd was the wife of Oswi (No. 62) and daughter of Ealdorman Brihtnoth (No. 25). Her will took the form of a letter to King Cnut written in triplicate, of which one version was kept at Ely, one at the king's treasury, and the third with Leofflæd. Upon her death she was buried at Ely, to which abbey Æthelswyth then released her life interest in Stetchworth, receiving in return the lease of *Coveneia* (Coveney), where she retired with her maidens to work at embroidery and weaving. See also p. 62.

69. N.D.   (1017 × 1049)   Will of LUSTWINE. *Dittune* (Fen

Ditton), *Burch parva* (Borough Green), *Westune* (Weston Colville), and *Cnopwelle* (Knapwell), except for half a hide there, to Ely Abbey. Lands in Suffolk and Essex.   *Lost.*

LE II, c. 89; ECEss No. 48. Dated after the will of Leofflæd (No. 68), and before that of Thurstan (No. 72). Cf. W pp. 189–90. See also p. 63.

70. (1020 × 1034)   TURKIL to Ramsey Abbey. The west part of *Ellesworth* (Elsworth).   Chron Rams pp. 129–34.

The story of this forfeiture is recorded in a Latin abstract of an OE law memorandum, which commences with the statement that after his accession King Cnut shared out the property of some English noblemen among his Danish followers (cf. Stenton p. 401 n. 1). One of these was Turkil, a man of high birth; he received among other places an estate at West Elsworth. His wife murdered her stepson and buried him secretly at *Lolleswrthe* (Lolworth). Turkil was an accessary to the crime, which was discovered. The king ordered an investigation and the body was found; Turkil surrendered the estate as part of his penance. The event occurred during the abbacy of Æthelstan and the episcopacy of Æthelric, whence the outside dates. It is conceivable that Turkil was in fact Turkil the Tall, who was present at *Assandun*, became earl of East Anglia, and was banished by Cnut in 1021, for what reason is unknown. The identification is accepted without discussion by Professor F. Barlow, who describes in some detail the legal procedure leading up to this transaction.—*The English Church, 1000–1066*, London, 1963, pp. 273–4. See, further, No. 325.

71. 1022   *CNUT, king of all the English, to Abbot Leofric, at the petition of Bishop Ælfwine, Abbot Leofric, and the brothers of Ely, in exchange for the wooded estate at *Chefle* (Cheveley). *Dittune* (Wood Ditton).   K 734.

LE II, c. 82. The surviving version of the charter has no bounds, and the hidation of the estates exchanged is not given. See, further, LE p. 417.

(33) N.D.   (1029 × 1035)   *Abbot LEOFSIGE of Ely, with the consent of King Cnut, settles the food-rents due to the monastery from its estates in Cambs., Hunts., Essex, Norfolk, and Suffolk. Those from Cambridgeshire comprise: *Stapelford* (Stapleford), *Havechestune* (Hauxton), *Neutune*

(Newton), *Thoftes* (Toft), *Cotenham* (Cottenham), and *Wive-lingeham* (Willingham), which each provide one week's food farm; *Sceldford* (Shelford), *Tripelaue* (Triplow), *Meldeburne* (Melbourn), *Grantedene* (Little Gransden), *Dittune* (Fen Ditton), *Horningeseie* (Horningsea), *Stevech-worde* (Stetchworth), and *Belesham* (Balsham), which each provide two weeks' food farm; and *Suefham* (Swaffham Prior) which provides three days' farm.   Lost.

LE II, c. 84. See also pp. 34, 65, and 81.

(35) N.D.   (1042 × 1057)   *EDWARD, king of the English, to Ely Abbey. Confirmation of estates, including, in Cambridgeshire, the Isle [of Ely], with its two hundreds; and outside the Isle, *Suafham, Horningeseie, Dittune, Havechestune, Neutune, Stapelford, Sceldford, Triplaue, Meldeburne, Erninge-ford, Grantedene, Stevechwrde, Belesham, Fuelburne, Theveres-ham, Westlai, Trumpintune, Wratinge, Sneilewelle, Dittune, Hardwic, Middeltune, Impetune, Cotenham*, and *Wivelingeham*, and a quarter of all the fines in the province of *Grantecester* (Cambridge), and land in the same town. The gift of sake and soke over all Ely lands is confirmed. Land in Hunts., Suffolk, Norfolk, Essex, and Herts.   K 907.

LE II, c. 92. The Cambridgeshire estates are: Swaffham Prior, Horningsea, Wood Ditton, Hauxton, Newton, Stapleford, Great Shelford, Triplow, Melbourn, Armingford (hundred name), Little Gransden, Stetchworth, Balsham, Fulbourn, Teversham, Westley Waterless, Trumpington, West Wratting, Snailwell, Fen Ditton, Hardwick, Milton, Impington, Cottenham, and Willingham. Of these, only Westley Waterless does not appear in other pre-Conquest records of Ely estates. See also pp. 34, 67, and 84.

72. N.D.   (1043 × 1045)   *Will of THURSTAN. The estate at *Cnapwelle* (Knapwell) to Ely, except land held by Ordeah and the monk Æthelric; *Westone* (Weston Colville) to Æthelswyth, with reversion to Ely, except the land which Sæwine holds, which is to go to the village church; *Bidicheseye* (Bottisham) to be sold; the land at *Burg* (Borough Green) to Ulfketel, if he should live longer, except half a hide at *Westle* (Westley Waterless) and a hide at *Dullingham*

(Dullingham), which he grants to his servant Viking. Land in Essex, Norfolk, and Suffolk.   ♦W XXXI.

♦EHD II, pp. 837–8. The testator is called *vir strenuus heing Thurstanus filius Wyne* in BBL; for Wine see ECEss No. 48. *Westone* is identified in ECEss I, p. 28. *Bidicheseye*, previously unidentified, can hardly be other than Bottisham, which lies next to Weston, Westley, Borough, and Dullingham. The name means "the *eye* (piece of dry ground in the fen, cf. PN Elements I, p. 147) by the dykes," the first two elements being identical with those of Biddick, Durham (*Bidich* c.1190; cf. Ekwall p. 40), the dykes in our example being the River Cam and its tributaries. The identification rests on sound topographical considerations, which must override any etymological objections to the sound change –i– → –o–. In the case of Dinnington, Somerset, the change –i– → –u– → –o– is recorded (*Dinnitone, Dunintone* DB; *Doniton* 1201, *Dunington* 1254 Ass); the change in the reverse direction –o– → –i– is more common. But it is not difficult to conceive that the original element *Bidiches* was confused at an early date with a lost personal name *Beoduc* (cf. Ekwall p. 52), and that "Bidiches eye," later "Bidiches ham," and "Boduc's ham," ran together as alternative forms of the name, possibly for centuries, until the latter form gained the ascendancy. See also pp. 70 and 85.

(41) N.D. (c.1044)   Grant in reversion by WULFWINE the son of Ælfwine to Ramsey Abbey, in consideration of a life lease of other lands. An estate at *Abbintune* (Abington). Lands in Hunts., Suffolk, and Essex.   *Lost.*

Chron Rams pp. 152–3. See also pp. 36 and 70.

73. 1049   *Writ of King EDWARD to Westminster, granting to the abbey the estates of Datchworth and Watton (both in Herts.), as fully and as completely as Ælfwynn the nun held them and committed them to Abbot Edwin and the monks, and as King Edgar granted them to the monastery, and as they were adjudged in the assembly of the nine shires at *Wendelbury* (Wandlebury).   ♦H 79.

A nun named Ælfwynn became abbess of Barking in the mid-eleventh century (ECEss II, p. 6), but there is no evidence to identify her with the Ælfwynn of King Edward's writ. The assembly of the nine shires cannot be dated more closely than 957 × 1049, the former date being that of the accession of King Edgar to Mercia. Dr Harmer (*op. cit.*, pp. 503–4) does not offer a definite location for *Wendelbury*, but it can hardly be other than the Iron-Age hill fort near Cambridge; see No. 54.

(47) N.D.   (C.1062)   ***King EDWARD confirms the estates of Ramsey Abbey. Lands in Lincs., Hunts., Beds., Norfolk, Suffolk, Northants., and Herts.   K 809.

The Cambridgeshire estates include those mentioned in the spurious charter of Edgar (No. 18), together with Girton, the east part of Elsworth, Bottisham, Over, Knapwell, and Burwell. See also pp. 39, 77, 95, and 106.

CHAPTER III

THE EARLY CHARTERS OF
SUFFOLK

(48) (895) ****ALFRED, king of the Anglo-Saxons, to Bishop Burric of Rochester. Land at *Ffrekeham* (Freckenham), in Suffolk, free of all royal dues. Land in Cambs.   CS 571.

R. Rainbird Clarke, *East Anglia*, London, 1960, p. 165, quotes this charter as the earliest evidence for the division of East Anglia into Norfolk and Suffolk; but the only authentic evidence for this division earlier than the eleventh century is No. 49, which shows that although there was a single bishopric for the whole of East Anglia in the mid-tenth century, it had a Suffolk centre at Hoxne as well as a Norfolk centre at North Elmham, cf. W p. 102. (The evidence presented by S. E. Rigold in *Medieval Archaeology*, VI–VII, 1962–3, pp. 67–8, for the existence of two separate dioceses in East Anglia at the beginning of the ninth century appears to me to be inconclusive.) See also p. 40.

(49) N.D.   (942 × 951)   *Will of THEODRED, bishop of London. The estate at *Myndham* (Mendham) to his sister's son Osgot, except that the minster and one hide of land there shall go to the church; the estate at *Scotford* and *Mydicaham* (Shotford and Mettingham) to the community at Mendham church; estates at *Sulham* (Syleham), *Isestede* (Instead in Weybread), *Chikeringe* (Chickering), *Aysfeld* (Ashfield Green), and *Wrtinham* (Wortham), together with the small pieces of land (? strips) attached to them, are granted to Osgot; estates at *Horham* (Horham) and *Elyngtone* (Athelington) to the community at St Ethelbert's church at Hoxne; the estate at *Luthinglond* (Lothingland) to his sister's son Offa and his brother: half the men there and at Mendham are to be freed; the estates at *Bertune* (Barton), *Rucham* (Rougham), and *Pakenham* (Pakenham) to his kinsman Osgot, Eadulf's son; the estates at *Newetune* (Nowton), *Horninggeshæthe* (Horningsheath), *Ikewrthe* (Ickworth), and

Wepstede (Whepstead) to the community at St Edmund's church (Bury St Edmunds) for his soul; an estate at *Wald-ringfeld* (Waldringfield) and the house which he bought at *Gypeswich* (Ipswich) to his sister's son Osgot; an estate at *Wrtham* (Wortham) to Wulfstan; ten pounds to be distributed for his soul at his episcopal demesne at Hoxne; and the stock there is to be divided, half for the minster, and half for his soul; and as much as he found on the estate is to be left on it, but the men are to be freed, for his soul. Lands in Essex, Cambs., Norfolk, Middlesex, and Surrey.

♦W 1.

Wrtinham, previously unidentified, can safely be located at Wortham. A second estate there occurs later in the text, under the name *Wrtham*. Ekwall (p. 511) states: "in early sources *worþ* and *worþig(n)* often interchange for the same name." Several of the BBL lists state that Bury St Edmunds subsequently exchanged Ickworth with a certain *miles* for Elveden. They also claim that Theodred's estate at Barton descended to Bury; a certain Edwin *dives* gave another part, and the remainder was acquired by Eric *prepositus* TRE. See also pp. 40 and 79.

74. 945   *EDMUND, king of the English, ruler of the other peoples round about, to Bury St Edmunds. Grant of privileges.   CS 808.

♦Lord Francis Hervey, *Corolla Sancti Eadmundi*, 1907, pp. 589–93. The basic formulae of this charter agree closely with those found in contemporary land-books, but in place of the usual donation of "*x* hides at *y*" is substituted a statement that the land surrounding the monastery is to be free of all tribute, such payment being rendered solely to the monastery. This appears to represent exemption from the three common dues—a rare privilege—together with exemption from the payment of taxes into the royal fisc; when a national tax is levied (based on the hidage) the inhabitants are to pay their levy to the monastery, and not to the king. The same privilege is granted, in more specific terms, in the charter of Cnut (No. 86). Apart from the phrases dealing with this privilege, the only unusual feature of the charter is the word *indeclinabiliter* after Edmund's name and title in the witness list; this appears in no other charter of Edmund, but is a regular feature of the charters of his successor Eadred. The indiction in the charter is correct for the year of grace, and the witness list is compatible with the date, the only suspicious name being that of Ælfgifu, Edmund's queen, who is usually thought to have died in 944. However, this date is derived from a passage in Æthelweard which has a rather muddled chronology, and which could be interpreted equally well as suggesting the year 946 for Ælfgifu's death. In any case, it is likely that Ælfgifu's name is a late addition to the witness list; it is not present in most of the surviving texts; cf. A. Campbell, *The Battle of Brunanburh*, London, 1938, p. 51; *The Chronicle of Æthelweard*, 1962, p. xliii; *Encomium Emmæ Reginæ*, R. Hist. Soc., 1949, p. 62 n. 2.

Ever since the time of W. H. Stevenson, the charter has been considered as spurious because of the special privileges it purports to give to the abbey.—Lobel p. 2 n. 7; H p. 144 n. 1. The arguments against it, however, do not strike me as conclusive.

The charter incorporates a boundary clause giving the limits of the area of special jurisdiction granted to the abbey. Whatever the authenticity of the remainder of the charter, there can be no doubt that this boundary clause was drawn up in the OE period; the only point at issue is whether it is contemporary with the date claimed for the remainder of the charter, or has been borrowed from a later statement of the bounds, drawn up after the refoundation of the monastery by Cnut. The former hypothesis seems the more likely.

In the absence of any detailed place-name study of the town, it may be considered that Mrs Lobel, *op. cit.*, p. 3, was not over-cautious in refusing to offer locations for the boundary marks in this charter. In fact, however, with the aid of her map, *ibid.*, p. 200, it is not difficult to establish beyond reasonable doubt that the OE bounds were identical with those of the medieval *banleuca* of the abbey, which coincides with the modern borough boundary, except that the parishes of Westley and Fornham All Saints, which now lie within the borough, were originally outside the *banleuca*. The text used in the following account is taken from the version of the charter printed in Dugdale III, p. 137, and Memorials I, pp. 340–1; this is far superior to the perambulation in CS 808, which omits several words, including a whole passage describing one landmark (no. 6), and contains some important spelling errors. We must also accept the extraordinary fact that whoever drew up the bounds had only the haziest notion of where the points of the compass lay in relation to the territory; he consistently repeats a 90° error clockwise, so that for "south" in the bounds we must read "west," and for "east" we must read "south." This is highly unusual in an OE boundary description, but no other explanation will fit the facts.

We are now ready to start the perambulation, which may be followed on the 2½-in. OS sheet TL 86—

1. First south by the eight trees.

This is described as *terra apud Excetros* in the *Pinchbeck Register*, I, p. 354. The reference is to a stone boundary cross known as *eyght cross*, lying, according to a reference temp. Ed. I, *iuxta acquam que venit de Saxham*, which must be the River Linnet; cf. John Gage, *History of Thingoe Hundred*, London, 1838, p. 475. In her map Mrs Lobel placed the cross rather too far to the west; the correct position appears to be grid reference 839635, the east end of the stretch of the river which formed the *banleuca* boundary at this point. Note that the starting-point lies w. of the town, and not s. as given in the bounds.

2. Up by Ealhmund's trees.

Proceeding up river to the point where the boundary turns sharply N. (837635).

3. And so to Osulf's lea.

A water-meadow beside the river (837636).

4. Then to the right of many hills.

The *banleuca* boundary proceeds N. up a hill, crossing the 300-ft contour; from the water tower at the top several hills can be seen lying to the w., although the area is now being built over (838641).

5. Then up *Hamarlunda*.

Continuing in the same direction, first downhill to cross the Risby road, then following Beeton's Footpath up along the w. wall of the military barracks. *Hamarlunda* is derived from ON *hamarr, lundr* "a small wood or grove containing a smithy."—PN Elements I, p. 231; II, pp. 27–8. The name recurs as *Hamerlound* in a deed of c. 1260–70 (Bodleian Suffolk Charter, no. 84), which shows that it was by then an open field divided into strips.[1] It lay somewhere w. of Tayfen meadows (844655), and it is no doubt

---

[1] In this charter, Richard son of Katherine of St Edmunds releases Prior Robert and the brothers of the hospital of St Peter outside the gate of Ryseby in the town of Bury St Edmunds from the obligation to pay an annual rent of 6d for a small piece of land. The context is as follows: ". . . *de una acra terre arrabilis In Hamerlound Jacente inter terram Johannis le Jeuene ex parte una et terram galfridi sprot ex altera et abbutat ad unum capud super terram luce filii Johannis et ad aliud capud super terram prædicti hospitalis . . .*"

merely a coincidence that this is near the site of the Northgate Iron Works. See further, Fo p. 175.

6. To four *hogas*.

Fo p. 175 n. 4 notes that this probably represents ON *haugr* = hill, hillock, mound. The four mounds were at 845657, the point where the bounds turn sharply w. In medieval times this was the site of *Henhowe Mill*, which took its name from *Thingoe*, the assembly mound of the eight and a half hundreds in Saxon times. The second element of *Thingoe* is clearly derived from one of the four *haugr* mentioned at this point in the bounds.

7. So to the way to *Litlandtune*.

The "little tun" was Little Fornham, which according to BBL lists was also given to Bury by King Edmund. The road is reached at a point near Babwell Friary (851659).

8. Then over the river.

The boundary runs along the River Lark for a short distance, then crosses it (853660).

9. Following the way to Barton valley (*Bertunedene*).

This appears in the *Pinchbeck Register*, I, pp. 353–4, as (*in*) *dala de Berton*. The road to Barton Shrub and East Barton is named *Berton Weye* in a rental of c.1334, and *Barton grene way* in Thomas Warren's map of 1791. Grid reference 872652.

10. And so eastwards to *Hole(e)gate*.

ON *gata* here means a road, and Bury St Edmunds still has North, South, East, and West gate streets, together with Risbygate, Churchgate, and Abbey gate. If we amend the direction given in the charter bounds from E. to S., we arrive at Rougham Road (earlier *Wolpetweye*). This runs near *Eldohouse* Farm; in the fifteenth century the name was *Holdhawe*, the site of a boundary cross, but ultimately this name goes back to *Aldehage* c.1182 (*Kalendar of Abbot Samson*, p. 86), so that it cannot, as some have thought, easily be identified with *Holegate* in the charter. Whether or not there is an etymological connection between Eldohouse and Holegate, there is little doubt of the topographical identity (876635).

11. A furlong eastwards to *Bromleage*.

The wood, now called Broom Plantation, lies a furlong to the *south* of the road (877628).

1 2. Then south to *Niwantune meaduwe*.

Amending the direction once more, the *banleuca* bounds run westwards, crossing the River Lark, to the N. end of the grounds of Nowton (formerly Newton) Court, at 866625.

The bounds do not return to their starting-point, and it is possible that a passage has dropped out of the text here.

(50) N.D.   (946 × 951)   *Will of ÆLFGAR, ealdorman [of Essex]. Estates at *Cokefeld* (Cockfield) and *Lauenham* (Lavenham) to his daughter Æthelflæd, for their two souls, and those of her mother and brother; Cockfield is to descend afterwards to Bury St Edmunds, and Lavenham to Æthelflæd's child, if she have any, or else to [the community at] Stoke[-by-Nayland], for the souls of his ancestors; the estate at *Illey* (Eleigh) to his youngest daughter for life, with descent first to Brihtnoth [later ealdorman of Essex], then to their children, then to his daughter Æthelflæd, and then to the community at Christ Church, Canterbury; the woodland at *Aisfeld* (Ashfield) as Eakild himself bought it, to Stoke; the state at *Ryssebroc* (Rushbrook) to his mother if she survives him, and then to Winehelm, if he serve Æthelflæd loyally. Estates in Cambs. and Essex.   ♦W II.

See also p. 40.

75. 962   **WULFSTAN, with the consent and licence of King Edgar, to God and to the church of the holy martyr Edmund in the place called *Beodrichesworth* (Bury St Edmunds). 4 "cassati" at *Palegrave* (Palgrave), exempt from all but bridgework and *fyrd* service.   CS 1084.

Cf. R p. 443. A unique charter, by which a private person (of whom no other record survives) makes a grant couched in the phraseology of contemporary royal diplomas. The land is said to be exempt from all but two of the three common dues, but *burh* work is not mentioned. In surviving versions the bounds of the estate are omitted. The indiction is given as 6, which could be correct if the Caesarean computation was used. The witness list is compatible with the date, and the forms of subscription of the bishops are noteworthy; they resemble those appearing in CS 1112, a rare Yorkshire charter of the same indiction. That the Palgrave charter is modelled on a contemporary text cannot be doubted, but it is not possible in our present state of knowledge to pronounce with any assurance on its authenticity.

76. 962 †EDGAR, ruler of all Britain, to Æthelflæd. 7 "mansae" at *Ceorleswyrðe* (Chelsworth), free of all but the three common dues. CS 1082.

BM Facs III, 25. The recipient is Æthelflæd of Damerham, the daughter of Ealdorman Ælfgar of Essex, and second wife of King Edmund. She gave the reversion of Chelsworth to Bury St Edmunds in her will (No. 58). The bounds of this estate have as yet not been worked out.

77. 970 *EDGAR, king of all Britain, to Ely Abbey, at the request of his wife Ælfthryth. 10 "cassati" at *Stoche* (Stoke, near Ipswich), free of all but the three common dues.
CS 1269.

LE II, c. 39. The *Liber* states that the property included two mills located on the south side of the estate, and that Bishop Æthelwold gave the king 100 (mancuses) of gold. The bounds of this estate have not as yet been worked out.

(55) 970 †EDGAR, king of the island of Albion, and ruler of the Scots, Cumbrians, and Britons, and all the regions thereabout, to the monastery at Ely. Lands and privileges, including soke over the five and a half hundreds at *Wicklawan*. Lands in Cambs. and Norfolk.
CS 1266 (Latin) and ♦R XLVIII (OE).

These were the hundreds of Plumesgate, Loes, Wilford, Carlford, and Colneis, and the half hundred of Parham, cf. H. Cam, *Liberties and Communities*, pp. 88–9, and Feud Docs pp. cli–clii. See also pp. 42 and 79.

78. N.D. (975 × 979) Will of GODWINE. The vill of *Hoo* (Hoo) to Ely Abbey. Lost.

LE II, c. 69. Brother of Ælfmær (No. 80). For the DB holding, see VCH *Suffolk*, I, p. 525. See also No. 339.

(58) N.D. (975 × 991) *Will of ÆTHELFLÆD. Estates at *Cohhanfeldæa* (Cockfield), *Cæorlesweorðe* (Chelsworth), *Polstede* (Polstead), *Strætforda* (Stratford St Mary), *Lauanham* (Lavenham), *Byligesdynæ* (Balsdon Hall nr Lavenham), and

Ylmesæton (Elmsett) to Ealdorman Brihtnoth and to her
sister; after their deaths the first two estates are to go to
Bury St Edmunds, the last to Edmund, and the remainder
to (the community at) Stoke(-by-Nayland); *Hwifer(mer)sce*
(Withermarsh) to Stoke; one hide at *Þorpæ* (Thorpe
Morieux) to Hadleigh; *Wæaldingafelda* (Waldingfield) to
her kinswoman Crawe. Lands in Berks., Wilts., Essex,
Herts., and Cambs.   ♦W xiv.

ECEss No. 17; LE ii, c. 64. See also p. 44.

(24) N.D.   (989)   †Will of ÆLFHELM POLGA. *Hwipstede*
(Whepstead), and *Wealtune* (? Walton near Felixstowe) to
his son Ælfgar for his lifetime, and then to wherever (i.e.
whichever religious community) he pleases, for the souls
of them both; confirmation that he has given *Strætford*
(? Stratford St Andrew) to his wife, as part of her *morgengifu*; the estate at *Trostingtune* (Troston) to be divided
among his three brothers, except that Ælfwold is granted
that which Æthelric had; and half the stud there is to go
to his wife, and half to his riding companions; and his wife
is to have half the woodland there, and his daughter the
other half. He grants *Byornham* (Barnham) to Wulfmær.
Lands in Cambs., Essex, Herts., Beds., and Hunts.
                                                      ♦W xiii.

Just before making this will, Ælfhelm made a grant of Potton,
Beds., to his goldsmith (R lxxi), which was witnessed by Æthelric of *Hernicwelle*, hitherto unidentified. This must be Herringswell, near Barnham and Troston. See also pp. 31 and 45.

79. 991   ***Ealdorman BRIHTNOTH [of Essex] to Christ
Church, Canterbury. *Hæðleh* (Hadleigh) and *Illaleh* (Monks
Eleigh). Land in Essex.   MS. Lambeth 1212, p. 326.

Texts: Twysden, *Decem Scriptores*, col. 2223, l. 60–col. 2224,
l. 2; Essex Arch. Soc. *Trans.*, xxx, p. 175 n. 1. Discussions:
Palgrave, *The Rise and Progress of the English Commonwealth*, 1921
edn, Part ii, p. 314; W p. 107; R p. 430; ECEss i, p. 18; Dugdale
i, p. 96. The Chronicle of Gervase of Canterbury assigns the gift
of Hadleigh to Ælfflæd, the widow of Brihtnoth, saying that it
was given "with the consent of King Æthelred," but assigning to it
the impossible date 835.

(25) N.D. (991) Will of Ealdorman Brihtnoth. *Acholt* (Occold) and *Fineberge* (Finborough) to Ely. Land in Hunts., Cambs., Norfolk, Essex, and Northants. *Lost.*

LE ii, c. 62; Chron Rams pp. 116–17. For the DB holdings, see VCH *Suffolk*, i, p. 519, and IE pp. 153 (Occold) and 157 (Finborough). See also pp. 31, 46, and 80.

80. N.D. (996 × 1001) Will of Ælfmær. *Hecham* (Hitcham) to Ely. *Lost.*

LE ii, c. 70. Dated before the death of Bishop Æthelstan of Elmham, and during the abbacy of Ælfsige. See also No. 339.

81. N.D. (c.1000) Will of Æthelric. His son Æðelmær is to become a monk at Ely, and with him is to be given *terram calciatoriam* called *Ceaddeberi* (Chedburgh). *Lost.*

LE ii, c. 68, which states that the OE will was kept at Ely. Æðeric was the brother of Oswi (No. 62) and Ufi (No. 63). For the DB holding, see VCH *Suffolk*, i, pp. 521–2, and IE p. 155. *Terram calciatoriam* translates OE *scoh land*, "shoe land," i.e. land used to provide footwear for the monks (EHR lxxiv, 1959, pp. 664–5); the leather probably came from cattle on the estate. By the twelfth century the name *solanda* was applied only to small demesne estates which were owned by the canons of St Paul's *ad prebendam*. Cf. ECEss ii, pp. 38–9, and *Notes and Queries*, N.S., iv, 1957, pp. 327–9.

(64) N.D. (1000 × 1002) *Will of Ælfflæd, widow of Ealdorman Brihtnoth. Lands (æt) *Ylmsætun* (Elmsett), (æt) *Bucyshealæ* (Buxhall), *Stredfordæ* (Stratford St Mary), *Fresantun* (Freston), *Wiswyþetun* (Wiston), *Lauanham* (Lavenham), *Bylesdyne* (Balsdon Hall), *Polstyde* (Polstead), *Wifærmyrsc* (Withermarsh), *Illanlege* (Monks Eleigh), *Cæorlesweorþæ* (Chelsworth), *Cochanfelde* (Cockfield), *Hnyddinge* (Nedging nr Bildeston), and (æt) *Wealdingafelda* (Waldingfield). Lands in Essex, Cambs., and Herts. ♦W xv.

ECEss No. 34. The Ely bequests are recited in LE ii, c. 63. The bounds of the 5 hides at Balsdon, and of Withermarsh and Polstead, all of which were given to the religious foundation at Stoke-by-Nayland, are recited at the foot of the will. As yet they have not been worked out in detail. See also p. 47.

82. N.D.   (1001)   Will of Bishop ÆTHELSTAN (of Elmham).
Dringestune (Drinkstone) to Ely.   *Lost.*

   LE II, c. 65.

(65) N.D.   (1002 × C.1016)   LEOFWINE son of Æthulf to Ely.
Cingestune (Kingston), *Undeleia* (Undley) with its fisheries,
land in *Lachingeheðe* (Lakenheath) called *Oswaradala*, and
Glemesford (Glemsford). Land in Cambs., Essex, and London.   *Lost.*

   LE II, c. 60. See also p. 48.

83. N.D.   (C.1005)   *Declaration of a grant by ULFKETEL
to Bury St Edmunds. Estates at *Rikinghale* (Rickinghall),
Rucham (Rougham), *Wlpet* (Woolpit), and *Hildericlea* (Hin-
dercley), and *Redfaresthorpe*, with their produce and men,
and with sake and soke, as he owned them.   ♦R LXXIII.

   This OE record was possibly made at Bury soon after the transaction was completed; it survives only in late copies. For Ulfketel, see No. 86. He is said to have given Redgrave, Felsham,
   Hessett, and part of Bradfield to Bury, according to BBL, which
   date the gifts variously 1005 and 1009. There can be little doubt
   that *Redfaresthorpe*, hitherto unidentified, represents Redgrave,
   which is close to Rickinghall, Rougham, Woolpit, and Hinder-
   cley. The form before the copyist was probably *Redgrafesthorpe*,
   which became *Redgrafe* (No. 108).

84. N.D.   (1006)   ***ÆTHELRED, king of the English, to
Christ Church, Canterbury. Confirmation of estates, in-
cluding *Hædleh* (Hadleigh) and *Illaleh* (Monks Eleigh).
Lands in Kent, Sussex, Surrey, Essex, and Bucks.   K 715.

   ECEss No. 40. The end of the witness list is printed as the last
   four lines of K 847; cf. H p. 453.

(28) N.D.   (C.1007)   Will of ÆLFWARU. *Ratlesdene* (Rattlesden) to Ely. Lands in Cambs., Hunts., Norfolk, and Herts.
                                                           Lost.
   Chron Rams pp. 84–5; LE II, c. 61. See also pp. 32, 48, and 80.

(67) 1015   †Will of the Ætheling ÆTHELSTAN. The estates
which he obtained in East Anglia, and the estate *æt Peaces-*

dele, to his brother Edmund; and each year on the festival of St Ætheldreda (23 June) one day's food rent and 100 pence are to be paid to the community at Ely from the revenue of these estates, for 100 poor people to be fed that day at the monastery. Lands in Cambs., and many other counties. ♦W xx.

It is possible that among these unnamed estates in East Anglia was Lakenheath, which Edmund gave to Thorney (No. 85), but which Edward the Confessor later granted to Ely (No. 35). The estate *æt Peacesdele* was tentatively identified by Mawer with the valley of the Peak, Derbyshire (W p. 171), but Ekwall's suggestion of Pegsdon in Bedfordshire (*op. cit.*, p. 343) is to be preferred, as this is much nearer to Ely. When the Ely food rents were reorganized about 15–20 years after the time of this charter, outlying estates were exempt from the farm (No. 33). See also p. 48.

85. N.D. (1015 × 1016) *EDMUND Ironside to Thorney Abbey. 5 "mansae" *æt Lacingahiðe* (Lakenheath). CS 809.

Edited on p. 198.

(68) N.D. (1017 × 1035) *Will of LEOFFLÆD. Her daughter Leofwaru is to have *Weðeringesete* (Wetheringsett), provided she remains chaste until her marriage. Lands in Cambs. LE ii, c. 88.

Leofwaru married Lustwine (No. 69). See also p. 48.

(69) N.D. (1017 × 1049) Will of LUSTWINE. *Chidingtune* (Kedington) to Ely Abbey. Lands in Essex and Cambs.

Lost.

LE ii, c. 89. See also p. 48.

86. N.D. (1022 × 1023) *CNUT, king of the whole island of Britain, to Bury St Edmunds. The monastery at *Beadrichesworthe* shall always be inhabited by monks, and free from domination by the bishops of that shire; the monks are to elect their abbot freely, as granted by King Edmund. When *censum Danis* is levied, either for ships or for arms, the inhabitants of Bury are to pay their share to the monas-

tery, for its own use. He grants the fish due to him annually by way of fine, and the fishery which Ulfketel had in *Welle* (Upwell and Outwell, Cambs. and Norfolk), and the profits of justice from all the vills belonging to the monastery, now or in the future. He confirms the queen's annual gift of 4,000 eels to the monastery, which was rendered to her from the *villa* called *Lakingheðe* (Lakenheath).   K 735.

Memorials, I, pp. 342–3. Comment: H pp. 433–4; C. W. Goodwin, *Norfolk Archaeology*, IV, 1855, pp. 93–117; Lobel p. 5; Feudal Docs pp. 50, 59, 62; *Kalendar of Abbot Samson*, Camden 3rd, LXXXIV, 1954, pp. xxv–xxvi.

This charter is generally considered spurious, but at our present state of knowledge this is an unsafe assumption, at least as far as the Latin text is concerned. There is no authority for the date 1028 claimed for the charter in a late entry in the margin of a copy of Marianus Scotus (*Memorials*, I, p. 342), and as the charter contains no dating clause, it must be dated from the witness list. It is witnessed by Bishop Ælfwine of Elmham, whose predecessor Ælfgar died on 25 December 1021 (ASC (D)). Another witness is Wulfstan, archbishop of York, who died on 28 May 1023 (D. Whitelock, *Sermo Lupi ad Anglos*, p. 7 n. 2). The remaining witnesses are all compatible with these outside dates. One of them, Archbishop Æthelnoth of Canterbury, was in Rome on 7 October 1022 (ASC (D)), and King Cnut himself was also out of the country for part of this period.

It is worthy of comment that the bishops and earls in this witness list are identical with those of No. 125, King Cnut's foundation charter to St Benedict at Holme; moreover, they appear in precisely the same order. If these two charters are authentic (and on one has yet proved otherwise), then they were witnessed on the same occasion. The close connection between the foundation of the two houses is further brought out in the Holme Register (BM Cotton Galba E. I, fo. 7b; cf. Dugdale III, p. 135). Holme was established before Bury, which was colonized from it. Although the monks are said to have been placed at Bury by Cnut in 1020, at the petition of Queen Emma and of Earl Turkil (who was banished on 10 November 1021), the erection of the monastic church there could not have started before 1022, if the Holme Register is to be believed, for the direction of the work was placed in the hands of Bishop Ælfwine of Elmham, who could not have been consecrated until that year. It is noteworthy that the date suggested by the witness lists is one which means that (if authentic) these two charters were drawn up soon after the death of the diocesan bishop; on this, see V. H. Galbraith, 'The East Anglian See and the Abbey of Bury St Edmunds', EHR XL, 1925, pp. 222–8.

87. N.D. (1022 × 1029) *The Lady GODIVA to Ely. The land of *Berchinges* (Barking), which she had inherited from her parents. LE II, c. 83.

For Godiva or Godgifu, see ECEss I, p. 23.

(33) N.D. (1029 × 1035) *Abbot LEOFSIGE of Ely, with the consent of King Cnut, settles the food rents due to the monastery from its estates in Cambs., Hunts., Essex, Norfolk, and Suffolk. Those from Suffolk comprise *Herdherst* (Hartest), *Drenchestune* (Drinkstone), *Necdinge* (Nedging), and *Wederingesete* (Wetheringsett) which each provide one week's food farm; and *Ratelesdene* (Rattlesden), *Hecham* (Hitcham), and *Berechinge* (Barking), which each provide two weeks' food farm. *Lost.*

LE II, c. 84. See also pp. 34, 49, and 81.

88. N.D. (1035 × 1038) †Will of Bishop ÆLFRIC II of Elmham. *Wilrincgawerþa* (Worlingworth) to Bury St Edmunds as he had received it from King Cnut; *Mulantune* (Moulton) to Sibriht; fenland worth a thousand pence to the priests at Hoxne. Land in Norfolk. ♦W XXVI.

BM Facs IV, No. 21. Miss Harmer (H p. 549) establishes the dates of the bishops named Ælfric at Elmham as follows: Ælfric I, temp. King Edgar; Ælfric II, c. 1023 × Christmas 1038; Ælfric III, 1039 × 1042–3. Since this Ælfric says in his will that he acquired his estates in the time of King Cnut, he is presumably Ælfric II, for he is unlikely to have obtained these estates before he became bishop. See also p. 82.

89. N.D. (1035 × 1044) *Will of LEOFGIFU. Hintlesham to Bury St Edmunds, except that Æthelsige is to have every third acre in the wood there; the estate at *Bromforde* (Bramford) to her kinsman Ælfric, Wihtgar's son; *Willauesham* (Willesham) to Stigand; *Stonham* (Stonham) and *Waldingfeld* (Waldingfield) to her brother's son Æthelric; *Hagele*

C

(Haughley) to her daughter Ælfflæd; the "reeve land" at Stonham to Æthelmær; land at Waldingfield to her reeve Godric. Lands in Essex and Norfolk.   ♦W XXIX.

ECEss No. 47. See also p. 82.

90. N.D.   (before 1038)   *Will of THURKETEL of Palgrave. *Palegrave* (Palgrave) and half of *Witingham* (Whittingham near Fressingfield) to Bury St Edmunds; the other half of Whittingham to the bishop (of Elmham); *Wingefeld* (Wingfield) to his brother's sons, Ulfketel and Thurketel; 15 acres and a homestead at Palgrave to Leofcwen; land at *Thrandestone* (Thrandeston) to Osbeorn. Land in Norfolk.
                                                                    ♦W XXIV.

BBL lists date the gift 1013, and call Thurketel "*nobilis heros.*" See LT p. 62. See also p. 82.

91. N.D.   (c.1040)   *Agreement concerning an estate at *Playford* (Playford). Stigand, the owner, leases the estate to his priest Ælfgar for his lifetime, and after Ælfgar's death it is to revert to Stigand, if he survives. Upon the death of both of them, it is to pass without controversy to (Bury) St Edmunds, with its men and produce. And he (i.e. Ælfgar) can neither lose it by lawsuit, nor forfeit it.   ♦R XCII.

For Stigand, see R p. 424. He is called *Lauerd* in BBL, probably to distinguish him from Bishop Stigand. The gift is dated 1039–40 in BBL. This estate did not descend to Bury; TRE it was held by Godwine, son of Alfer, under Edward's queen (VCH *Suffolk*, I, p. 454). It is tempting to identify the DB *Alfer* with the Ælfgar of this charter.

92. N.D.   (1040 × 1042)   ***King HARTHACNUT to Bury St Edmunds. Confirmation of King Cnut's charter to the monastery, and grant of additional privileges.   K 761.

Facsimile: Hervey, *Corolla Sancti Eadmundi*, 1907, facing p. 598. H pp. 434–5.

93. N.D.   (1040 × 1042)   †THURKETEL to Bury St Edmunds. The land at *Culeforde* (Culford) which was his own, with men and produce and with sake and soke; the whole of the

land at *Wridewellan* (Wordwell); and the land at *Gyxeweorðe* (Ixworth), with men and produce. ♦R XCIII.

BM Facs IV, No. 44. Distinguished in BBL from other men of the same name by the description "*dreing inclitus.*"

94. N.D. (C.1040 × 1057) *Will of EDWIN. 4 acres to the church of *Blitleford* (Blyford). Land in Norfolk.

♦W XXXIII.

Dated before King Edward's confirmation charter to Ely (No. 35), if this is accepted as a genuine record (cf. LE pp. 161, 147). The earliest date cannot be established. Edwin was still alive in 1066 (cf. RE p. 291 n. 5). He is called "*vir gloriosus lauerd Edwinus*" in BBL. See also p. 83.

95. N.D. (1042 × 1043) *Writ of King EDWARD in favour of Bury St Edmunds. Abbot Ufi is to have the monastery there, which is to retain unaltered the freedom granted to it by Kings Cnut and Harthanut; and he forbids any bishop to appropriate to himself anything therein. ♦H 8.

Dr Harmer concludes: "the authenticity of the final passage in the writ must remain an open question."

(35) N.D. (1042 × 1057) *EDWARD, king of the English, to Ely Abbey. Grant of estate at *Lachingeheðe* (Lakenheath), and confirmation of estates and jurisdiction, including in Suffolk: *Hertest* (Hartest), *Glamesford* (Glemsford), *Hecham* (Hitcham), *Ratelesdene* (Rattlesden), *Drinchestune* (Drinkstone), *Neddinge* (Nedging), *Berchinges* (Barking), *Bercham* (Barham), *Weðeringesete* (Wetheringsett), *Livremere* (Livermere), *Achold* (Occold), the 5½ hundreds of *Wichelaue* (Wicklaw), *Sutburne* (Sudbourn), *Meltune* (Melton), *Kingestune* (Kingston), *Hoo* (Hoo), *Stoche* (Stoke near Ipswich), *Debham* (Debenham), *Brithwelle* (Brightwell), *Oddebruge* (Woodbridge), and *Brandune* (Brandon). Estates in Hunts., Cambs., Norfolk, Essex, and Herts. K 907.

LE II, c. 92. Of these estates, the acquisition of Melton is not recorded elsewhere. See also pp. 34, 50, and 84.

96. N.D. (1042 × 1065) King EDWARD in favour of Bury St Edmunds. Writs granting sake and soke and commendation

over freemen at Wetherden, Harleston, and Onehouse.
Lost.

So in DB II, fo. 360*b*; cf. VCH *Suffolk*, I, p. 496, and H pp. 441, 545. The number of writs is not recorded. They were in the possession of the abbey at the time of the Domesday Inquest.

97. N.D.   (1042 × 1065)   King EDWARD in favour of Eadric of Laxfield. Writ restoring to him the lands he had owned before his outlawry, and granting that whosoever of his freemen under commendation may choose to return to him, by his grant they may return. Land in Norfolk. *Lost.*

DB II, fo. 310*b*; cf. VCH *Suffolk*, I, p. 450; EHR LIX, p. 303; H p. 545. Eadric was perhaps the greatest landowner in Suffolk TRE, next to the king and the abbey of Bury. His estates were mainly in the N. and E. of the county. Most of them passed to William Malet after the Conquest, and were used by him to found the honour of Eye.—VCH *Suffolk*, I, p. 395. See also p. 84.

98. N.D.   (1042 × 1065)   The abbot of Bury St Edmunds to Edith. Lease of the manor of Norton, with reversion to the abbot after her death. *Lost.*

So in DB II, fo. 286; cf. VCH *Suffolk*, I, p. 425, and RE p. 160. Edith was still in possession at the time of the Confessor's death.

99. N.D.   (1042 × 1065)   The abbot of Bury St Edmunds to a freeman (unnamed). Lease of half a carucate of land at Pakenham, on condition that after the freeman's death the whole of his land there shall revert to Bury. *Lost.*

So in DB II, fo. 361*b*; cf. VCH *Suffolk*, I, p. 497, and RE pp. 161–2.

100. N.D.   (1042 × 1065)   The archbishop of Canterbury to Leveva. Lease of half a carucate of land in Topesfield, on condition that after Leveva's death it is to revert to Christ Church, Canterbury, together with another half a carucate which she held there. *Lost.*

So in DB II, fo. 372*b*; cf. VCH *Suffolk*, I, p. 509, and RE pp. 161–2.

101. N.D. (1042 × 1065)   The abbot of Ely to Beorn, a free
man. Lease of land at Little Bealings, with reversion to the
abbey after Beorn's death.   *Lost.*

So in DB II, fo. 373; cf. VCH *Suffolk*, I, p. 510, and RE pp.
160, 166 n. 2. The *Inquisitio Eliensis* has the entry: "In *litelbelings*
Beorn holds 50 acres of St Ætheldreda (of Ely), which he may
not sell" (IE p. 151). It seems that a lease is implied in most of
those cases in IE, and possibly in DB, in which the tenant "*non
potuit vendere.*"

102. N.D. (1042 × 1065)   ***King EDWARD to Bury St Edmunds. The monastery and town are to enjoy the freedom
granted by Kings Cnut and Harthacnut; no bishop in Norfolk or Suffolk shall have authority within the boundaries
of the town, marked out by four crosses; the king confirms his previous grant of sake and soke to the monastery.
                                              K 895, 910.

H p. 141 n. 2; Lobel p. 5 n. 8 for the boundary crosses.

103. N.D. (1042 × 1065)   King EDWARD to Bury St Edmunds. Land at Risby and Stanton; and Woolpit, which
was *de socagio*.   *Lost.*

Recorded in BBL and *Memorials*, I, p. 364, which states that
the charters were preserved in the monastery. The individual
gifts may have been made on different occasions. Woolpit was
already an abbey property (No. 83), and King Edward's gift *de
socagio* there is probably represented in DB by the 40 *liberi
homines* who held between them only one carucate; they could
give or sell their land to whom they pleased, but the soke and
all services, including fold-soke, remained with the abbey.

104. N.D. (1042 × 1065)   EDMUND the priest to Ely, with
his wife's consent. Grant of the reversion of Clopston and
Brandeston, which he had received from his wife (upon
their marriage).   *Lost.*

DB II, fo. 431*b*; IE p. 152; cf. VCH *Suffolk*, I, p. 566.

105. N.D. (1042 × 1066)   *Agreement concerning the payments due from the residents of Bury St Edmunds to
Orderic, the cellarer of the Abbey.   ♦R CXIX.

106. N.D.   (1043 × 1044)   *King EDWARD to Bishop Grim-
ketel [of East Anglia], Ælfwine, and Ælfric. Writ declaring that the land at *Mildenhale* (Mildenhall) and the sokes
of the 8½ hundreds belonging to *Thinghog* (Thingoe) are
to belong to (Bury) St Edmunds as fully as his mother
possessed them.   ♦H 9.

   According to a later writ (H 18), Ælfric son of Wihtgar administered these sokes on behalf of King Edward's mother,
Ælfgifu Emma. For Ælfwine, see H p. 552.

(72) N.D.   (1043 × 1045)   *Will of THURSTAN. *Wetheringsete*
(Wetheringsett) to Ely; *Kydingtone* (Kedington) to his
wife Æthelgyth, with reversion to the three priests Ælfwig, Thurstan, and Ordheah. Lands in Cambs., Essex, and
Norfolk.   ♦W xxxi.

   This will contains the earliest recorded reference to Suffolk
by name (*Suffolke*). See also pp. 50 and 85.

107. N.D.   (1043 × 1047)   *Agreement between WULFGEAT
and his wife, and the abbot and community of Bury St
Edmunds, that two estates, of which one is at *Gyselingham*
(Gislingham), shall pass to (Bury) St Edmunds after the
deaths of Ælfwine and his wife. Land in Norfolk.   ♦R c.

   Cf. RE p. 162. Could Ælfwine in this agreement be an error
for Ælfsige? See No. 109. See also p. 85.

(41) N.D.   (c.1044)   Grant in reversion by WULFWINE the
son of Ælfwine to Ramsey Abbey, in consideration of a
life lease of other lands. An estate at *Weldingefeld* (Waldingfield). Lands in Hunts., Cambs., and Essex.   *Lost*.

   Chron Rams pp. 152–3. See also pp. 36 and 51.

108. N.D.   (1044 × 1065)   *Assessment of food rents due to
Bury St Edmunds. Increase of assessment for *Niwentune*
(Nowton), and assessment of the following estates: *Wir-
lingaweorthe* (Worlingworth), *Saham* (Soham), *Pallegrafe*
(Palgrave), *Thorpa* (Westhorpe), *Redgrafe* (Redgrave),
Ricyncgahale (Rickinghall), *Stoca* (Stoke), *Brocaforde*
(Brockford), *Byrtune* (Barton), *Ruhham* (Rougham), *Elmes-
wella* (Elmswell), *Wulepettas* (Woolpit), *Grotene* (Groton),

Koccefelda (Cockfield), *Ceorlesworthe* (Chelsworth), *Hwip-stede* (Whepstead), *Bradefeldæ* (Bradfield), *Horningasearthe* (Horringer), *Rysebi* (Risby), *Lecforde* (Lackford), *Hyrningc-wylle* (Herringswell), *Culeforde* (Culford), *Fornham* (Fornham), *Paccenham* (Pakenham), and *Stantune* (Stanton). Lands in Norfolk.   ♦R CIV.

Cf. D. C. Douglas in EHR XLIII, 1928, pp. 376–83. See also p. 91.

109. N.D. (1044 × 1065)   LEOFSTAN, abbot of Bury St Edmunds, to Ælfsige and his wife. Lease of Gislingham, with reversion to Bury after their deaths, together with Euston, another manor of Ælfsige's.   *Lost.*

DB II, fo. 444*b*; cf. VCH *Suffolk*, I, p. 578; RE pp. 161–2. See No. 107.

110. N.D. (1044 × 1065)   ÆLFRIC son of Wihtgar to the secular canons at Clare. Foundation charter.   *Lost.*

BBL accounts run: "The famous earl Ælfric, son of Wihtgar, gave to Bury St Edmunds *Meleford* (Long Melford), and built the church of St John the Baptist at *Claram* (Clare), and instituted clerks there; and he gave the manor of this church to Bury St Edmunds, and he gave half the church to Abbot Leofstan (of Bury), and his son Wihtgar dwelt in a certain tower where the hospital now is, and confirmed the gift of Melford for the use of the sick." For Ælfric, a kinsman of Æthelwine the Black and Leofgifu (No. 89), see W p. 188, R p. 425, and DB II, fo. 389*b*, which refers to his foundation charter.

111. N.D. (1045 × 1047)   *King EDWARD to Bishop Stigand and Earl Harold. Writ declaring that he has given the estate of Pakenham, formerly owned by Osgot, to Bury St Edmunds.   ♦H 14.

Cf. R p. 445; *Memorials*, I, p. 364.

112. N.D. (1045 × 1066)   Abbot WULFRIC of Ely to his brother Guthmund. Lease in reversion of *Livremere* (Livermere), *Nachentune* (Nacton), and *Acholt* (Occold). Lands in Norfolk and Essex.   *Lost.*

LE II, c. 97, and pp. 424–5; ECEss I, p. 29; Miller's *Ely*,

p. 25 n. 2; p. 51 n. 6; RE pp. 160–1. Guthmund required these lands to make up the 40 hides needed to establish himself as a *procer*, without which he could not fulfil his desire to marry the daughter of Earl Ælfgar of East Anglia. The entries for Nacton in DB II, fo. 406b, and IE p. 144, show that Guthmund held the lease only of this estate, with reversion to Ely after his death. The DB and IE entries for the other estates are less specific, but probably the same form of tenure was adopted. See also p. 91.

113. N.D.   (1046)   *Will of WULFGYTH. *Sumerledetune* (Somerton) to her two daughters Gode and Bote; *Cheartekere* (Chadacre) to her daughter Ealdgyth; *Friþetune* (Fritton) to Earl Godwine and Earl Harold. Lands in Essex, Norfolk, and Kent.   ♦W XXXII.

ECEss No. 64. Professor Whitelock points out that Somerton is near Chadacre; the alternative identification is Somerleyton, near Lowestoft. Fritton is either the place of that name near Lowestoft, or Fritton near Long Stratton, Norfolk. See also p. 91.

113A. N.D.   (1047 × 1065)   ***King EDWARD to Bishop Æthelmær, Earl Harold, Earl Gyrth, Abbot Leofstan [of Bury St Edmunds], and all his thegns in Suffolk. Writ declaring that he intends to have possession of land *æt Iccawurðe* (Ickworth), as his right to it has been testified, for [the endowment of] Westminster.   ♦H 80.

114. N.D.   (c. 1051)   *King EDWARD to Bishop Æthelmær, Earl Ælfgar, and all the thegns and sheriffs of Norfolk and Suffolk. Writ declaring that the *inland* of (Bury) St Edmunds is to be exempt from payment of heregeld and every other render.   ♦H 15.

A later writ by William I shows that the *inland* referred to in the Confessor's writ refers not only to the *banleuca* of the abbey, which was exempt from the geld by Cnut's charter (No. 86), but to all the other demesne lands of the abbey; cf. H p. 139.

115. N.D.   (1051 × 1052, or 1053 × 1057)   *King EDWARD to Bishop Æthelmær, Earl Ælfgar, and Toli. Writ declaring that the land at *Cunegestone* (Coney Weston) is to

belong to (Bury) St Edmund's monastery, with sake and soke and all lawful appurtenances. ◆H 20.

116. N.D. (1051 × 1057) Earl ÆLFGAR [of East Anglia] to Abbot Wulfric of Ely, for 25 marks of gold. *Bercam* (Barham). *Lost.*

LE II, c. 97.

117. N.D. (1052 × 1066) King EDWARD to Christ Church, Canterbury. Grant of Chartham, Kent, and Walworth, Surrey; confirmation of Hadleigh, Monks Eleigh, and lands in other shires.

Ego Eduuardus gratia dei Rex Anglorum gubernator et rector, instinctu dei concedo Christi ecclesie in Dorobernia et monachis in eadem ecclesia deo seruientibus ad uictum eorum pro salute anime mee terras nomine Certaham et Walewrthe iuxta Lundoniam. Omnibus quoque uolo esse notum me esse prouisorem et defensorem eiusdem ecclesie nec uelle consentire, ut aliquis hominum inde aliquam terram auferat, quam tempore patris mei eadem ecclesia habuit, siue sit donum regis, seu archiepiscopi, episcopi, ducis, comitis, thegenes. Uolo ut donum omnium cuiuscumque sexus uel ordinis sic stabile permaneat, et ecclesia Christi iam predicta omnium dona firmiter habeat et teneat. Siquis autem aliquid horum a iure eiusdem ecclesie abstulerit, faciendo aut consentiendo, perpetuo anathemate feriatur, et cum iuda traditore dampnetur. Hec sunt nomina terrarum quas ut michi indicatum est ad presens . . . [erasure][1] ecclesia habet: Sanduuic, Estreia, Folcestan, Tenet, Edesham, Iocaham, Certaham, Godmæresham, Wielle, East ceart, Other ceart, Beruuican Broce, Werehorn, Apeldre, Merseham, Orpinctun, Preostantun, Meapaham, Culinges, Fryningaham, Hytha, Hollingeburnan, Fearnleage, Peccham. On suthsexan: Pæccingæs et Wdetun. On suthrygan: Walauurthe, Mersætham, Ceiham, Hosrlege. On Estsexan: Suthcyrcan, Lagefare, Middeltun, Lællinges, Boccinges, Cicce, Stigestede. On Est engla: Hæthlege, Illelege.

[1] C and D have *christi*, not erased.

c*

In Buccingahamscire: Hrisbeorgan. In Oxoniafordscyre: Niuuantun et Bruteuurthe.[1]

TEXTS

A. BM Cotton Claud., A iii, fo. 6b (old numbering, fo. 5b). The first part of this MS. consists of fragments from a ninth-century Gospel Book which once belonged to Christ Church. The MS. is described in Ker p. 240. The charter appears in an OE version, entered in three different hands, of which the first is mid-eleventh century, and the other two are dated later in the same century.

B. Lambeth Palace MS. 1212, fo. 331. A composite thirteenth/fourteenth-century cartulary of the see of Canterbury (cf. Davis, No. 159). This contains a Latin version of A.

C. Canterbury, D & C, Muniments, "Reg.P." ff. 16–16b (Davis, No. 163A). Thirteenth century.

D. Canterbury, D & C, Muniments, "Reg.I." ff. 58b–59 (Davis, No. 165). Thirteenth century.

EDITIONS

(1) R xcv, from A. This lists earlier editions, which it supersedes.

(2) This edition is from B, which as far as I can discover has not previously been published. Contractions are extended, and minimal punctuation is introduced. C and D are inferior versions, with later place-name forms, but supply a word erased in B.

DATE

King Edward reigned 1042 × 1066. Miss Robertson (R p. 427) says that the OE version "gives the impression of having been drawn up soon after Edward the Confessor's accession." Ker p. 240 notes, however, that lists of Christ Church benefactors assign the gift of Chartham to the year 1052, and Stisted, too, could not have descended to the abbey before that date (W xxxiv; cf. ECEss I, No. 66). But these considerations are dependent upon the authenticity of the charter, which is discussed below.

DIPLOMATIC

In ECEss I, p. 27, I expressed the opinion that the OE version was derived from the Latin text, but more careful collation shows that this is not the case; the Latin version is in fact a

---

[1] interlined—*welle* in a later hand.

straight translation of the OE charter, except that for obvious reasons it omits one passage, which states that King Edward dedicated his bequest on the altar at Christ Church, "with my own hand on this Gospel Book."

The diplomatic has therefore to be compared with contemporary OE charters, and not Latin ones, which employ different formulas. The OE version commences with the unique royal title "*Ic Eadwerd cyng 7 Englalandes wealdend under Criste an heofenlican cyninge,*" which is a development of the title given to King Æthelred in another Christ Church charter entered earlier in the eleventh century in the same Gospel Book (K 715; cf. Ker pp. 239–40): ". . . *Ic Æðelred mid Godes gyfe Angel eode cyning, and wealdend eac oðra iglanda ðe her abutan licgað* ;" in the same series we find the title ". . . *Cnut ðurh Godes geue Ængelandes kining* . . ." attributed to Cnut in the Sandwich charter of Christ Church (R LXXXII; cf. H p. 177 n. 1).

Following the king's title, the phrase ". . . *for mine sawle þan hirede to fosterlande þe þærinne Gode þeowað*" is paralleled in two other Christ Church charters, R LXXXVI ". . . *Godes ðeowum to fosterlande for his sawle,*" and R XCVI ". . . *þan hirede to fosterlande for uncre beigra sawle.*" Next, the phrase "*ic eom þæs mynstres mund 7 upheald*" recalls similar passages in two writs (H nos. 2 and 7), and see p. 89 below. The rest of the text is less easy to parallel, but reference to "the traitor Judas" is characteristic of contemporary charters (see p. 89).

AUTHENTICITY

In default of any statement to the contrary in her edition, one assumes that Miss Robertson considered the OE version to be genuine, but Miss Harmer (H p. 175 n. 5) states: "The charter is not in its present form authentic, though it may contain authentic material." It seems to me that the first and earliest hand of the entry, which records the Confessor's gift of Chartham, is probably an authentic text. It is this section which shows the most convincing parallels with the diplomatic found in other charters of the period. It is simple and self-contained, and of similar form to three other short vernacular charters entered above it on the same folio (R XCVI, LXXXIX, and LXXXVIII, in that order; see Ker p. 240).

To this, a second hand (commencing *7 ic wille*) adds a general confirmation of all the possessions of Christ Church, ending with a double anathema, and I would consider this to be a post-Conquest addition, made possibly at the time of the Penenden Heath litigation in 1072 or 1076, when Lanfranc was engaged in recovering, from Odo of Bayeux and others, lands which were once the property of the archbishopric (H pp. 167–8 and the authorities there cited).

A third hand, of similar date, adds a list of the estates alleged to have been confirmed to the abbey by the Confessor. It is clear that the compiler used as one of his sources a list of estates in the OE version of the charter of Æthelred to Christ Church which has already been referred to (K 715). Compare, for example, the entries for Monks Risborough; in Æthelred's charter this appears as "*Hrisebyrgan be Cilternes efese*;" in Edward's charter it becomes "*be Cilternes efese. Hrysebyrgan.*"

A number of the estates entered in this section of the charter were subsequently erased (cf. B. Kissan in EHR LIV, 1939, p. 287) and the chief interest of the Latin version here edited lies in the fact that its own list of estates, which is recited in the same order as the OE list, shows no sign of erasure. It must, therefore, have been copied from the OE text after the erasures had been made. Moreover, six additional estates are included in the Latin list, at positions which do not correspond with the erasures in the OE list. In the following list of the estates, the positions of the erasures in the OE list are shown by dots, and the six additional estates inserted in the Latin list are printed in italic:

In Kent: Sandwich, Eastry, *Folkestone*, Thanet, Adisham, Ickham, ..., Chartham, ..., Godmersham, ..., Westwell, Great Chart, Little Chart, Berwick in Lympne, *Brook*, Warehorne, Appeldore, Mersham, Orpington, ..., Preston, ..., Meopham, Cooling, Farningham, *Hythe*, Hollingebourne, Farleigh, ..., Peckham.

In Sussex: Patching, Wooton.

In Surrey: Walworth, Merstham, Cheam, Horsley.

In Essex: Southchurch, *Laver*, Milton, Lawling, ..., Bocking, *St Osyth*, *Stisted*.

In East Anglia (Suffolk): Hadleigh, Monks Eleigh.

In Buckinghamshire: Monks Risborough.

In Oxfordshire: Newington, Brightwell Baldwin.

It will be seen that the erasures and interpolations are confined to estates in Kent and Essex; in Kent there are six erasures and three interpolations, and in Essex one erasure and three interpolations.

In ECEss I, p. 27, I erroneously inferred that the interpolations restored names which had been erased, but the above list forbids so simple an explanation. Moreover, the Latin version has an additional interpolation in the body of the charter, by which Edward is made to grant Walworth, in addition to Chartham, to the abbey. The interpolated phrase, *Walewrth iuxta*

Lundoniam, is similar to the entry for Walworth in the Latin text of Ethelred's charter (K 715): *iuxta Lundoniam Wealwyrð*. We have therefore a very complicated series of modifications to the text of the original (and probably authentic) gift by the Confessor of Chartham to Christ Church. It is probable that they were all made at the time of the Penenden Heath litigation, and one can only repeat the remark by Dr Harmer (H p. 169 n. 1): "Scribes copying charters into the Christ Church registers frequently took liberties with their texts." This extensive rewriting, of which the charter under review is but one example of many, makes the early Christ Church muniments probably the most difficult to deal with of all the pre-Conquest monastic houses.

118. N.D. (1052 × 1066) *Will of KETEL. He records agreements with his sister Bote concerning *Somerledetone* (Somerton or Somerleyton), with his sister Gode concerning *Prestone* (Prestone near Lavenham), and with his stepdaughter Ælfgifu concerning *Anhus* (Onehouse); he grants *Rissewrthe* (Rushford) to his priest and relation, Ælfric. Lands in Essex and Norfolk. ♦W xxxiv.

ECEss No. 66. See also p. 95.

(47) N.D. (c.1062) ***King EDWARD to Ramsey Abbey. Confirmation of estates, including *Laugetsille* (Lawshall). Lands in Hunts., Lincs., Cambs., Beds., Norfolk, Northants., and Herts. K 809.

See also pp. 39, 52, 95, and 106.

118A. 1065 ***King EDWARD to Westminster Abbey. Confirmation of privileges and estates, including *Icceweorthe* (Ickworth), which had been granted to the abbey in the king's presence by his *miles* Bricsige.

Widmore, *Westminster*, App II.

See H pp. 291, 317; ECEss No. 69.

119. N.D. (1 Aug. 1065 × 5 Jan. 1066) *King EDWARD to Bishop Æthelmær, Earl Gyrth, and Toli. Writ declaring that he has granted to Abbot Baldwine (of Bury St Edmunds) a moneyer within (the borough of) Bury St Edmunds. ♦H 25.

120. N.D.   (1 Aug. 1065 × 5 Jan. 1066)   Writ of King ED-
       WARD in favour of Baldwine, abbot of Bury St Edmunds,
       giving him sake and soke over the abbey's land and men
       in the *ferding* of Elmham.   *Lost.*

   DB II, fo. 379; cf. VCH *Suffolk*, I, p. 516; H p. 545.

CHAPTER IV

THE EARLY CHARTERS OF
NORFOLK

(49) N.D. (942 × 957) *Will of THEODRED, bishop of London. *Illyntone* (Illington) to the king, as part of his heriot; *Suthereye* (Southery) with the fishing that belongs to it to the community at St Paul's church (London), and the men are to be freed, for his soul. Lands in Essex, Suffolk, Cambs., Middlesex, and Surrey. ♦W I.

See also pp. 40 and 53.

(55) 970 †EDGAR, king of the island of Albion, and ruler of the Scots, Cumbrians, and Britons, and all the regions thereabout, to the monastery at Ely. Lands and privileges, including the manor of *Norðwold* (Northwold). Lands in Cambs. and Suffolk.

CS 1266 (Latin) and ♦R XLVIII (OE).

LE II, c. 4, gives the hidage of this estate as 12. See also pp. 42 and 59.

(18) (28 Dec. 974) ***Foundation Charter of Ramsey Abbey. King EDGAR confirms the gifts of various donors, including Hilgay, Walsoken, Brancaster, and an annual rent of 6,000 eels from 20 fisheries at *Welles* (Upwell and Outwell, in Cambs. and Norfolk). Lands in Hunts., Cambs., and Northants. CS 1310, 1311.

See also pp. 27 and 44.

121. N.D. (c.990 × 1066) *Will of SIFLÆD. *Marþingforð* (Marlingford) to Bury St Edmunds.

♦W XXXVII, W XXXVIII.

The two wills are very similar; the second mentions Christchurch and St Mary's Church, both at Norwich. There is no means of arriving at a closer dating, but resemblances between this gift and No. 133 suggest that it was made towards the end of the period assigned.

(25) N.D.   (991)   Will of Ealdorman BRIHTNOTH of Essex. *Chrochestune* (Croxton) to Ely. Lands in Essex, Cambs., Suffolk, Hunts., and Northants.   *Lost.*

LE II, c. 62; Chron Rams pp. 116–17. Subsequently Croxton and Methwold were leased to Archbishop Stigand (RE p. 163 n. 1). See also pp. 31, 46, and 61.

122. N.D.   (995 × 1001)   *WULFGIFU to Ramsey Abbey. The vill of *Bramcestria* (Brancaster), to descend to the abbey after her death. There are three copies of this grant, of which one is to remain with Wulfgifu, one is to go to Ramsey, and one to Bishop Æthelstan [of Elmham].
CS 1059.

She was the third wife of Ealdorman Æthelwine, and survived him. The dates given for her charter are those of Æthelstan's episcopate, the earlier being derived from K 688, witnessed by his predecessor Theodred II. Wulfgifu's obit is entered under 994 in Cart Rams III, p. 166, but this is less reliable than K 688.

(28) N.D.   (c.1007)   Will of ÆLFWARU. *Brigeham* (Bridgeham), with all that appertains to it, within the vill and without, in land and water, in wood and field; land at *Teodford* (Little Thetford, Cambs.), and the fisheries in the nearby marshes; *Hengeham* (Ingham or Hingham), *Vetinge* (Weeting), and *Mundeford* (Mundford): all to Ely. Lands in Suffolk, Hunts., Cambs., and Herts.   *Lost.*

Chron Rams pp. 84–5; LE II, c. 61. See also pp. 32, 48, and 62.

(29) N.D.   (c.1007)   *GODRIC to Ramsey Abbey. Land at *Turingtona* al. *Tiringetona* (Terrington), to acquit the heriot of his brother Eadnoth, abbot of Ramsey. Land in Hunts.
K 928.

Chron Rams pp. 111–12; CAS LVI–LVII, 1964, p. 64. Godric died in 1013 (Cart Rams III, p. 167). The gift was made probably before Eadnoth became bishop of Dorchester in 1007. The alternative identifications, Torrington in Lincs, and Thorington in Suffolk, are less likely, because the Norfolk vill was near to existing holdings of Ramsey. See also p. 32.

123. N.D. (1017 × 1021) AILRIC to Ramsey Abbey, on becoming a monk there. 5 hides at *Berewick* (? Barwick).

Lost.

Chron Rams p. 147. The location is not certain, as no further references have survived to Ramsey property at a place bearing this name. Ailric's grant was witnessed by Lyfing, archbishop of Canterbury, Ætheric, bishop of Dorchester, Brihtwold, bishop of Ramsbury, Ælfsige, bishop of Winchester, Turkil, earl of East Anglia, and Eilaf, a Viking whose earldom is unknown.

124. N.D. (c.1020 × 1050) *Will of THURKETEL HEYNG. Land at *Castre* (Caister St Edmunds) and Thorpe to be divided between Bury St Edmunds and St Benedict at Holme; *Ormisby* (Ormesby) to his daughter Ælfwyn, with reversion to Holme; *Scrouteby* (Scratby) to his nephews' children, the sons of Sweyn and Ealhmund. ♦W xxv.

All the estates lie in East Flegg hundred.

125. N.D. (1022 × 1023) *CNUT, king of the English, to (St Benedict at) Holme. The vill at *Horningga* (Horning), with its meadows and woodland, and the adjacent land at *Ludham* (Ludham) and *Netheshird* (Neatishead), which belonged to it. K 740.

Better edited by J. R. West, *The Eleventh and Twelfth Century Sections of Cotton MS. Galba E ii*, Norfolk Record Soc., 1932, I, p. 5; II, p. 199. On the date and witness list, see No. 86. *Huc* among the witnesses in K 740 is an error for Earl *Yric*. According to a late record of benefactors, Cnut's gift included Irstead, Heigham, Thurne, Ashby, and Worstead.—Dugdale III, pp. 88–9.

(33) N.D. (1029 × 1035) Abbot LEOFSIGE of Ely, with the consent of King Cnut, settles the food-rents due to the monastery from its estates in Cambs., Hunts., Essex, Norfolk, and Suffolk. Those from Norfolk comprise *Brecheham* (Bridgeham), *Pulham* (Pulham), *Thorpe* together with *Dirham* (Thorpe Abbots together with East Dere-

ham), *Nordwolde* (Northwold), *Feltewelle* (Feltwell), and *Merham* (Marham). Each of these is to supply two weeks' food farm, with the exception of Marham, which is to provide carrying services between the Norfolk estates and the abbey, in lieu of food farm.   *Lost.*

LE II, c. 84. Dr Blake, LE p. 152 n. 5, identifies *Brecheham* tentatively with Barham, Suffolk, and since this estate did not descend to Ely until the time of Leofsige's successor (No. 116), he thinks that "some suspicion must attach to this version of Leofsige's allocation of farms." But the estate in question is clearly Bridgeham, Norfolk, acquired by the will of Ælfwaru, dated c.1007 (No. 28). See also pp. 34, 49, and 65.

(88) N.D.   (1035 × 1038)   †Will of Bishop ÆLFRIC [II] of Elmham. The estate at *Hunstanestune* (Hunstanton) east of the brook, and including the estate at Holme (Holme-next-the-sea), to Bury St Edmunds; *Ticeswelle* (Tichwell) and *Doccynge* (Docking) to Bury for the sum of sixty pounds; *Grimastune* (Grimston) to Leofstan the dean; *Walsingaham* (Walsingham) and *Fersafeld* (Fersfield) are to be sold; thirty acres at *Eggemera* (Egmere) are to go to Ælfwine, his priest at Walsingham, and the rest to Ufi the prior; Edwin the monk is to have the mill at *Gæssæte* (Guist) which Ringwaru owned; the estate at *Rygedune* (Roydon, near Diss) which he bought from Leofwyn is to go to Ælfwig the priest; the messuage at *Norðwic* (Norwich) is to go to Bury St Edmunds. Land in Suffolk.
                                                        ♦W XXVI.

According to BBL, the church of St Laurence was built on the site of the messuage at Norwich, and made an annual render to Bury of one last of herrings. See p. 65.

(89) N.D.   (1035 × 1044)   *Will of LEOFGIFU. One hide at *Forendale* al. *Frendenhale* (Fundenhall) to Æthelric the priest. Lands in Essex and Suffolk.   ♦W XXIX.

See also p. 65.

(90) N.D.   (before 1038)   *Will of THURKETEL of Palgrave. Land at *Reydone* (Roydon, near Diss) to the church; *Simp-

lingham (Shimpling) and half of Roydon to his wife Leofwyn; twenty acres at Roydon to his nephew Leofric, his
kinswoman Godwine, and Godwine's brother Wulfwine.
Land in Suffolk. ♦W xxiv.

See also p. 66.

126. N.D. (1041 × 1042) *King HARTHACNUT to Æthelwig
and all the burgesses of *Tedfordia* (Thetford). Writ declaring that Abbot Æthelstan of Ramsey shall have his *mansus*
(house or messuage) in Thetford as fully and freely as he
had it in the days of King Cnut. ♦H 56.

(94) N.D. (c.1040 × 1057) *Will of EDWIN. *Eskeresthorp*
(Algarsthorpe in Melton) to Ely, 10 acres for the church
there, and 3 acres to Leofric; *Lithle Meddletone* (Little
Melton) to St Benedict's at Holme, and 10 acres to the
church; land south of King's Street at *Beorh* (Bergh) to
Ely, except the northern enclosure at *Appelsco*; 10 acres
south of the street to Bergh church, and 10 acres north
of the street to *Apetune* (Apton) church; 4 acres to *Hulue-
stone* (Holverston) church, and 10 acres to *Sparham* (Sparham) church. The survivor of the two brothers Wulfric
and Edwin is to have *Thorp* (Thorpe near Fundenhall) and
Middletone (Great Melton), then upon his death Melton is
to go to St Benedict's and Thorpe to Ketel, then to Bury
St Edmund's; and land at Melton is to go to the church
which Thurward owned; 8 acres from the estate at Thorpe
to *Aescewelle* (Ashwell) church, and 10 acres from *Wreningham* (Wreningham) to the old church, 2 acres to *Funden-
hale* (Fundenhall) church, and two to *Neolondes* (Naylond
in Wreningham, lost) church. Land in Suffolk.
♦W xxxiii.

Little Melton was leased back to Edwin by the abbey of St
Benedict at Holme, with reversion to the abbey after his death.
—DB ii, fo. 204*b*; RE p. 161. See also p. 67.

127. N.D. (1042 × 1043) *Will of ÆLFRIC MODERCOPE.
Lodne (Loddon) to Bury St Edmunds; *Birthe* (Bergh Apton)
to Ely; *Berton* (Barton Turf) to St Benedict's at Holme.

Thurwineholm is granted with Loddon, and *Fuglholm* with Bergh Apton.   ◆W XXVIII.

The late list of Bury benefactors printed in Dugdale III, p. 139, has *Beorch*, which confirms the identification with Bergh Apton.

(35) N.D. (1042 × 1057) *EDWARD, king of the English, to Ely Abbey. Confirmation of estates, including, in Norfolk, *Feltewelle* (Feltwell), *Brugeham* (Bridgeham), *Meðelworde* al. *Meðelwolde* (Methwold), *Crochestune* (Croxton), *Watinge* (Weeting), *Mundeford* (Mundford), *Berc* (Bergh Apton), *Westfled* (Westfield), *Fingeham* (Fincham), *Notwelle* (Northwold), *Walepol* (Walpole) with appendages, *Merham* (Marham), *Derham* (East Dereham), *Thorp* (Thorpe Abbots), and *Pulham* (Pulham). Land in Hunts., Cambs., Suffolk, Essex, and Herts.   K 907.

LE II, c. 92. The acquisition of Methwold, Westfield, and Fincham is unrecorded elsewhere. See also pp. 34, 50, and 67.

(97) N.D. (1042 × 1065) King EDWARD in favour of Eadric of Laxfield. Writ restoring to him the lands he had owned before his outlawry. Land in Suffolk.   *Lost*.

DB II, fo. 310b. Eadric had extensive Norfolk estates. See also p. 68.

128. N.D. (1042 × 1065) King EDWARD to Bury St Edmunds. Land at *Castre* (Caister St Edmunds).   *Lost*.

Recorded in BBL, and in *Memorials*, I, p. 364, which says that the charter survived in the monastery.

129. N.D. (1042 × 1065) A person unnamed to St Benedict at Holme. Grant of land in Smallburgh; he is to hold it as life tenant, with reversion to the abbey after his death.
                                                        Lost.

DB II, fo. 219b; RE p. 161.

130. N.D. (1042 × 1065) EADRIC to St Benedict at Holme. Grant of his half of the land at Honing; the abbot grants him the lease of this for his lifetime, together with the lease of the other half, which was already the property of

the abbey; after Edwin's death, both halves are to revert to the abbey. *Lost.*

DB II, fo. 219b; RE pp. 161–2. Identified as Eadric *stiresman* in No. 134.

131. N.D. (1042 × 1065) TOLI the sheriff [of Norfolk and Suffolk] to Bury St Edmunds. Grant of land in Broome, which he is to hold of the abbey for two days' food farm. *Lost.*

DB II, fo. 211b; RE p. 161.

132. N.D. (1043 × 1044) *Abbot UFI and the community of Bury St Edmunds to Æthelmær, the bishop's brother, for one mark of gold. Lease of the little estate at *Swanetone* (Swanton Novers), and half the estate at *Heldoluestone* (Hindolveston); upon his death the estate is to revert, with produce and men, to Bury. Witnessed by Bishop Stigand (of Elmham) and others, including the abbots and communities of Bury, Ely, and St Benedict's [at Holme], Ulf of *Welle* (possibly Upwell and Outwell, Norfolk and Cambs.), and Godwine at *Cringelforð* (Cringleford).   ♦R XCVII.

RE p. 162. See also No. 136.

(72) N.D. (1043 × 1045) *Will of THURSTAN. To his wife Æthelgyth, everything he has in *Norfolke* (Norfolk); the north hall at *Sculham* (Shouldham) to Bury St Edmunds after their two deaths; the middle hall at Shouldham to be divided after their two deaths, half to Ramsey and half to St Benedict's at Holme. Lands in Cambs., Suffolk, and Essex.   ♦W XXXI.

This is the earliest recorded reference to Norfolk by name. See also pp. 50 and 70.

(107) N.D. (1043 × 1047) *Agreement between WULFGEAT and his wife, and the abbot and community of Bury St Edmunds, that two estates, of which one is at *ffakenham* (Fakenham), shall pass to St Edmunds after the death of Ælfwine and his wife.   ♦R C.

See also p. 70.

133. N.D.   (1044 × 1052)   *Agreement between Osulf and
Leofrun concerning land at Dickleburgh and Semer.

OLD ENGLISH VERSION

Her kith and with song wrthe write þat forwarde þat
osulf and Leofroun wrouhte hem bitwen himbe þat lond
at dicleburg and at semere swa ful and swa forth swa it
hem on honde stod, on wode and on felde crist to loue
5 and sancte marie and alle cristes halgen here soules to
alesenesse. He it willetӡ þat þer singetӡ foure prestes, to
after osulf and to after leofroun is day, and ilke woke to
singen tuelue messes. And we willetӡ þat qwo so betӡ
abbot at sancte edmondes bery þat he betӡ þis minstres
10 mund and her prestes þat he ne mowen neyþer for hem[1] ne
for here kin ferren ne forwerken. Þise sindon þise prestes
names Godric and alfric and tweyne þat leofstan abbot
and leofroun reden hem bytwen, quilke he monn ben. He
hauen gode stoundes þat up schulen holden. And qwo so
15 nouth[2] ne dotӡ as[3] oure wille was, in helle flod mote he
drinklen witӡ þe traytour iudas. fiat. fiat.

TRANSLATION

Here in this document is announced the agreement that
Osulf and Leofrun made between themselves concerning
the land at Dickleburgh and at Semer [that it should descend after their deaths to Bury St Edmunds] as fully and
completely as it stood in their possession, in woodland
and in field, for the praise of Christ and St Mary and all
Christ's saints [and] for the redemption of their souls.
They wish that four priests should sing, two after Osulf's
day, and two after Leofrun's day, and each week [they are]
to sing twelve masses. And we desire that whoever is abbot

---

[1] Beneath *hem* in the MS. appear three dots to indicate an erasure, but beside
these appears *st'*, probably for *stet*.

[2] Before this word appears *nouht*, dotted underneath to indicate an erasure.

[3] After *as* appears *h*, dotted underneath and crossed through to indicate an
erasure.

of St Edmunds bury should be the guardian of the minsters, and their priests must never transfer or surrender them [the minsters] to themselves or their kin. These are the priests' names: Godric and Alfric, and two that Abbot Leofstan and Leofrun shall choose between them. [May] they that uphold [this agreement] have good fortune. And whoever does not carry out our intention, may they drink in the river of Hell with the traitor Judas. May it be so.

LATIN VERSION

Ecce consistunt osulf et leofroun meditantes animarum suarum necessitatem, id est quod post uite sue decessum has terras dicleburg et semere federe firmo concedunt christo et sancto edmundo, ut semper sint libere, pro animarum suarum redemptione. Et abbas Leofstanus sancti edmundi uel quicumque sit illius sancti monasterii gubernator tam sit patronus uenerabilis no'ue quam terrarum nec quisquam censeat in aliud uertere dona sua quam constituerunt. Et si aliquis fecerit, sit ipse sub stigi fluminis unda cum iuda proditore mersus si ad emendationem non uenerit. ✠ Hec sunt duorum presbitorum nomina qui debent ecclesie perficere officia, id est, Godricus et alfgarus. Et adhuc duo quos abbas leofstanus et illa leofroun elegerunt. Et qui celebrent per septimanam xij missas pro uiuis et mortuis.

TEXT

BM MS. Harl. 1005, fo. 195 (old foliation, fo. 188). This Bury St Edmunds register, known as the *Liber Albus* (Davis, no. 105), was compiled in the early fifteenth century by a number of different hands. The contents, which are very varied and include the Chronicle of Jocelin de Brakelond (ff. 127–92), are summarized in Dugdale III, pp. 122–4. It was this summary which led me to the discovery of the text here edited, in which the OE charter appears under the rubric *Prima fundatio iiijor rectorum ecclesie de Dicleburg* (probably supplied by the fifteenth-century copyist), and is followed by a Latin translation which is almost certainly pre-Conquest. No other texts of the agreement are known, and it is evident that the original charter was separated at an early date from the rest of the OE material preserved at Bury, nearly all of which was entered in the Sacrist's Register (CUL MS. Ff.2.33) early in the fourteenth century.

EDITION

In this edition abbreviations introduced by the copyist are extended in italic. Throughout the MS. OE *þ* is written *y* or *ẏ*, as is common in fifteenth-century texts, but the original sign is restored in the present edition. No other alterations have been made in the spelling, but minimal punctuation has been introduced. I am indebted to Miss F. E. Richardson for helpful advice on both text and translation.

DATE

Between 1044, when Leofstan became abbot of Bury, and 1052, when King Edward issued a writ concerning Semer (see below).

COMMENTARY

The fifteenth-century copyist appears to have made a fairly accurate rendering of the OE original, preserving northern and eastern spellings such as *qwo*, *qwilke*, and *preste*, and the northerly verb inflection *tȝ* for *th*. The only obvious corruption is in the opening sentence of the agreement, but the precise sense of some other passages is obscure. The Latin translation shows that in the process of transcribing the original, a complete line of text was dropped out. It seems probable that the original record of the transaction had a witness list, which has not survived.

l. 1. *Her kith and with song wrthe write* appears to be a corruption of *her kith an þison gewrite*, a common introductory phrase in vernacular charters of the period, the nearest spelling being from Harold Harefoot's charter to Sandwich (R xci).

ll. 1 f. *þat forwarde þat osulf and Leofrun wrouhte hem bitwen himbe þat lond at...*, cf. *... þe forward þe Wlfric and Eadwine þa tueye brethere wroughten hem bitwen, ymb þa to lond at...* in the will of Edwin (W xxxiii). Similar phrases occur in other Bury documents of the period (R xcii, xcvii, c, civ) and in those of a few other houses.

l. 3. The Latin translation shows that a line is missing here in the OE text; probably it stated that Dickleburgh and Semer should descend to Bury St Edmunds after the deaths of Osulf and Leofroun.

ll. 3 f. *swa ful and swa forth swa it hem on honde stod*. Dr Harmer (*Writs*, p. 86) says: "formulas such as *swa ful ⁊ swa forð swa he hit me to handa let . . .* were evidently in common use" in charters, writs, and wills.

l. 4. *on wode and on felde* is another common phrase discussed by Dr Harmer (*ibid.*, pp. 86, 91), who observes: "they are not merely conventional sequences . . . they bear some relation to the actual physical features of an estate." DB records woodland at both Dickleburgh and Semer.

ll. 4 ff. *crist to loue and sancte marie and all cristeshalgen, here soules to alesenesse* is an old formula, e.g. . . . *Gode to loue and saint Marie and alre Godes halgen, mine saule to þearue* in a bequest of King Alfred to Shaftesbury (R xiii). The new stone church at Bury, begun by order of Cnut, was dedicated to Christ, St Mary, and St Edmund.

ll. 6 ff. *He it willetȝ þat þer singetȝ foure prestes, to after osulf and to after leofroun is day, and ilke woke to singen tuelue messes* recalls the will of Edwin (W xxxiii) . . . *after here boþere day . . . for here eyþeres soule ilke day ane messe . . .*, and of Mantat (see p. 204) . . . *he sculen elke geare don for us twa hundred messen. . .*

ll. 9 f. *þat he betȝ þis minstres mund*, cf. R xcv *ic eom þæs mynstres mund*, and see further H p. 427.

ll. 10 f. *he ne mowen neyþer for hem ne for here kin ferren ne forwerken*, cf. another Bury charter (R xcii) . . . *he it may neyþer ne forsegen ne forwerken*, and the will of Thurketel Heyng (W xxv) . . . *he it ne may forwirken*. The intention was to forbid the mass-priests to treat the churches as their own hereditable property, as could and did happen elsewhere, even at this late date.

l. 13. *monn* from ON *mon*, "must."

l. 14. *stoundes* apparently from OE *stund*, "time"; *gode stoundes* would therefore seem to mean "good times," "good fortune" in this context.

ll. 15 f. *in helle flod mote he drinklen*. I can find no biblical or patristic warrant for the concept of a river in Hell. The Latin translation renders the phrase *sub stigi fluminis unda* (using a formula which appears in charters of the previous century—e.g. the Yaxley charter edited on p. 159), and it does seem likely that whoever drew up the charter had in mind the River Styx in the Hades of classical mythology, the waters of which were deadly poison. *drinklen* in our passage is therefore possibly better rendered as "drink" than as "drown," its alternative meaning, adopted in the Latin version.

l. 16. *witȝ þe traytour iudas*; cf. R xxiii . . . *be hey Judan feyre Christes traytour on helle*. The OED has nothing earlier than ME for "traitor," through the OF *traitre*.

PERSONAL NAMES

Leofstan was abbot of Bury St Edmunds 1044 × 1065. *Osulf* and *Leofrun* appear in a BBL entry as *Osulf þe Syre* and his wife, the lady *Leueruna*, who gave Bressingham near Dickleburgh to Bury. The nickname probably derives from OE *sӯfre*, "sober," "morally pure." Evidently they were without issue, for there is no provision in the charter for masses for other members of the family. DB shows that both died TRE. *Godric* and *Alfric*, priests, do not occur elsewhere. There were still two priests serving the church of Dickleburgh at the time of DB.

HISTORY

Although the charter is entered under the late rubric "First foundation of 4 rectors at the church of Dickleburgh," the text itself does not make it clear where the priests were to sing. The reference to minsters (plural) suggests that it was intended that two should sing at Dickleburgh, and two at Semer. On fo. 82 recto of Harl. 1005 appears the statement *quedam matrona dedit Semere*, and it could well be that Semer was Leofrun's gift, and Dickleburgh Osulf's. If this is the case, then the two named priests were probably appointed to Dickleburgh, and at the time the charter was drawn up the arrangement for Semer had not been completed.

This must give cause for reconsideration of Writ No. 17 in Dr Harmer's collection (No. 139 below), dated by her March–September 1052, by which King Edward declares that St Edmunds is to possess Kirby (Cane) in Norfolk, with all the rights, as his mother had bequeathed it to that house. The writ then goes on: "*And ic bidde ihu alle þat ge deme me swilc dom of Semere þat haueð þider inne faren mid unlage swilk ge for Gode witen þat me mid rithte to bireð.*" Dr Harmer translates this: "And I pray you all that you pronounce for me a judgement concerning Semer, who has illegally occupied it (i.e. Kirby), such as you, in the sight of God, know to be my lawful right." Dr Harmer takes *Semere* to be a personal name, representing OE *Sæmær*, and includes it among her biographical notes on p. 571, with the remark "otherwise unknown"; she indexes it under "Semer of Kirby" (p. 599). It will be noted that this translation implies that the king had already prejudged the issue by declaring "Semer's" act to be illegal without awaiting the result of the investigation which his writ ordered; this does not fit in with what we know of OE law.

It seems to me, however, in the light of the charter now under discussion, that the passage in this writ could be construed to make *Semere* a place-name; it is the identical spelling in the charter, and Semer (Norfolk) is quite near to Kirby Cane.

If this is indeed the case, then the writ deals with the affairs of two separate estates in the same locality; possibly the descent of both of them to Bury was being contested at the time. By this thesis, our charter should be dated 1044 × 1052, and we must assume that Semer descended to Bury, was temporarily alienated, and was restored by King Edward's writ. That might account for the fact that although two priests held Dickleburgh of the abbot at the time of DB, none are mentioned at Semer, which was held by the abbey in demesne. Some connection between the two holdings persisted as late as 1194, when a Hugh de Semer held one carucate of land from the church of Dickleburgh.—*Pinchbeck Register*, I, p. 430.

AUTHENTICITY

It seems probable that the OE text here presented is a late but reliable version of an authentic agreement of 1044 × 1052, in which the copyist corrupted the introductory clause, and omitted a short passage in the body of the text.

(108) N.D. (1044 × 1065) *(a) List of the holdings of Bury St Edmunds in the following hundreds: *Elsingtun* (Islington), *Spelhoge* (Spellow), *Clencware* (Clenchwarton), *Lynware* (Lynn), and *In*, *Fuwelege*, *Ærnehogo*, unidentified. (b) Statement that "from Athulf's 'Sutton' to the old 'Walbeck', from *Watlingetune* (Watlington) north to the sea, (Bury) St Edmund has a share of the land with his neighbours." (c) Note regarding food-rent due to Bury St Edmunds from *Runcgetune* (Runcton). (d) Inventory of the stock at *Eggemere* (Egmere) "after Cole left it." Notes on food-rents in Suffolk. ♦R CIV.

Athulf's Sutton is probably Sutton St Edmund in Holland, Lincs. Athulf may have been the father of Leofwine (p. 177), who owned part of Whittlesey Mere, not so very far away. See also p. 70.

(112) N.D. (1045 × 1066) Abbot WULFRIC of Ely to his brother Guthmund. *Gerboldesham* (Garboldisham), and part of *Merham* (Marham), with *curia ville* (? soke). Lands in Essex and Suffolk. *Lost*.

LE II, c. 97. This was probably a lease; see p. 71.

(113) N.D. (1046) *Will of WULFGYTH. *Karltune* (East Carleton), *Walsingham* (Walsingham in East Carleton),

and *Herlingham* (East Harling) to her sons Ulfketel and Ketel; *Sexlingham* (Saxlingham) to her daughters Gode and Bote. Lands in Essex, Suffolk, and Kent. ♦W XXXII.

See also p. 72.

134. N.D. (C.1047) ***King EDWARD to St Benedict of Holme. Confirmation of lands and privileges, including: the church and vill of *Hornigge* (Horning); the (soke of the) hundred of Tunstede; the churches and vill of *Netheshirda* (Neatishead); the churches of Hoveton and *Belhae* (Belaugh), with the vill of Hoveton; the land of *Sutwalsham* (South Walsham), which was Ralph the Staller's; the church and vill of *Wrðestede* (Worstead); the church of *Hanninge* (Honing), with land there which belonged to Eadric *stiresman*; the church and vill of *Thurgartun* (Thurgarton); the church and vill of *Thweyt* (Thwaite); the church of *Caleðorp* (Calthorpe), with land which belonged to Eadric *stiresman*; the church of *Totingtonne* (Tottington), with land which belonged to Æthelwine *alderman*; the churches of Erpingham and Antingham, with land in those vills which belonged to Eadric *stiresman*; the church and vill of *Norðwalsham* (North Walsham), which belonged to Sket; the church of *Swaneton* (Swanton Abbot), with land which belonged to Saxy; the churches of *Scoteho* (Scottow) and *Lammesse* (Lamas), with land which belonged to Æthelwine *alderman* in those vills, and in *Estone* (Easton); land which belonged to Æthelwine *alderman* in *Hobbesse* (Hautbois); the church and vill of *Ludham* (Ludham), with its appurtenances; the church of *Bestone* (Beeston St Lawrence), with land there belonging to Æthelwine *alderman*; the church of *Stalham* (Stalham), with land which was Odulf's; the church of *Waxtonesham* (Waxham), with land which belonged to Eadric *stiresman*; the churches of *Wintertun* (Winterton) and *Sumerton* (East and West Somerton), with land which was Godric's; the churches of *Thirne* (Thurne) and *Askeby* (Ashby), with land in those vills and in Rollesby which belonged to Æthelwine *alderman*; the church of *Castra* (Caister next Yarmouth), with

land in that vill which belonged to Grimolf the Dane;
land at *Redham* (Reedham) and *Nortuna* (Norton Sub-
course), which belonged to Æthelwine *alderman*; the
church of *Bastwick* (Woodbastwick), with land in that vill
which belonged to Æthelwine *alderman*; the church of
Randewrðe (Ranworth), with land which belonged to
Æthelward the priest; the church of St Martin of Shotes-
ham, with land in that vill and in *Grenesvilla* (Grenvills in
Stoke Holy Cross) which was Brihtric's; land in *Tybenham*
(Tibenham) which belonged to Æthelwine *ealdorman*.

K 785.

Best edited in *The Eleventh and Twelfth Century Sections of Cotton
MS. Galba E ii* (the Register of the Abbey of St Benet of Holme),
ed. J. R. West, Norfolk Record Society, nos. 2, 3 (1932), I,
p. 5; II, p. 199. Dr Harmer (H pp. 42–3) mentions doubtful
features, and thinks it not unlikely that the charter was fabricated after the Conquest. The charter is undated, and there are
anachronisms in the witness list, which, for example, includes
both Bishop Ælfwine of Winchester and Bishop Æthelmær of
Thetford (*sic* for East Anglia). But Æthelmær did not succeed
to East Anglia until his predecessor Stigand was translated to
Winchester, and this did not occur until after the death of
Bishop Ælfwine on 29 August 1047. However, the charter's list
of lands and their original owners contains information which is
independent both of DB and of the early list of benefactors who
were admitted to the confraternity of the abbey (Dugdale III,
p. 89), and it appears likely that this part of the charter is based
on authentic material.

Among the landowners whose names appear in the charter,
perhaps the most interesting is Æthelwine *alderman*, who held
land in thirteen of the places which descended to the abbey.
Is he to be identified with Ealdorman Æthelwine of East Anglia,
the patron of Ramsey, who died in 992 and was buried at Ramsey
(Chron Rams p. 106)? This Æthelwine is known to have held
land in Norfolk (No. 122) and it would have been possible for
other property of his to have been given to St Benedict of Holme
by his descendants. But a more likely hypothesis is that the two
Æthelwines are not identical, and that the title *alderman* given
in the Holme charter is a courtesy title, not implying high office;
thus Grimolf the Dane, the donor of Caistor, is called *Grynolfus
laicus aldermannus* in another Holme text (Dugdale III, p. 81).
Moreover, the charter says Æthelwine *alderman* gave Scottow to

the abbey, and the list of Holme benefactors already cited records that "Alfwinus" the donor of Scottow was buried at Holme
(*ibid.*, p. 89). See further H pp. 555–6, where he is identified
with Æthelwig of Thetford.

Names appearing in this list of benefactors which do not appear in the charter include Wulfric, who gave Heigham, and
who is possibly identical with men of the same name who gave
Hardley and Waxham; Edgiva Swanneshals, who gave Thurgarton; Ernwald, who gave Witchingham; Osfryth, who gave Fel-
mingham; and Leofward, who gave Tibenham. All of these
donations are to be dated 1022 × 1066.

135. N.D.   (c.1047)   ***King EDWARD to Archbishop Stigand, Bishop Æthelmær, Earl Gyrth, and Toli the sheriff.
Writ declaring that he has given to Ramsey Abbey judicial
and financial rights and shipwreck and what is cast up by
the sea at *Bramcæstre* (Brancaster) and *Ringstyde* (Ring-
stead), the soke within *Bichamdic*, the market at *Dunham*
(Downham Market), and judicial and financial rights in
every shire in which St Benedict of Ramsey has land.

♦H 61.

See also No. 45.

136. N.D.   (1047 × 1070)   *Bishop ÆTHELMÆR of Elmham
to Bury St Edmunds. Estates at Hindringham, Langham,
Hindoluestone (Hindolveston), and *Suanetone* (Swanton
Novers), and half a hundred marks of silver.   ♦W xxxv.

BBL lists have "lx" marks, so the measure would seem to be
the long hundred. See also No. 132.

137. N.D.   (Sept. 1051 × March 1052)   *King EDWARD to
Bishop Æthelmær and Earl Ælfgar. Writ declaring that
his mother is to have the estate at *Kirkeby* (Kirby Cane)
as fully as her retainer Leofstan had it.   ♦H 16.

138. N.D.   (1051 × 1052, or 1053 × 1057)   *King EDWARD
to Bishop Æthelmær and Earl Ælfgar. Writ testifying to
Ælfric Modercope's grant of *Lodne* (Loddon) after his
death to the monastery of Bury St Edmunds.   ♦H 22.

139. N.D.   (1052 × 1057)   *King EDWARD to Bishop Æthel-

mær and Earl Ælfgar and all his thegns in Norfolk. Writ declaring that the land at *Kirkeby* (Kirby Cane) is to belong to (Bury) St Edmunds with sake and soke as fully as any man had it, and as his mother bequeathed it to that house. And they are to pronounce the king's lawful judgement upon whoever has illegally occupied *Semere* (Semer).

♦H 17.

See the notes to No. 133 above.

(118) N.D. (1052 × 1066) *Will of KETEL. *Herlinge* (East Harling) to Archbishop Stigand; he records agreements with his uncles Edwin and Wulfric concerning *Meþeltune* (Great Melton), and *Thorpe* (Thorpe near Fundenhall), and with his sisters Bote concerning *Keteringham* (Ketteringham), and Gode concerning Walsingham (in East Carleton); his brother Godric is to have *Hemfordham* (Hainford), and also *Strattune* (Stratton Strawless), for which he is to pay Ælfwig, Ketel's servant, two pounds. Earl Harold is to have *Moran* (? Mousehold Heath). Lands in Suffolk and Essex.   ♦W XXXIV.

See also p. 77.

140. N.D. (1053 × 1057) *King EDWARD to Bishop Stigand, Bishop Æthelmær, Earl Ælfgar, and all his thegns in Norfolk. Writ declaring that the soke within *Bichamdic* (the dyke at Beechamwell) is to belong to St Benedict of Ramsey as fully and completely as it was first given to that church, and he forbids anyone to usurp the rights there. And they are to assist Abbot Ælfwine and the brothers of Ramsey to obtain justice.   ♦H 60.

The soke *infra Bichamdic* was the soke of the hundred and a half of Clacklose, which was appendant to the Ramsey manor of Wimbotsham.—Cart Rams I, p. 241.

141. N.D. (? c.1060) *THURKIL and ÆTHELGYTH to Bury St Edmunds. The reversion of *Wigorham* (Wereham).

♦W XXXVI.

(47) N.D. (c.1062) ***King EDWARD to Ramsey Abbey.

Confirmation of lands in Norfolk, and in Lincs., Cambs., Beds., Hunts., Northants., and Herts.   K 809.

The Norfolk estates are the same as those appearing in the spurious charter of Edgar (No. 18). See also pp. 39, 52, and 77.

ADDENDUM

120A. 942   **EDMUND, king of the English and ruler of the peoples round about, to Theodred, bishop of London. 400 "arvi segetes" in the isle of *Suthereye* (Southery), free of all but the three common dues.   CS 774.

It seems probable that "arvi segetes" means acres, and that the long hundred is intended, i.e. 4 carucates of 120 acres. Bury St Edmunds, to whom part of this estate descended (Dugdale III, p. 140), held 2 carucates there at the time of DB; the remainder was left to St Paul's (cf. p. 79, No. 49).

CHAPTER V

THE EARLY CHARTERS OF
LINCOLNSHIRE

(1) 664 ****WULFHERE, king of the Mercians and of the Middle and Southern Angles, to the monastery of *Medeshamstede* (Peterborough). Confirmation of privileges and lands including: *Hrepingas* (? Rippingale), *Cadenac* (? Cadney), *Swynesheved* (Swineshead), *Lodeshale* al. *Lodeshac* (? Louth), *Barchanig* (Bardney), *Wassingburge* (Washingborough), *Langeledenham* (Leadenham), *Fiskerton* (Fiskerton), *Refham* (Reepham), *Scotere* (Scotter), *Scalthorpe* (Scotterthorpe in Scotter), *Scotton* (Scotton), *Thorpe* (Northorpe), *Iolthorpe* (Yawthorpe), *Risum* (Riseholme), *Messingham* (Messingham), *Malmiton* (Manton), *Cletham* (Cleatham), *Hibaldstowe* (Hibaldstowe), *Ragenildetorpe* (Ravensthorpe), *Holm* (Holme in Bottesford), *Riseby* (Risby near Market Rasen), *Walcote super Humbram* (Walcot in Alkborough), *Alkebarue* (Alkborough), *Normanby* (Normanby—one of the five holdings of this name in the county), *Alethorpe* (Althorpe), *Thurleby* (Thurlby), *Osgoteby* (Osgodby in Lavington), *Walcote juxta Trickingham* (Walcot near Folkingham), *Breidesthorpe* (Bowthorpe in Manthorpe), *Manthorpe* (Manthorpe), *Carletun* (Carlton Scroop), and *Quadaveringge in Hoyland* (Quadring in Holland). Lands in Leics., Rutland, Notts., Yorks., Hunts., Soke of Peterborough, Kent, and Salop.   CS 22, 22a.

♦*Shrops. Arch. Soc. Transactions*, 4th series, I, 1911, p. 2. ECWM No. 426. For the names as far as Washingborough, see Stenton's *Medeshamstede* and Nos. 144, 145, 146, and 147. *Lodeshale* al. *Lodeshac*, previously unidentified, is probably Louth (DB *Ludes*), where there was a monastery in 790 (ASC F). If so, we seem to have here another colony of Peterborough. For *Langeledenham*, see Fo p. 75. The remaining names appear roughly in the same order as the Peterborough holdings in the Lincs. DB, which was no doubt the forger's source for details of these estates. See also pp. 21, 107, and 110.

142. N.D.   (669 × 672)   King WULFHERE of Mercia to Bishop Ceadda of Lichfield. 50 hides to build a monastery at *Adbearw* (Barrow-on-Humber), in the province of Lindsey.

Lost.

HE IV, c. 3. A charter of King Ethelbald of Mercia dated 743 "*on þam cynehame þe is ge cyged Bearuwe*" was probably drawn up at Barrow-on-Humber, cf. CS 165; ECWM No. 23.

143. N.D.   (675 × 691)   **King ÆTHELRED of the Mercians, when on a visit to the brethren of *Medeshamstede* (Peterborough), gave them for the health of his soul 30 "manentes" in the place called *Leugttricdun* (? Laughterton), and shortly afterwards, when some of the brethren visited him, in his own chamber and before many witnesses he placed a turf taken from that land upon a gospel book as a confirmation and evidence of his gift. There were present Saxulf, bishop of the Mercians; Wecca and Berthhun, monks; Hosthrytha the queen; Herifrit and Eadfrit, *principes* of King Æthelred. An anathema follows.

CS 840.

♦Stenton's *Medeshamstede*, pp. 315–16, the source of the above translation. On the identification, which is not certain, see Ekwall p. 276.

144. N.D.   (675 × 691)   **The *princeps* FRIDURIC to Hædda, abbot of Breedon (Leics.). 31 "manentes" called *Hrepingas* (? Rippingale). For confirmation of his gift, at Friduric's request, King Æthelred and Bishop Saxulf [of the Mercians] joining their hands placed a turf from the land on a gospel-book before a multitude of people, and confirmed the testimony of this writing by subscribing in their own hands.   CS 842.

♦Stenton's *Medeshamstede*, p. 316. For the identification, see Ekwall p. 370. Stenton thinks this too far from Breedon, but against this it may be argued that Peterborough, the mother house of Breedon, held at an early date land at Swineshead and Sempringham, both near Rippingale (Nos. 146, 147, 149).

145. N.D. (675 × 691)   *King ÆTHELRED of the Mercians
to Hædda, abbot of Breedon (Leics.). 15 "manentes" called
Cedenan ác (? Cadney). For this Hædda gave to King Æthelred 500 *solidi* and a number of presents (detailed). When
this was done, King Æthelred in his chamber in his own
vicus called *Tomtun* (Tamworth, Staffs.), joining hands with
the queen and Bishop Saxulf, placed a turf from the land
on a gospel-book before many witnesses in confirmation.
An anathema follows.   CS 843.

   ♦Stenton's *Medeshamstede*, p. 316. The form of the place-name
given in No. 146 is *Cadenac*, which could be "*Cada*'s oak." Cadney was *Cada*'s island (Ekwall p. 77).

146. (680)   ***Pope AGATHO to Æthelred, king of the Mercians; Theodore, archbishop of Canterbury; and Saxulf,
bishop of the Middle Angles or Mercians. Letter granting
privileges to *Medeshamstede* (Peterborough), with confirmation by King Æthelred of privileges and lands including
Hrepingas (? Rippingale), *Cadenac* (? Cadney), *Swinehafed*
(Swineshead), *Lodeshale* (? Louth), and *Bardunig* (Bardney). Lands in Shrops., Leics., and Kent.
                                    CS 48 (Latin) and 49 (OE).

   See Stenton's *Medeshamstede*, p. 314; Levison p. 201; ECWM
No. 427. For the identifications, see No. 1.

147. N.D. (787 × 796)   *BEONNA, abbot of Peterborough,
with the consent of the monks, to the *princeps* Cuthbert.
Lease of 10 "manentes" *æt Suinesheabde* (Swineshead), with
the pasture, meadows, and woodland belonging to it.
Cuthbert pays 1,000 *solidi*, and renders one day's food-
rent or 30 *sicli* each year. And after Cuthbert's death, his
heirs are to observe the terms of the agreement, both in
money and in food-rent, and upon their death the estate
is to be returned intact to the abbey. Witnesses: Offa,
king of the Mercians; Ecgfrith, king of the Mercians;
Hygberht, archbishop [of Lichfield]; Ceolwulf, bishop [of
Lindsey]; Unwana, bishop [of Leicester]; Abbot Beonna;
Wigbald, priest and archdeacon; Beornwald and Eanred,
priests; Tilþegn.   CS 271.

Dates: between 787 when Ecgfrith, Offa's son, was anointed king of the Mercians (Stenton p. 217), and 796 when Offa died. Hygberht first appears as archbishop as a witness to a reliable and datable charter in 788 (CS 253, cf. Stenton p. 216). On the authenticity of this lease, see Stenton's *Medeshamstede*, pp. 313–14, and for further comment see Stenton p. 477 and RE p. 168. For the term *sicli*=shekels, cf. ECWM pp. 104–5 and CS 513.

148. N.D.   (825)   ****ALGARUS the son of Vorthangia to Syward, abbot of Crowland. The manor and 4 carucates at Baston.   CS 383.

This Crowland forgery does not appear in the pseudo-Ingulf.

149. N.D.   (852)   *Agreement between CEOLRED, abbot of Peterborough, and Wulfred. The abbey leases *Sempinga-ham* (Sempringham) to Wulfred for two lives, reserving for themselves the estate at *Slioforda* (Sleaford, which appears from the agreement to be appended to Sempring-ham). And after the death of Wulfred and his heir, 12 hides at *Forde* and *Cegle* (Cheal in Gosberton) are to be given to the abbot. Wulfred is granted two hides at *Leh-cotum* (unidentified, but probably one of the Lincolnshire Cotes), with the right that it should descend to his heirs. Land in Rutland.   ♦R VII.

Authenticity: see Stenton's *Medeshamstede*, pp. 313–14. *Forde* is unidentified; R. Lennard has suggested tentatively Greatford in Ness Wapentake, Lincs.—*Econ. Hist. Rev.*, XIV, 1944–5, p. 57 n.7. See also p. 107.

150. 971   *EDGAR, king of the whole island of Britain, to Bishop Æthelwold, for the endowment of the newly re-founded monastery at Peterborough. The estate *æt Bearuwe* (Barrow-on-Humber) which was once the possession of St Ceadda, before its destruction by the pagans. For this, Æthelwold gives the king 40 pounds in silver, a golden cross, and many other costly gifts.   CS 1270.

The hidage is not given. The estate was lost by Peterborough in the period 1005 × 1041; cf. HC p. 64.

151. N.D.   (971 × 983)   *Will of ÆTHELMÆR, ealdorman [of

Hampshire]. One pound to *Burnan* (? Bourne). Lands in Wilts. and Rutland. ◆W x.

Presumably there was a minster at Bourne, if this identification is correct. The church and priest appear in Lincs. DB (pp. 162–3), and later there was a small Augustinian priory there. See also p. 107.

(15) 972 ***EDGAR, king of Great Britain, at the petition of Bishop Æthelwold, to the monastery once called *Medeshamsted* and now, being restored, called *Burch* (Peterborough). Confirmation of lands and privileges, including the estate at *Baruue* (Barrow-on-Humber). Lands in Hunts. and the Soke of Peterborough.

CS 1258, 1280 (Latin), 1281 (OE).

An alleged confirmation of this charter by Edward the Confessor reads: "and I concede freely the vill of *Fiskertune* (Fiskerton), which Abbot Leofric at my request gave (or surrendered its jurisdiction) to my queen, with land, woods, waters, and other appurtenances. Similarly other lands which were added in my time, namely *Æstuna* (Ashton Wold, Northants.), *Flettuna* (Fletton, Hunts.), *Overtuna* (Orton Waterville, Hunts.), *Aluultuna* (Alwalton, Hunts.), and *Osgotebi* (Osgodby in Lavington)." See also pp. 26 and 112.

(21) N.D. (986) Will of ÆTHELSTAN MANNESSUNE. Land at *Haggethorn* (Hackthorn) to his youngest daughter Ælfwenna, and after her death to Ramsey Abbey. Lands in Cambs., Hunts., Beds., and Norfolk.

Chron Rams pp. 59–60, 192; LE p. 91.

DB records that TRE Hackthorn was divided into several holdings, none of them being then in the possession of Ramsey. The particular holding given by Æthelstan to Ramsey can be identified, however, in a roundabout way, with the 3 bovates held at Hackthorn in 1086 by Auti, the man of Archbishop Thomas of York (Lincs. DB, p. 27, no. 17). It was claimed by Robert of Stafford that the land of Auti ought to lie in the soke of his (Robert's) predecessor Lepsi (*ibid.*, p. 227, no. 16). Now the only place in which Lepsi had been Robert's predecessor was Metheringham (*ibid.*, p. 188, no. 19), and Lepsi is to be identified with the Leofsige the Deacon of No. 154 below, who gave estates near Metheringham to Ramsey Abbey; it seems likely, therefore, that Ramsey granted the soke of Hackthorn to

Leofsige in return for his gifts of land to the abbey. See also pp. 29 and 45.

152. N.D.   (1002 × 1004)   *Will of WULFRIC SPOTT. *Taða-wyllan* (Tathwell) to the abbey of Burton-on-Trent. Lands in Glos., Staffs., Lancs., Yorks., Derbys., Leics., Worcs., Notts., Cheshire, and Warwicks.   ♦W XVII.

OS Facs III, Anglesey 2. Tathwell is a long way from the other estates of Wulfric, but his brother held lands in Northants. (No. 347) and no other example of the name is known. There is no record in DB of the abbey possessing land in Lincolnshire.

153. N.D.   (1016 × 1034)   ÆTHELRIC, bishop of Dorchester, to Ramsey Abbey. The estate called *Offerthun* in Holland, to provide beans, salt, and honey for the monks.   *Lost.*

Chron Rams p. 145. In the spurious confirmation charter of King Edward (No. 73) this estate is called *Orfyridtune*. Thorpe p. 383 n. 8 quotes an inspeximus, source not given, with the variant *Osfyrðtunæ*. In the confirmation charter of William I (Chron Rams p. 202) the spelling is *Osfirdetune*. This suggests that the original name was "Osferth's tun," with later misreading of OE 's' as 'r' and 'f'. The place-name is now lost, but the site can be located, for the Ramsey account of the transaction goes on to say that the estate passed into the hands of Alan the Red after the Conquest. It must therefore be the carucate at Drayton in Swineshead which had belonged to Ramsey, but which was usurped by Count Alan at the time of DB. The jurors of Kirton wapentake bore witness that Ramsey had leased the estate to Bishop Wulfwig (of Dorchester, 1053 × 1067); at the inquest the estate was claimed by his successor, Bishop Remigius (of Lincoln, to which the seat of the bishopric had been removed). The DB description of the estate mentions a saltpan, and there can be no doubt that the beans and honey for the monks were also provided in kind from the holding there.— Lincs. DB p. 68, no. 59; p. 235, no. 1. The journey by road would be about 40 miles. This is an early example of the food farm supplied by a monastic estate; cf. RE pp. 130–41.

154. N.D.   (1040 × 1041)   LEOFSIGE the Deacon to Ramsey Abbey. Land at *Langetune* (Langton by Horncastle), *Wipsin-tone* (Wispington), *Mertona* (Martin), and *Wathingworthe* (Waddingworth).   *Lost.*

Chron Rams pp. 153–4. Dates: during the episcopate of Eadnoth II, bishop of Dorchester 1034 × 1049, who was at Ramsey when the transaction was completed; in the abbey chronicle it is included among the gifts made in the time of King Harthacnut, 1040–1. The Ramsey account says that before he was ordained, Leofsige had a son called Morcar, who was sent to school at Ramsey, and eventually became a monk there. At the time of the gift, the brothers of Ramsey granted to Leofsige the monkhood, and to the mother of the boy the veil in Ramsey, whenever they wished to change their state of life. Upon the death of Leofsige, Morcar successfully claimed the estates on behalf of the abbey at a court held at Lincoln in the presence of Edward of Salisbury (sheriff of Wiltshire after the Conquest), and farmed them as a monk, paying a yearly rent to the abbey, until they were seized by Odo, bishop of Bayeux (cf. RE p. 158 and n. 2).

DB shows that Leofsige's estate at Langton passed to Odo (Lincs. DB p. 43, no. 51), but Martin, Waddingworth, and Wispington were obtained by Eudo, son of Spirewic (*ibid.*, p. 135, nos. 5 and 6; p. 136, no. 7). The remaining estates of Leofsige the Deacon, at Grainsby, Riseholme, Bag Enderby, and Metheringham, were all in the hands of the Conqueror's followers by the time of DB (*ibid.*, p. 63, no. 20; p. 118, no. 2; p. 134, no. 38; p. 188, no. 19).

155. N.D. (1053 × 1055)   *Agreement between Bishop Wulfwig [of Dorchester] and Earl Leofric and his wife Godgifu, concerning the endowment of Stow St Mary.
♦R cxv.

♦H. E. Salter, *The Cartulary of the Abbey of Eynsham*, Oxford Hist. Soc., I, 1906–7, pp. 28–9; see also F. Harmer, 'Chipping and Market', in *The Early Cultures of North West Europe*, ed. Sir Cyril Fox and Bruce Dickins, Cambridge, 1950, pp. 358–60; RE pp. 297–8. For a list of the estates used for this endowment, see No. 156.

156. N.D. (1055 × 1057)   ***Pope VICTOR [II] to Godgifu, wife of Earl Leofric [of Mercia]. Confirmation of her endowment of *Stou* (Stow St Mary) with estates at *Newarcha* (Newark) and *Flatburche* (Fledborough, Notts.) and *Brandon* (Brampton in Torksey) and *Martine-Welle* (Marton in Well wapentake).   K 818.

The dates assigned to this spurious charter are those of the papacy of Victor II, but the name of Ealdred appears among the witnesses as archbishop of York, to which see he was not appointed until 1060. Another anachronism in the witness list is the presence there of both Siward (died 1053) and Tostig, his successor to the earldom of Northumbria. The list of estates said to have been used by Godgifu for the endownmet of Stow appears, however, to have been based on a reliable tradition. See No. 155 and Lincs. DB p. 47. no. 7/1 ; p. 48, no. 10 ; p. 243, no. 1.

157. N.D. (1055 × 1060) ***King EDWARD to Peterborough Abbey. Confirmation of a gift to the abbey by his thegn Askil, upon his journeying to Rome, of his land at *Walecote quae est iuxta fluvium Humbrae* (Walcot-on-Trent, near Alkborough); and he frees the land of all service except the three common dues.   K 806.

   Printed by Kemble from the Black Book of Peterborough; the pseudo-original survives in the Marquess of Exeter's collection at Burghley House, Stamford, as a separate membrane in a late eleventh-century hand, bearing the contemporary endorsement: *Landboc of Walecote by humbre.* The charter has no dating clause, but claims to be witnessed *inter alia* by Tostig, who was appointed earl of Northumbria in 1055, and by Archbishop Cynesige of York, who died in 1060. In one of the Peterborough cartularies Askil is called the son of Toke (cf. HC p. 71 n. 1), and he witnesses No. 158 as *Askill Tokes sune.* F. M. Stenton suggests that he was killed at Stamford Bridge or Hastings (Lincs. DB p. xli). On the authenticity of this charter, see No. 159.

158. (1060) ***King EDWARD to Peterborough Abbey. Confirmation of a gift to the abbey, by the will of Leofgifu of London, of the vill of *Fiskertun* (Fiskerton). Upon Leofgifu's death on a pilgrimage to Jerusalem, the estate had been acquired by Eadgyð, Edward's queen, who declared that it had been given her by Leofgifu; whereupon Abbot Leofric of Peterborough purchased the estate from Eadgyð, with the consent of her brothers Harold and Tostig, for 200 marks of gold, and ornaments of the church worth a further 20 marks.   K 808.

   The witness list is compatible with the date. On Eadgyth's interests in the area, see p. 247 and Barlow p. 52 n. 2. On the authenticity of this charter, see No. 159.

159. (1060 × 1066)   ***King EDWARD to Abbot Leofric of Peterborough. Confirmation of an agreement made in the king's presence, by which the monk Brand leased to his brother Askil three estates, namely *Scottun* (Scotton), which Brand himself had bought; *Scottere* (Scotter), which his brother Siric had given him; and *Malmetun* (Manton), which his father had given him by word of mouth. The lease had been on these terms: that Askil should pay a yearly rent as long as he held them; after his death, the two first-named estates should revert to the monastery, together with another estate called *Thorp* (Northorpe) in the place of Manton.   K 819.

The charter has no dating clause, but claims to be witnessed by Ealdred, who succeeded Cynesige as archbishop of York in 1060. It appears together with Nos. 157 and 158 on successive pages of the Black Book of Peterborough, and as these three charters have certain features in common, it is convenient to discuss their authenticity as a group.

Stenton (Lincs. DB p. xli) and Lennard (RE pp. 167–9) both appear to consider these charters authentic. Barlow (Vita Edwardi p. 69 n. 1) quotes No. 159 as evidence for a pilgrimage to Jerusalem. Oleson (pp. 153–4) also accepts all three charters as genuine; but his tests of authenticity appear to be restricted to whether or not the dates of witnesses to a charter are compatible one with another, and with the charter's dating clause. But genuine charters of confirmation (as opposed to donation) by King Edward are uncommon, and the occurrence of three such examples in the archives of a single house gives immediate cause for suspicion. The diplomatic they employ is unusual, but because of the rarity of authentic confirmation charters, one cannot press this point very far. The reference in No. 158 to "sake and soke" is, however, highly suspicious, as is the freeing of the estate from services except fortification and military service, without reference to bridges.

The basic information in the three charters appears in various passages in Hugh Candidus (HC pp. 40–2, 67, 71), and there is no reason to doubt that the transactions actually took place. It seems likely, however, that the charters themselves were forged after the Domesday Inquest, to support the claims of Peterborough to the estates concerned. The pseudo-original of No. 157 is in a late eleventh-century hand. The information within No. 159 looks as if it is modelled (incorrectly) on an

D*

entry in the Lincolnshire *clamores* (Lincs. DB 71-15). Moreover, the minor names in the three witness lists are all those of Lincolnshire thegns who had dealings with Peterborough, and who figure prominently in DB. Further doubtful features in the witness lists are the descriptions of the bishop of Dorchester's see as Lincoln, to which place the seat of the bishopric was not transferred until after the Conquest; and the description of the stallers Ralph and Esgar as "dapifers," a term which does not appear elsewhere in pre-Conquest texts. Considering the three charters together, Nos. 157 and 158 could have been drawn up on the same occasion, but No. 159 (if authentic) must have been witnessed at a later date, after Ealdred's accession to York. The concentration of Lincolnshire names, to the exclusion of all others, among the minor witnesses in all three charters could only mean that if they were authentic, King Edward must have been in Lincolnshire, or at least in Peterborough, on the occasion when each was drawn up. When one considers this in relation to the rarity of Edward's authentic charters of confirmation, it seems unlikely that these particular examples are genuine instruments. It is safer to assume that they are late eleventh-century forgeries by a monk of Peterborough, having access both to the returns of the Domesday Inquest and to the material at Peterborough lying behind the Chronicle of Hugh Candidus. Leofgifu's alleged pilgrimage to Jerusalem (No. 158) should be compared with Askil's alleged pilgrimage to Rome (No. 157). The forger possibly got his idea from the pilgrimage to Jerusalem of Ulf and Madselin, whose (authentic) will, dated 1066 × 1069 (W xxxix) is entered together with these doubtful charters in the Peterborough Black Book.

(47) N.D.   (c. 1062)   ***King EDWARD to Ramsey Abbey. Confirmation of estates, including *Orfyridtune* in Holland, Langton by Horncastle, Wispington, Martin, Mareham on the Hill, and Quarrington. Lands in Cambs., Norfolk, Suffolk, Hunts., Beds., Northants., and Herts.   K. 809.

For *Orfyridtune*, see No. 153. See also pp. 39, 52, 77, and 95.

CHAPTER VI

THE EARLY CHARTERS OF
RUTLAND

(1) 664   ****WULFHERE, king of the Mercians and of the Middle and Southern Angles, to the monastery of *Medeshamstede* (Peterborough). Confirmation of privileges, and lands including: *Glathestune* (Glaston), *Tynewelle* (Tinwell), *Ingeðorp* (Ingthorpe), *Rihale* (Ryhall), and *Belmesthorpe* (Belmesthorpe). Lands in Leics., Lincs., Notts., Yorks., Hunts., Soke of Peterborough, Kent, and Salop.

CS 22, 22a.

See also pp. 21, 97, and 110.

(149) N.D.   (852)   *Agreement between CEOLRED, abbot of Peterborough, and Wulfred. The abbey leases *Sempingaham* (Sempringham, Lincs.) to Wulfred for two lives, and every year 60 fothers of wood, 12 of brushwood, and 6 of faggots are to be given to the monastery from the wood at *Hornan* (Horne). Other lands in Lincs.   ♦R VII.

Evidently the wood at Horne was part of the Sempringham estate. See also p. 100.

(151) N.D.   (971 × 973)   *Will of ÆTHELMÆR, ealdorman [of Hampshire]. *Cottesmore* (Cottesmore) to his youngest son (unnamed). Land in Wilts.   ♦W x.

Cottesmore is a long way from Æthelmær's other estates, but no other example of the name is known. TRE it belonged to "Goda" (DB fo. 293b), who is probably to be identified with Gytha, the wife of Earl Ralph of Hereford (VCH *Rutland*, 1, p. 134). See also p. 101 for a bequest to Bourne, Lincs.

160. N.D.   (1042 × 1055)   *GODGIFU to Peterborough Abbey. *Righale* (Ryhall) and *Beolmesðorp* (Belmesthorpe).

K 927.

This entry in the Peterborough Black Book takes the form of

a straightforward history of the estates, which runs: "The widow Godgifu gave to St Peter of Burch two vills called Ryhall and Belmesthorpe for the redemption of her soul, with the consent of King Edward. Afterwards she married Earl Siward [of Northumbria and Hunts.], and not long after, she died. An agreement was then made between Earl Siward and Abbot Leofric and the brethren [of Peterborough] that Siward should hold the vills for as long as he lived, after which they should revert to the abbey. Upon Siward's death [in 1055] his son Waltheof made an agreement with Abbot Leofric, in the presence of King Edward, by which Waltheof received 5 marks of gold, and he was to hold Ryhall for life; but by the judgement of King Edward, Belmesthorpe was to remain in the possession of Peterborough Abbey.[1] But after King Edward's death, Waltheof broke this agreement. Subsequently repenting of this, Waltheof went to the monastery, and granted to St Peter the reversion of the two estates, after his own lifetime." The entry copied into the Black Book ends with an anathema. Waltheof was executed in 1076. In spite of the anathema, the abbey did not obtain the reversion of the estates, which remained in the possession of Waltheof's widow, the Countess Judith (VCH *Northants.*, 1, p. 350; VCH *Rutland*, i, p. 142). It is not known how Godgifu obtained the estates, which had previously been given to Peterborough by Halfdene (No. 350). She was the donor to Peterborough of lands in Northants., Yorks., and Lincs. (No. 353), and it could well be that Ryhall and Belmesthorpe had been given to her by Peterborough as a life lease in return for these favours. See also VCH *Rutland*, ii, p. 269, and D. Whitelock in Clemoes, p. 84 n. 4.

161. 1046   *EDWARD, king of all Britain, to his minster Æðelstan. 3 "cassati" at *Æðelstanes tun* (Ayston), free of all but the three common dues.   K 784.

[Professor Finberg contributes the following commentary on the bounds of this charter.]

The boundary is covered by sheet SK 80 of the 2½-inch OS map.

It runs as follows:

1. From Thornham Brook

Starting at the point (Grid ref. 877015) where the road from

---

[1] That Peterborough held Belmesthorpe for a short period TRE is confirmed by an entry in the Lincolnshire Domesday.—DB i fo. 366d: Lincs. DB p. 176, no. 4.

Preston to Glaston crosses a brook. The brook has no name on the modern map, but there are hawthorns growing near it.

2. to Thursley Brook;

following the line of the present parish boundary southward to 882008, and there turning westward.

3. then to Martin's-hoe (i.e. spur or heel);

Now Castle Hill (850005). This promontory forms the westward end of the plateau on which Ayston stands. Its Saxon name must be connected with the former church of St Martin in Martinsthorpe, 2¾ miles away to the NE., and with Martinsley, the hundred in which it stands.

4. Then to Holbrook (i.e. sunken brook, brook in a ravine);

This brook flows down the valley below Castle Hill, and for part of its course still forms the parish boundary of Ayston (845007).

5. Then to Brockholes (=badger holes);

? 844012. The boundary climbs up the plateau again, and crosses A47, the main Uppingham–Leicester road.

6. Then to Red Way;

843019. This is the lane leading to Ridlington; the name Red Way was probably suggested by the underlying ironstone. It leads to the Thornham Brook, along which the parish and charter boundaries now turn eastward.

7. From Red Way then to Wing Ford,

868014, where the road from Preston to Uppingham crosses the brook.

8. And then again to Thornham Brook.

Back to the starting-point.

162. N.D.   (1053 × 1066—possibly 28 Dec. 1065 × 5 Jan. 1066)   *King EDWARD to Bishop Wulfwig [of Dorchester], Northman the sheriff [of Northamptonshire], and Ælfwine, Merefinnes son, and all his thegns in Northamptonshire. Writ declaring that he has given to Westminster Abbey *Roteland* (Rutland) and all that belongs to it; and Queen Edith is to have it for her lifetime, and annually enrich the monastery therefrom.   ♦H 94.

RE pp. 169–70.

CHAPTER VII

THE EARLY CHARTERS OF
THE SOKE OF PETERBOROUGH

(1) 664 ****WULFHERE, king of the Mercians and of the Middle and Southern Angles, to the monastery of *Medeshamstede* (Peterborough). Confirmation of privileges, and lands including: *Thorpe* (Thorpe Hall), *Dodesthorpe* (Dogsthorpe), *Estfelde* (Eastfield), *Newerke* (Newark), *Carton et Eye* (Garton End and Eye), *Wytherintgon* (Werrington), *Gunthorpe* (Gunthorpe), *Peichirche* (Peakirk), *Glinton* (Glinton), *Depingge* (Deeping Gate), *marisca de Peichirche* (Peakirk Marsh), *marisca de Eye* (Eye Marsh), *Hermitorio de Senglesholt* (Singleshole Farm in Eye), *Castre* (Castor), *Eylesworthe* (Ailsworth), *Sutton* (Sutton), *Upton* (Upton), *Milton* (Milton Park), *Bernake* (Barnack), *Suthorpe* (Southorpe), *Walcote* (Walcot Hall in Southorpe), *Pilesgate* (Pilsgate), *Ufforde* (Ufford), *Badington* (Bainton), *Aiston* (Ashton in Bainton), *Torpel* (lost, in Ufford), *Thornhawe* (Thornhaugh), *Sibertone* (Sibberton Lodge in Thornhaugh), *Walmesforde* (Wansford), *Witheringge* (Wittering), *Wirthorpe* (Wothorpe), *Burle* (Burghley House), *Makeseye* (Maxey), *Loholm* (Lolham Hall in Maxey), *Nunton* (Nunton Lodge in Maxey), *Helpeston* (Helpston), *Northburge* (Northborough), *Etton* (Etton), *Wodecroft* (Woodcroft Castle in Etton), *Paston* (Paston), *Walton* (Walton), and *Marham* (Marholm). Lands in Leics., Rutland, Notts., Yorks., Hunts., Lincs., Kent, and Salop. CS 22, 22a.

This list was compiled in the late eleventh or early twelfth century, and comprises almost the whole of the two hundreds of Nassaburgh in Northants., which became the Soke of Peterborough. See also pp. 21, 97, and 107.

163. 948 *EADRED, king of the English, to his thegn Ælfsige. 3 "mansae" at *Ægelsuurð* (Ailsworth), free of all but the three common dues. CS 871.

Bounds: PN *Northants.*, p. 288 n. 1. The formulas in this charter agree in many places with those found in contemporary texts. The reason for the grant is given in No. 12, where it is recorded that the estate was in the hands of an unnamed woman and her son, who tried to bring about the death of Ælfsige by witchcraft. When this was discovered, the woman was taken and drowned at London bridge, the son was outlawed, and the estate passed to the king, who gave it to Ælfsige.

(12) N.D. (963 × 975) *WULFSTAN UCCEA to Æthelwold, bishop [of Winchester], in exchange for Washington, Sussex. Yaxley, Hunts., and *Ægelswurðe* (Ailsworth).

♦R XXXVII.

See also p. 25.

(13) N.D. (963 × 984) *Bishop ÆTHELWOLD's gifts to Peterborough Abbey upon its restoration. The list includes *Medeshamstede* (the site of the monastery), with its berewicks, and *Anlafestun* (lost) with its berewicks. The seed tithes from *Macuseige* (Maxey), *Nunnetune* (Nunton Lodge in Maxey), *þan oþren Macuseige* (the other Maxey), *Æstune* (Ashton in Bainton), and *Pilesgete* (Pilsgate in Barnack) are also listed. Lands in Hunts. and Northants.

♦R XXXIX.

For the site of *Anlafestun*, see No. 164. See also p. 25.

164. N.D. (963 × 984) List of sureties for Peterborough estates, including: *Æsctune* (Ashton in Bainton), *Anlafestune*, *Badingtune* (Bainton), *Beornican* (Barnack), *Burh* (Peterborough), *Castre* (Castor), *Hylpestune* (Helpston), *Macusige* (Maxey), *Mylatune* (Milton Park in Castor), *Oxanige* (Oxney in Peterborough), *Pilesgate* (Pilsgate in Barnack), *Theorp* (Longthorp), *Uptune* (Upton), *Waltune* (Walton), *Wiðeringa eige* (Wittering), *Wyðreðe cross* (Wittering Cross), and *Wylmesforda* (Wansford). Lands in Northants.

♦R XL.

The sites of *Wyðreðe* cross, a hundred meeting-place, and *Anlafestune*, a lost place-name, have not hitherto been located. The sureties for *Anlafestune* included men from Longthorp, Barnack, and Helpston, and the name occurs also in No. 13, in a context suggesting that it lay close to the monastery itself; the site may have been near the watercourse known in 1753 as *Allerton Gull*, whence the modern *Alwalton Gull Road* in Peterborough; cf. PN *Northants.*, p. 226. The late association with Alwalton, Hunts., is misleading.

(15)   (972)   ***EDGAR, king of Great Britain, at the petition of Bishop Æthelwold, to the monastery once called *Medes-hamstede* and now, being restored, called *Burch* (Peterborough). Confirmation of privileges, and lands including *Dodethorp* (Dogsthorp), *Aege* (Eye), *Pastone* (Paston), *Thorp* (Thorp Hall), *Waltun* (Walton), *Witheringtun* (Werrington), and a mint at *Stanforde* (Stamford). Lands in Hunts. and Lincs.   CS 1258, 1280 (Latin), 1281 (OE).

See also pp. 25 and 101.

165.   1015   *EDMUND IRONSIDE to New Minster, Winchester. Land *æt Pegecyrcan* (Peakirk), and 3 virgates at *Wealtun* (Walton).   K 726.

See notes on pp. 202–3.

166.   N.D.   (1052 × 1066)   Abbot LEOFRIC of Peterborough to Ælfgar, the chaplain of Queen Edith. Life lease of *Burchle* (Burghley), with reversion to the abbey.   *Lost.*

HC p. 67 and n. 13, which states that when Ælfgar died, King Edward and Queen Edith tried to take the estate away from the abbey. Abbot Leofric established the abbey's right to the land by a payment of 8 gold marks to the king. See, further, RE pp. 162, 168.

167.   N.D.   (1055)   **Exchange of lands between ÆLFWINE, abbot of Ramsey, and LEOFRIC, abbot of Peterborough. Leofric gives to Ælfwine 9 virgates (named) at Lutton, Northants., for which Ælfwine gives to Leofric land at *Marham* (Marholm). In addition Ramsey gives to Peterborough 4,000 eels annually during Lent, for which in return Ramsey is to receive as much building stone as it needs from Peterborough's quarries at *Bernech* (Barnack),

and wall-stone from *Burch* (Peterborough), free from toll by water and by land. *Lost.*

Recited in a spurious writ (H 62), the compiler of which used materials (probably authentic) which are now lost. According to Hugh Candidus (HC p. 70), Marholm (*Marham, Mariham, Martham*) was given to Peterborough by Wulfric Cild some time in the eleventh century.

PART II

CHAPTER VIII

THE EARLY CHARTERS OF
BARKING ABBEY[1]

BEDE's account of Erkenwald's foundation of the monasteries of St Mary at Barking and St Peter at Chertsey does not supply a date,[2] but we know that it occurred during the reigns of King Egbert of Kent[3] (664 × 4 July 673) and King Sebbi of Essex (664 × 694), and probably after the East Saxons had been brought back from their lapse into idolatry in 665. It may well be, therefore, that the traditional foundation date of 666, which appears in the Chertsey Register,[4] is the correct one. Erkenwald himself became the first abbot at Chertsey, and he placed his sister Ethelburga as abbess at Barking, which from Bede's description was evidently a double monastery. Soon afterwards,[5] Erkenwald was enthroned as the fourth bishop at St Paul's; his see was coterminous with the East Saxon province, which then included the whole of the modern counties of Essex and Middlesex, and a large part of south-east Hertfordshire. In addition, his diocese embraced Surrey, which by Erkenwald's day had long since ceased to be part of the East Saxon kingdom.

Erkenwald, who was probably of royal blood,[6] became one

[1] This chapter incorporates a much revised version of parts of my *Early Charters of Barking Abbey*, a limited edition of which was printed privately in 1953: it is now unobtainable.

[2] HE IV, c. 6. Bede's information came from Nothelm, then a priest at St Paul's, later archbishop of Canterbury. He had available also a *Miracula S. Ethelburgae*, now lost.

[3] CS 34; EHD I, pp. 440–1; cf. F. M. Stenton, *Medeshamstede*, p. 313 n. 2.

[4] BM MS. Cotton Vit. A xiii, fo. 19.

[5] After 673: cf. CS 34. The traditional date is 675.

[6] Founders of monasteries—particularly double monasteries—at this period were nearly always members of a royal house. Erkenwald's name, and that of his sister, alliterate with those of the Kentish dynasty. Professor Deansley makes Erkenwald the son of Frithwald, sub-king of Surrey (*The Pre-Conquest Church in England*, 1961, p. 206), but CS 34 establishes that this was not the case.

of the great leaders of the English Church.[1] Dr Myres has pointed
out that the foundation of Chertsey Abbey is the earliest evidence
of Christian enterprise in Surrey;[2] in the East Saxon province
his episcopate was marked by the decline of Celtic usage, and a
return to the Romanizing policy of St Augustine.[3] The tiny and
remote early communities which had been set up by St Cedd at
Tilbury and Ythancestir[4] were allowed to fade into obscurity,
and the new influence was reflected by the growing prestige, both
spiritual and temporal, of the Benedictine rule at Barking Abbey.

Erkenwald was zealous in obtaining gifts of land for his new
foundations. From the king of Kent and the sub-king of Surrey
he received an endowment of over 300 hides for Chertsey,[5] and
the charters now under discussion show that over a period of
some twenty years he persuaded the kings of Essex, Wessex, and
Mercia to endow Barking with lands amounting to a similar
hidage.[6] It was a period of great instability in south-east England,
in which the overlordship of the various kingdoms changed
hands with bewildering rapidity.[7] It might be thought that these
conditions were hardly propitious for the founding of new
monasteries, but such was not the case. Setting aside all question of pious motives, monastic endowments resulted in the
creation of a new, peaceful, and trustworthy class of large here-
ditary landowners, which made for stability within a kingdom,
and it is noteworthy that when political control of a province

[1] His life by Stubbs in the *Dictionary of Christian Biography* was a masterly
exposition of the knowledge then available, but it is now ninety years old, and
a new assessment is needed.

[2] *Roman Britain and the English Settlements*, 1937 edn, p. 370.

[3] In this, Erkenwald aligned himself with Wilfrid and Theodore. For an
account of the differences between the Celtic and Roman usages, see Plum-
mer's *Bede*, II, pp. 348 f, and *Encyclopædia Britannica*, s.v. Easter. The Celtic
influence in the East Saxon Church is traceable to St Cedd's Northumbrian
upbringing. The change to Roman usage was initiated by Cedd just before his
death, when he abandoned the Celtic computation of Easter.

[4] St Peter's-on-the-Wall, near Bradwell-on-Sea.   [5] CS 34.

[6] There is some evidence that 300 hides was regarded as suitable provision
for a major monastery at the end of the seventh century. Gloucester and
Pershore each received an endowment of this size (CS 60), and Malmesbury's
benefactions amounted to a similar total (ECW pp. 69–70). Wenlock received
at least 222 hides (ECWM pp. 204–6).

[7] See p. 119.

changed hands, the new overlords customarily confirmed the monastic land charters of their predecessors.[1] When one considers that at this period the whole East Saxon kingdom was rated at only 7,000 hides,[2] the political importance of these large land gifts to Barking and Chertsey at once becomes apparent.

It is fortunate that of the three land charters relating to the early endowment of Barking for which texts have survived, one of them, which for convenience of identification may be called Erkenwald's Charter, gives a complete list of the abbey's possessions some twenty years after its foundation. The other two charters relate to individual endowments recited in Erkenwald's charter. Taken together, these charters supply much reliable and important information concerning south-east England in the second half of the seventh century, which has been little used by historians in the past. In the edition which follows, the main object has been to discuss the authenticity of the charters, to identify the place-names, and to supply as precisely as possible the dates of the transactions concerned.

ESSEX AND THE HEPTARCHY

If Erkenwald's Charter is to be believed (and for convenience we make this assumption in what follows), Barking Abbey was endowed with no less than eight gifts of land within two decades of its foundation. The donors included kings of Wessex and Mercia as well as Essex, and some of the land lay in Kent and Surrey. It is impossible, therefore, to discuss the gifts in any detail without some reference to the rapidly changing relationships between these kingdoms at the time. The necessary information is available in a reliable form in the pages of the *Anglo-Saxon Chronicle* and Bede's *Historia Ecclesiastica*, and only the briefest outline need be given here.

A convenient date for beginning the period under review is 653, when the mission of the Northumbrian priest Cedd brought back the faith to pagan Essex. Oswiu of Northumbria was already the overlord of Kent and Essex. In 655 he invaded Mercia, which until then had been an insignificant kingdom, and converted it

[1] E.g. CS 89 (Hoo); CS 101 (Abingdon).
[2] Tribal Hidage, cf. Stenton pp. 292–3.

to Christianity. When Wulfhere succeeded in restoring Mercian independence in 658, he maintained the new Christian tradition. He also inherited Oswiu's interest in the East Saxons, to whom he sent the successful mission of Jaruman which overcame their second lapse into paganism in 665. By 669 Wulfhere was sufficiently in control of East Saxon affairs to be able to sell their bishopric to Wine, an exile from Wessex.

It is against this background that Erkenwald's foundation of the twin monasteries of Chertsey and Barking must be placed, for their initial endowments by King Egbert of Kent and King Suidfrid of Essex were a direct result of the current political environment.

After Wulfhere's defeat of Oswiu in 658, Kent had been ruled by its own king without recognizing any foreign overlord, but there are grounds for believing that upon the death of King Egbert in 673 the Mercians under King Wulfhere or his brother Æthelred (who succeeded Wulfhere in 674) were able with the help of the East Saxons to establish a puppet named Oswin as king of part of Kent. King Oswin issued three charters, of which one dated July 674 is confirmed by King Æthelred of Mercia. A second is dated 17 January 675, and a third is undated, but is to be assigned to the same period.[1] All three are witnessed by a certain Suebhard, who makes no claim to a royal title at this time. It seems very probable, however, that Oswin was deposed in 675 or early in 676, for in the latter year King Æthelred invaded Kent, and established Suebhard as king in Oswin's place. By a charter dated 1 March 676, witnessed by Oswin (without royal title), and confirmed by King Æthelred on 8 June the same year, Suebhard repeated the two earlier benefactions of Oswin which had not been confirmed originally by King Æthelred.[2]

Suebhard's charter states that he was the son of King Sebbi, and it seems probable that this scion of the East Saxon royal

[1] CS 73, 35, and 40 respectively. The dates 689 and 690 are suggested for these charters by G. J. Turner (*Black Book of St Augustine's*, p. xxxiii) and F. M. Stenton (EHR 1918, p. 437 n. 22). The formulas and witness lists suggest rather that they should be assigned to the same period as CS 36 (dated 674–5), CS 42 (dated 676), and CS 45 (dated 679).

[2] CS 42. Turner's suggestion (*op. cit.*) that the date of this charter should be revised to 1 March 691 ignores the reference within the text to Archbishop Theodore, who died 19 September 690.

house was claiming a share in the Kentish kingdom by virtue of old family ties.[1] He appears to have been one of the *reges dubii uel externi* whom Bede describes as reigning in Kent at this period, and as late as July 692 when King Wihtred had "by piety and zeal delivered the nation from invasion," Bede tells us that Kent was ruled by Wihtred and Suebhard jointly.

Meanwhile Mercia had become involved in a war with its old enemy Northumbria, and for a time Mercian influence waned in the south. The situation was ripe for the rise of new leaders, and in 685 a young exile named Cedwalla seized power in Wessex. His brief and violent reign was marked by a great extension of Wessex rule. He seems to have formed the ambition of adding all south-east England to his kingdom. He invaded Sussex and Kent, and gained control of Surrey, formerly a subordinate province of Mercia.[2]

Although there is no direct evidence that Cedwalla's political influence ever extended north of the Thames, the general trend of events does suggest very strongly that the East Saxons came under his subjection.[3] Erkenwald soon became closely associated with him, witnessing his charters; conversely, the East Saxon charters CS 81 and 87 were witnessed by Cedwalla's own bishops Wilfrid and Haedde. According to William of Malmesbury his (Cedwalla's) successor Ine ravaged East Anglia;[4] to do this he must have passed through Essex. Moreover, when Ine drew up his code of laws,[5] he called Erkenwald "my bishop." Cuthburga, sister of King Ine, was a nun at Barking Abbey c.686.[6] Bishop Wilfrid, who had come to Sussex in exile in 681, continued his work under Cedwalla, and probably the reconciliation between Wilfrid and Theodore which took place in London in Erkenwald's presence in 686–7[7] was influenced to some extent by Cedwalla's victories.

[1] Suebhard was the great-grandson of Sabert, the nephew of Ethelbert of Kent, who had been overlord of Essex.

[2] Stenton pp. 68–70; PN *Surrey*, p. xiii; EHD I, p. 445.

[3] This may explain the enigmatic statement in ASC *s.a.* 823, that the men of Kent, Surrey, Sussex, and Essex had formerly owed allegiance to the king of Wessex.

[4] *Gesta Regum*, I, c. 2.   [5] EHD I, pp. 364–72.

[6] E. S. Duckett, *Anglo Saxon Saints and Scholars*, 1947, p. 61 n. 159.

[7] Eddius, *Vita Wilfridi*, c. XLIII.

One cannot date the Laws of Ine any closer than some time between his accession (in 688) and the death of Erkenwald (before June 693). Detailed examination of the Barking charters suggests that the power of Mercia over most of the territory north of the Thames had already been re-established by the second of these two dates, although it is not until ten years later that this impression is confirmed by other charters.[1] South of the river, however, Ine preserved and even extended Wessex influence during the whole of his long reign.

I

ERKENWALD'S CHARTER

IN nomine domini dei nostri et saluatoris Jesu Christi. Ego Ercnuualdus episcopus provinciæ East Saexanorum, seruorum dei seruus, dilectissimis in Christo sororibus in monasterio quod appellatur Berecingas, habitantibus, quod deo auxiliante construxi, concedo ut tam vos quam posteri vestri in perpetuum, ut constructum est, ita possideatis, et ne quis presul cuius libet sit ordinis, vel qui in locum meum successerit, ullam in eodem monasterio exerceat potestatem, nec sui iuris ditione contra canonum decreta inquietudines aliquas facere presumat. Ea vero tantum faciat in predicto monasterio, quæ ad utilitatem animarum pertinent, ordinationes sacerdotum, vel consecrationes ancillarum dei. Ipsa vero sancta congregatio, que propter dei amorem ibidem deo laudes exhibet, moriente abbatissa, ex seipsa sibi aliam eligat ad dei timorem. Omnes terras quæ mihi ex donationibus regum sunt concessæ ad nomen eiusdem monasterij, quem ad modum donatae sunt, ex integro et quieto iure possideant, sicut chartulae donationum continent, quas in presenti vobis tradidi. Et nequis forte improbus negator huius donationis erumpat, ideo singillatim has terras in hac chartul[a] enumerandas et nominandas optimum duxi. Quarum prima fuit, quae mihi a Suidfrido rege data fuerat .40. cassatarum et appellatur Berecingas et Beddanhaam. Secunda quae ab Oedilredo tradita fuerat .75. manentium et appellatur Ricingahaam, Bydinhaam, Dæccanhaam, Angenlabeshaam cum campo qui dicitur

---

[1] CS 111, 115; *Early Charters of St Paul's*, J 6, 7, and 8.

Uuidmundes felth. Terra tertia quae ab eodem Oedilredo data
fuerat .10. manentium appellatur Celta. Quarta, quae ab aedilredo rege data fuerat .53. manentium, et uocatur gislheres
uuyrth. Quinta iuxta Hydabur[nam] donata ab æduualla rege
70. manentium appellatur [Ba]doricesheah. Sexta iuxta Lundoniam unius manentis data a uulfhario rege. Septima supra
vicum Lu[ndo]niæ data a Quoenguyda uxore ......aldi[1] 10.
man[en]tium. Octava quae appellatur Suanescamp et earhyth
donata ab aedilredo rege 40. cassatarum. Siquis autem episcoporum cuius libet dignitatis fuerit, vel omnium secularium
potestatum, contra hanc chartulam, canonice ac regulariter
a me constitutam, contendere presumserit, vel aliquid exinde
subtrahere, sit separatus a consortio sanctorum in hoc saeculo
omnium, et in futuro coelestis regni portas clausas contra se
undique inueniat a sancto Petro clauiculario coelestis regni, a
quo mihi licentia huius priuilegij data et permissa fuerat per
os beatissimi Agathonis, apostolicæ sedis presulis, cum Romam
adij ante annos .10. anno ab incarnatione domini 677° indictione
prima, chartula autem haec a me dictata, confirmata in sua
stabilitate nihilominus maneat.

✠ Ego Ercnuualdus episcopus donator pro confirmatione
    subscripsi.
✠ Ego Uuilfridus episcopus consensi et subscripsi.
✠ Ego Haedde episcopus consensi et subscripsi.
✠ Ego Guda presbyter et abbas consensi et subscripsi.
✠ Ego Eggbaldus presbyter et abbas consensi et subscripsi.
✠ Ego Hagona presbyter et abbas consensi et subscripsi.
✠ Ego Hooc presbyter et abbas consensi et subscripsi.
    Sig✠num manus Sebi regis regis[2] Est Sæxanorum.
    Sig✠num manus Sigiheardi regis.
    Sig✠num manus Suebredi regis.

Endorsements:
    Exhib' ap' Berk' cor' J. de Colet' iiij non' Marcii Anno dni
    M°cccvi^{to} . Registu' in regis registr' an' d'ni 1535 J. Rhesens
    Regist's B.

    [1] (B) Ædilbaldi. The line beneath the first few letters suggests that they
were supplied by the copyist.
    [2] *Sic*.

TEXTS

A. BM MS. Cotton Vesp. A ix, ff. 112–13 (old numbering 142–3). A transcript by John Joscelyn, first half of the sixteenth century. It is shown below (p. 132) that Joscelyn was copying a separate membrane in charter form, not a cartulary text, and that this source survived in the Barking Abbey archives until the Dissolution. Joscelyn was an accurate copyist, but he made at least one demonstrable error (see p. 144), and he changed all the figures in the charter from roman to arabic numerals. Joscelyn's figure 10 in the dating clause is hidden by the binding, and was not transcribed correctly in subsequent MS. versions, from which all the accessible printed texts are derived. I am indebted to Dr C. E. Wright for drawing my attention to the correct figure, which is unmistakably 10.

B. BM MS. Cotton Vesp. B xv, fo. 100^{rv}. A hurried copy of A by John Joscelyn (hand identified by Dr C. E. Wright, personal communication), containing numerous inaccuracies, the most important being that Joscelyn was unable to read his own figure 10 (above) and reproduced it as 18. The existence of this text was known to Thomas Tanner (cf. *Notitia Monastica*, 1748 edn), and doubtless to scholars of the preceding century.

C. Soc. Antiq. MS. 128, Vol. B, fo. 193^{rv}. An early seventeenth-century copy of A, by John Weever. Weever also found difficulty in reading the part of the dating clause referred to above; first he omitted it entirely, and later he supplied it from B, thus perpetuating the inaccurate figure 18. The section of A which recites the gifts of lands is missing from Weever's version.

D. Soc. Antiq. MS. 128, Vol. B, fo. 335^{rv}. A corrupt translation of C in Weever's hand, in which Weever renders *ab æduualla* by "Caed-uualla." It is shown below (p. 144) that this correction is justified, but it is a pity that Weever made it silently, as in the past this has bedevilled the reconstruction of the transmission of the text.

E. Bodl. MS. Dodsworth 10, fo. 25^{rv}. A seventeenth-century transcript by Dodsworth, from (1). It is curious that although Dugdale relied to a large extent on the Dodsworth MSS. for his *Monasticon* (1st Edn, 1682), he did not print Erkenwald's Charter.

F. Smart Lethieullier, *History of Barking* (MS.), fo. 27. Photostat available at Essex Record Office. Early eighteenth-century. From (1), but the section omitted by Weever is added in parenthesis by Lethieullier, the source being A, very badly copied.

Texts C to F have no independent value, except that they reveal the origin of mistakes in the printed versions of the charter, listed below.

FACSIMILE

of part of A (fo. 112, comprising most of the text), facing page 9 of John Taylor's *Our Lady of Batersey*, 1925.

EDITIONS

(1) John Weever, *Ancient Funeral Monuments*, 1631, p. 600, from C, with numerals changed back from arabic to roman. This edition, therefore, perpetuates the dating error made in B. The published text carries the marginal note *Ex lib. Abb. de Barking in bib. Cott.*, but this note (which must be a reference to B) does not appear beside the MS. version.

(2) Henry Spelman, *Concilia*, I, 1639, p. 192, from (1), with the section omitted by Weever supplied from A.

(3) David Wilkins, *Concilia*, IV, 1737, Appendix p. 746, from (2).

(4) K 38, from (2) or (3).

(5) Dugdale I, p. 438, from (4).

(6) CS 87, probably from (4).

(7) ECBA pp. 9–10, from A, with some missing letters from C and D.

(8) In this edition the text is from A, with letters in square brackets supplied from B. Contractions have been expanded, and punctuation introduced.

TRANSLATION

ECBA pp. 10–11.

WITNESSES

The witness list is identical with that of Hodilred's charter, edited below, pp. 127–8. The names appear in the same order, and this implies either that the two charters were witnessed on the same occasion, or that the witness list of one was copied from the other.

PLACE-NAMES

See below, pp. 141–5.

DATE

There is no orthodox dating clause, but the charter ends with the statement that ten years previously in 677 and the first indiction Erkenwald had visited Rome. The indiction is correct for the year. The charter therefore claims to be dated 687, and the witness list is compatible with this date. If the charters of Erkenwald and Hodilred are both assumed to be authentic, then both are to be dated March 687 (see p. 133).

DIPLOMATIC

Erkenwald's charter, if genuine, is unique, for no other authentic general confirmation of the lands and privileges of a seventh-century English monastery survives. It is not be to wondered, therefore, that its formulas cannot be traced in the donation charters of the period. There are however suspicious features both in the phrasing and in the substance of the document.

AUTHENTICITY

Detailed examination of the eight land gifts listed within the charter leaves no room for doubt that these were authentic seventh-century endowments of the abbey. More controversial is the question whether or not Bishop Erkenwald went to Rome and there obtained orally from Pope Agatho the privileges for his foundation which are outlined in the charter. Benedict Biscop obtained similar privileges for his foundation of Wearmouth, as did Wilfrid for his monasteries of Ripon and Hexham, but in neither case by word of mouth.

In its general structure the charter is unique. The Latin itself however cannot be faulted as an example of contemporary prose. Not a single word has crept into the text which is known to have a later origin that the date claimed for the charter. On the other hand, the use of an incarnational date as early as 677 is improbable. Moreover, the earliest known use by a diocesan bishop of the papal title *servus servorum Dei* is in 780.[1]

The charter is certainly not a post-Conquest forgery, nor can one conceive any circumstance in which it could have been put together in its present form during the last century and a half of the Anglo-Saxon state. Of course, a monastic privilege said to have been derived from Pope Agatho would be of great use to a house threatened with outside interference in the seventh or eighth centuries; but one doubts if the possession of such a document would confer much advantage upon a nunnery reconstituted after the Danish settlement—certainly not after the Benedictine reform got under way, and still less after the introduction of the Regularis Concordia, which incorporated its own provisions for protection of the nunneries. Indeed, the reference to ordination of priests to serve the monastery would be an anachronism at any time after the abbey's refoundation in the first half of the tenth century,[2] for from then onwards it had ceased to be a double monastery, and was a house for nuns only.

The same considerations apply with reference to the recital of the land gifts. No one could have put together this list of lands and donors at any time after the Danish settlement and made it all up out of monastic traditions and his own imagination; he would surely have made some error easily demonstrable under modern critical scrutiny. Even the spelling of the personal and place-names could not well have originated after the eighth century.[3]

---

[1] Levison p. 238. I am indebted to Mr Eric John for this reference, and for other valuable comments on the charter's authenticity. While agreeing that the list of land gifts appears to be authentic, Mr John thinks the charter could well have been fabricated in the tenth century or later.

[2] There was a community at Barking before 951: W II.

[3] E.g. the spelling of Ethelred: cf. Crawf p. 38.

One is forced to the conclusion that if this charter is a forgery, then it was created within two centuries of the abbey's first foundation.

II

HODILRED'S CHARTER

IN nomine domini nostri Iesu Christi saluatoris. Quotiens sanctis ac uenerabilibus locis uestris *aliqu*id offerre uidemur, uestra uobis *reddimus non nostra largimur. Quapropter ego* Hodilredus parens Sebbi *prouincia* East sexanorum, cum ipsius consensu *propria uoluntate sana mente integroque consilio, tibi* Hedilburge abbattissae, *ad augmentum monasterii* tui quae dicitur Beddanhaam, perpetualiter trado *et de meo iure in tuo transscribo terram* quae appellatur Ricingahaam, Budinhaam, Deccanhaam, Angenlabeshaam, et campo *in* silua *quae dicitur* Uuidmundesfelt, quae *simul* sunt *coniuncta* .xl. *manentium usque ad termino*s quae ad eum pertinent, cum *omnibus* ad se *pertinentibus, cum campis siluis, pratis* et marisco; ut tam tu quam posteri tui *teneatis possideatis et qu*ae *cumque uolueris de eadem facere terra liberam habeatis* potestatem. *Actu*m mense *martio*, et *testes* conpetenti numero *ut scriberent rogaui. Siquis contra hanc donation*is kartulam *uenire temptauerit* aut corrumpere, ante omnipotentem dominum et Iesum Christum filium eius et spiritum sanctum, id est inseparabilem trinitatem, sciat se condemnatum et *separatum ab omni societate Christiana*, manentem hanc *kartulam donationis* in sua nihilominus firmitate. Et ut *firma et in concuss*um *sit* donum termini sunt autem isti huius taerre cum quibus accingitur: ab oriente Writola burna, ab aquilone Centinces triow et hanc hem stede, ab australe *flumen Tamis*a. Siquis autem hanc donationem augere uoluerit, augeat dominus bona sua in regione uiuorum cum sanctis suis sine fine. Amen.

✠ *Ego* Sebbi rex East saxanorum pro confirmatione sub scripsi. Ego Oedelraedus *donator subscripsi*

✠ Ego Ercnuualdus *episcopus* consensi et subscripsi. Ego Wilfridus episcopus consensi et subscripsi

✠ Ego Haedde episcopus consensi et subscripsi. Ego Guda presbiter et abbas consentiens subscripsi

✠ Ego Egcbaldus presbiter et abbas consensi et subscripsi.

Written on the dorse:

✠ Ego Hagona presbiter et abbas consentiens subscripsi.

✠ Ego Hooc presbiter et abbas consentiens subscripsi.

Sig✠*num manus* Sebbi regis.

Sig✠*num manus* Sigihaerdi regis.

Sig✠*num manus* Suebredi regis.

Endorsed in a contemporary hand. De terra quam donauit Odil
    redus .xl. manentium ✠ Karta de Con....... [*illegible.*]

In a late Anglo-Saxon hand. this is seo boc to beorcingon.

Later endorsements.

[*Early fourteenth century*]. Pro Stebbenh'
    Exhib' ap' Berk' cor' J. de Colet' iiij non' Marcii Anno dni
    M°cccvi^{to}.

[*Late fourteenth century*]. Carta Hodured regis.

[*Sixteenth century*]. [Registu' in regis registr' an' dni 1535 J.
    Rhesens Regists' B].

[*In the hand of John Joscelyn*]. Erkenwald fuit Anno 675.

Further endorsements are now illegible.

TEXTS

A. BM MS. Cotton Aug. II, 29. A single vellum membrane 18 inches
wide by 9 inches long, which was folded at an early date three times
vertically and twice horizontally, and was so preserved for many centuries until it was mounted flat and sealed between two glass sheets a
few years ago.[1]

B. BM MS. Cotton Vesp. A ix, fo. 114 (old numbering, fo. 144).[2]
An extended transcript of A, made by John Joscelyn in the early sixteenth century. Joscelyn's version is of value in supplying the text of
an important late endorsement, now almost illegible (see below), and
also in supplying letters to fill gaps produced in a few places by frag-
mentation of the manuscript. Later texts exist, but are of no critical
value.

ACSIMILES

(1) D. Lysons, *Environs of London*, IV, 1796, frontispiece. An excel-
lent and exceedingly accurate lithograph of A, made originally for
Smart Lethieullier the antiquary, in preparation for his projected
History of Barking, which was never published.

---

[1] Cf. E. A. Loftus and H. F. Chettle, *A History of Barking Abbey*, Barking,
n.d. (1954), p. 11.

[2] Following immediately after Erkenwald's Charter, see p. 124.

(2) J. Kemble, *Codex Diplomaticus Ævi Saxonici*, I, 1835, frontispiece. Another lithograph of A, comprising part of the first line only.

(3) BM Facs I, No. 2. An autotype photograph of A.

(4) J. O'Leary, *Book of Dagenham*, 2nd edn, 1949, block No. 2. A modern photograph of A, which is slightly too small for critical study. When compared with (1) above, this shows that there was no deterioration in the MS. in the next 154 years, except for discoloration produced by the mistaken application of gallic acid, ammonium sulphide, or some similar chemical, probably early in the present century.

(5) ECBA, facing p. 27. A reduced copy of (1). The frontispiece to this book is a photographic facsimile of the subscription of the last five witnesses, which appears on the dorse of the charter.

(6) E. A. Lowe, *English Uncial*, Oxford, 1960, pl. xxii.

EDITIONS

(1) K 35 from A.

(2) CS 81 from A.

(3) J. Earle, *A Hand-book to the Land-Charters and other Saxonic Documents*, 1888, p. 13, from A.

(4) ECBA pp. 27–8, from A, with letters supplied from B.

(5) In this edition the text is from A, with letters and an endorsement supplied from B; these supplied readings are not bracketed, since facsimiles of the charter are readily available. Contractions have been expanded, and punctuation introduced. Words and phrases found in CS 34, a Chertsey charter dated 673 × 675, are printed in italic.

TRANSLATIONS

(1) A pamphlet by F. J. Brand entitled *Who was Hodilredus?* dated March 1939 (BM 20032, p. 37).

(2) ECBA pp. 29–30.

(3) EHD I, pp. 447–8, with comments.

WITNESSES

It is extremely difficult to establish close dates for the witnesses, since of the few datable sources in which their names appear most are suspect. The East Saxon kings and bishops receive scant attention in ASC.

Sebbi was king of the East Saxons. According to Bede III, c. 30, and IV, c. 11, he acceded in 664 or 665, reigned for thirty years, and then became a monk, some time after Erkenwald's death.

Hodilredus was of royal rank, or he could not have granted an estate by charter at this early date (EHD I, p. 346). He is unlikely to have been in the direct line of succession of the East Saxon kings, for his name does not commence with the alliterative "S" which characterizes

E

the dynasty. *Parens* in the charter cannot mean "father," for Sebbi was the son of Saeward. It is just possible philologically that the spellings in the charter could represent the common OE *Ethelred*, but there are no historical grounds for supposing the donor to have been King Ethelred of Mercia (cf. ECBA pp. 31–2). He does not witness as a king.

Erkenwald was the first abbot of Chertsey, and some time after 673 became fourth bishop of the East Saxons, with his seat at St Paul's, London. He died in or before 695.

Wilfrid was bishop of York. Considerable biographical information about him has survived (Bertram Colgrave, *The Life of Bishop Wilfrid by Eddius Stephanus*, 1927) from which can be reconstructed the following itinerary: September 677–summer 680 abroad; summer 680–early 681 imprisoned in Northumbria; early 681–summer 686 in Wessex; 687–91 in Northumbria; 691–9 in Mercia. The precise date at which he went to Northumbria from Wessex is uncertain.

Haedde was consecrated the fifth bishop of Wessex in 676, and died in 705.—Bede IV, 12; V, 18.

Guda was presumably the priest of that name who witnessed CS 72, which is dated internally 688, but is assigned to 685 × 687 by Professor Whitelock (EHD I, p. 445), who says Guda became abbot of Hoo, Kent.—*ibid.*, p. 448 n. 4; no authority quoted.

Egcbald was abbot of Peterborough.—Stenton's *Medeshamstede*, p. 324 n. 1.

Hagona witnesses CS 72 and CS 89 as an abbot. Loftus, *History of Barking*, p. 13 n. 4, says he was probably abbot of Chertsey, but supplies no proof.

Hooc was presumably the priest of that name who appears in the *Vita Wilfridi* as Bishop Wilfrid's chaplain. His monastery is unknown.

Sigiheard and *Suebred* were the sons of King Sebbi, who succeeded jointly as kings of the East Saxons upon their father's death (Bede IV, c. 11). They style themselves kings already in the charter; the title was at that time a customary one for all active members of the royal house.—Stenton p. 66.

PLACE-NAMES

Hodilred gave "land called *Ricingahaam, Budinhaam, Daeccanhaam, Angenlabeshaam*, and the open country called *Widmundesfelt*, within the forest, which comprise altogether 40 hides within the bounds that contain them, together with their appurtenances, namely fields, woodland, meadow, and marsh." The bounds are given as "to the east *Writolaburna*, to the north *Centincestriow* and (then) *hem stede*, to the south *flumen Tamisa*."

Clearly these four settlements and the field were close together, from the hidage. *Budinhaam* was the site of what we now call Barking, and *Daeccanhaam* became Dagenham. As with *Budinhaam*, the names of

Ricingahaam and *Angenlabeshaam* went out of use at an early date, and the sites of these two settlements are unknown. It is very doubtful if *Ricingahaam* can be linked with Rainham,[1] which probably originates from *Roegingahaam* like its Kentish neighbour. The settlement of *Angenlabeshaam* was derived from *Angenlaf*, a personal name found only in early documents. *Widmundesfelt* was the lost Wyfields,[2] which lay within the forest of Essex, about a mile to the north of (Great) Ilford.

Flumen Tamisa in the bounds is obviously the River Thames. To the east is another river called *Writolaburna*, which must be a tributary of the Thames. I have argued elsewhere that this is probably to be identified with the River Beam.[3] Dr Reaney suggests that *Centincestriow* to the north means "tree of Centing," i.e. a man from Kent. It may well be the earliest form of the name Becontree Heath, which was the site of the hundred court. This development postulates first that the middle element dropped out,[4] then that the OE preposition *be* was added,[5] i.e. *Centincestriow*→*Centreow*→*Becentreow*.

Hem stede, the other northerly limit to the bounds, is probably to be located near the modern Fulwell Cross, if its identity with *Hampstede* in a deed of 1368 be accepted.[6]

No western boundary is quoted in the charter; this is probably because the land donated by Hodilred abutted westwards on land already in the possession of the abbey, from the foundation endowment by King Suidfrid.

ENDORSEMENTS

The endorsements to the charter are important for studying the history of the text. The late OE entry *this is seo boc to beorcingon* is dated about 1000 by Dr J. E. Oxley (personal communication), who points out that *beorcingon* shows a late form of the dative plural, normally *-um*. It is interesting as evidence that the charter was available, and its significance understood, at the abbey soon after its second foundation. The entry dated 1306 in a contemporary hand shows that the charter was at Barking at that date and was examined there by a representative of the bishop of London, who had a palace at Stepney (*Stebbenhithe*) at this period.

The most important entries, however, are the two dating from the sixteenth century, at the time of the dissolution of the monasteries. *J. Rhesens* is the signature of John ap Rice, or Sir John Prise, one of the commissioners appointed to visit the religious houses. A paper by N. Ker ('Sir John Prise', *The Library*, Fifth Series, x, 1955, pp. 1–24)

[1] Dr Reaney, personal communication.   [2] ECBA p. 38.
[3] *Ibid.*, pp. 39–40: cf. EHD I, p. 447.
[4] See Ekwall, p. ix, for parallels.   [5] PN Elements I, pp. 32–3.
[6] D and C Worcs. MS. B.85: cf. ECBA pp. 42–3, and K. I. Sandred, *English Place-Names in -STEAD*, Uppsala, 1963, pp. 164, 208–9.

shows that the register in which Prise entered details of the charters examined by him was known to Lambarde (who made some extracts which have survived) and to Stowe. The register itself, which would be of great value to present-day students of Anglo-Saxon charters, has unhappily vanished. It is not to be found in the British Museum, and a search kindly made for me by Mr Michael Roper at the Public Record Office has likewise drawn a blank. That Prise made a habit of endorsing charters examined by him, and of entering them in his register, is shown by the fact that two Bury St Edmunds charters (K 735 and K 761) now at King's Lynn bear very similar endorsements to the Barking charter under discussion, a discovery noted over a century ago by C. W. Goodwin (*Norfolk Archaeology*, IV, 1855, pp. 93–117). Obviously it would be of interest to examine other charters for similar endorsements.

Some time after Prise's visit to Barking Abbey, John Joscelyn the Latin Secretary also examined the charters and made his own endorsement on Hodilred's charter (hand identified by Dr C. E. Wright). He wrote *Erkenwald fuit Anno 675*. No doubt the date he had in mind was the enthronement of Erkenwald, as then recorded on his tomb in St Paul's Cathedral, which was much revered and visited by Londoners in medieval times. This endorsement is most important, for it shows that Joscelyn's very accurate transcript of Hodilred's charter was taken directly from the original. Now it is significant that Joscelyn's transcripts of the two charters of Erkenwald and Hodilred appear on adjacent sheets of MS. Cotton Vesp. A ix—the similarity of the script suggests that they were written on the same occasion. If he was transcribing Hodilred's charter from the original then in the abbey archives, what is more likely than that he transcribed Erkenwald's charter too from a seventh- or eighth-century membrane, now lost? In support of this, note the records of the identical endorsements of the fourteenth and sixteenth centuries, which appear in his copies of both charters.

DATE

Hodilred's charter is not dated internally; it was "done in the month of March" but no year is given. There is no evidence whatever to support the date 693 ascribed to it by Kemble and his successors. This appears to be derived from the date which they wrongly assumed for Erkenwald's charter.

If we consider the career of Bishop Wilfrid, it will be seen that our charter could have been drawn up either in the period 681–7 while he was in Wessex or in 691–4 during his stay in Mercia. The presence of Haedde of Wessex among the witnesses makes the former period more likely. The witness list is the same as that appended to Erkenwald's charter, which is dated internally 687. If the two charters are authentic (and there is no reason to assume otherwise), then both are to be dated March 687. It appears likely, from evidence which is discussed elsewhere (p. 121) that Wessex established some control over East Saxon affairs during the reign of Caedwalla (685–8); the presence of the two bishops Wilfrid and Haedde as witnesses to these Essex charters may well be a reflection of this.

DIPLOMATIC

Sir Frank Stenton was the first to point out the way in which this charter repeats the formulas in CS 34, the only reasonably authentic seventh-century charter surviving for Chertsey (EHR XXXIII, 1918, p. 435 n. 2; cf. EHD I, pp. 440–1). He remarks ". . . this similarity, which could only be brought out adequately by a parallel edition of the two texts, is so close as to suggest either that the Beddanham (i.e. Hodilred's) charter was the model by which the Chertsey charter was composed, or that both came from some common scriptorium. . . the latter theory is much the most probable." In the above edition, phrases shared between the two texts are printed in italic, and there can be no doubt as to their interdependence. It is important to note also that many of the formulas are repeated in CS 72, King Caedwalla's charter founding a monastery at Farnham in Surrey, dated 688, which shares a number of witnesses with Hodilred's charter, including the bishops Erkenwald, Wilfrid, and Haedde. These three charters form a distinct group, with general structure and formulas which separate them sharply from the early Kentish charters on the one hand and Mercian and West Saxon texts on the other.

AUTHENTICITY

Until the turn of the present century, no one doubted that this was an authentic text of the late seventh century, drawn up at the time of the transaction which it described. Since then it has come under heavy criticism, and it is interesting to trace the growth of this tradition.

It was not until 1918 that the first note of hesitation crept in. In that year Sir Frank Stenton called it "a charter which may be strictly contemporary, and in any case is one of the very earliest of extant English diplomas."[1] By 1933 these doubts were becoming crystallized, and K. Sisam was able to write: "I think palaeographers would now agree that a charter in these stiff imitative uncials is not an original of the late seventh, but a copy of the late eighth century."[2] Twenty years later Sir Frank was prepared to call it "plainly spurious,"[3] and he elaborated this judgement in the following remarkable statement: ". . . the

---

[1] EHR XXXIII, 1918, p. 435 n. 11.

[2] 'Cynewulf and his Poetry', in *Proc. Brit. Acad.*, XVIII, 1933, p. 325; reissued in his *Studies in the History of Old English Literature*, Oxford, 1953, p. 3, note.

[3] LC p. 92.

'imitative copy' of uncertain date is positively dangerous, both to the student of diplomatic and also to the student of language. For many years the abnormal forms of personal names in the uncial charter of Oedelraed of Essex, now relegated to this class, complicated discussion about the date of *Beowulf*."[1] In the same year, writing independently, Professor D. Whitelock declared: "The charter used to be considered an original, but is now generally believed to be about a hundred years later. It is in formal, rather stiff uncials, and the production of a copy of this kind at a later date is easier to understand if, as I suspect, it represents the first substantial grant to the house, which turned it from an obscure community to the important abbey it became."[2]

It was not until 1960, however, that a paleographer at last committed himself in print. In that year E. A. Lowe wrote: "the script . . . is somewhat artificial. . . . the identical crosses before the signatures suggest that this was a copy: the wide separation of words favours a date in the eighth century."[3]

Now we have here a formidably unanimous verdict, and it is with the utmost diffidence that I must record my disagreement. There is nothing known to me, after many years of study of the early history of Barking Abbey, which leads me to the conclusion that this text is "plainly spurious." Nor do I accept that it represents the "first substantial grant to the house, which turned it from an obscure community to the important abbey it became." Barking Abbey had certainly received over 200 hides of land in Essex, Kent, Surrey, Middlesex, and London before the date of this charter, and there is every reason to believe that Erkenwald's background ensured the importance of his foundation from the outset. As for the date of *Beowulf*, we may safely leave this problem on one side, with the observation that if the charter's script is imitative, then presumably the scribe copied the spelling of his exemplar.

This brings us to the crux of the matter, the criticism on paleographical grounds. It is relevant to point out that we have very little material for comparison, for only one other supposedly original English seventh-century charter survives, and as Dr Lowe himself admits, "the varied look of their uncial might be accounted for by the varying models available in the different localities, and by the varying skill of the scribes."[4]

The crosses before the signatures to Hodilred's charter do not appear to me to be any more identical and formalized than those of the seventh-century charter of Hlothere of Kent,[5] nor can I detect any wide separation of the words, whatever the implication of such a separation might be. Such criticism must be purely subjective, and any conclu-

[1] LC p. 10.   [2] EHD I, p. 447.   [3] *English Uncial*, p. 21.
[4] *Ibid.*, p. 7.   [5] CS 45.

sions derived therefrom ought surely to be framed in the most cautious form of words, bearing in mind the paucity of the materials.

That the text itself is a copy is of course highly likely. One imagines that several copies of the exemplar were made at the time the trans-action was drawn up; this was certainly the case in later centuries. Criticism of the script as "imitative" is to this extent groundless. Nor can I satisfy myself that it is possible to pronounce with confidence as to the probable date of any such copy. The criticism is in fact a general one of all supposedly 'original' charters. If we accept it, there does not seem much point in trying to use any of them as historical materials. For myself, I prefer to take them at their face value, and assume these early texts to be authentic and contemporary, until proved otherwise. The fact remains that on purely historical grounds the material within Hodilred's charter has yet to be faulted.

III

THE BATTERSEA CHARTER

☧ IN nomine domini nostri Jesu Christi saluatoris. Ea que secundum decreta canonum et statuta synodalia salubriter definiuntur, quamuis sermo solus ad testimonium sufficeret, at tamen ob incertam futurorum temporum condicionem firmis-sima scripturarum syngraffat et cautionum cyrografis sunt ro-boranda. Qua propter ego E[rcnuualdus] absque meritorum pre-cedentium prerogatiua pontificali nomine functus, aliquam ter-ram aecclesiae beatae [dei genetricis Mariae] libenter impendere decreui, his locorum limitibus designatum. Idest in Batrices ege .xxviii. manentes, et alibi in uillam quae uocabulo fungitur Watsingaham .xx. Ex occidentali uero plaga fluminis cuius uocabulum est Hidaburna .xx. cassatas. Quam uidelicet terram a uenerando rege Ceduuala acceptam, *et ab Æthelredo regali cul-mine freto roboratam*, in cassatas sexaginta .viij. regulariter re-ciperam, sub testificatione plurimorum, quorum nomina infra tenentur asscripta. Siquis uero hanc donationis munificentiam augere et amplificare uoluerit, augeat deus partem eius in libro uitae. Siquis uero tirranica potestate irritam facere nisus fuerit, nouerit se in tremendo uiuorum et mortuorum examine coram Christo singulorum facta aequa discretionis lance liberante. Nouemque angelorum ordinibus zizaniorum fasciculos seque-strata beatorum caterua colligantibus rationem districte reddi-

turam. Scripta est autem haec cartula *idibus iunii mensis .indic-*
tione .vi. anno ab incarnatione domini sexcentisimo *nonagesimo*
.iji. Ego [Ercnuualdus] propria manu subscripsi. ✠ Ego Wilfridus episcopus consentiens subscripsi. ✠ Ego Haedde episcopus consentiens subscripsi. ✠ *Signum manus Æthelredi regis.* ✠

Signum manus Hagona abbatis. ✠

Signum manus Hooc presbiter. ✠

Signum manus Eadberht. ✠

Ego Haedda episcopus consentiens subscripsi. ✠

Ego Tirtil episcopus crucem infeci. ✠

Ego Eadgar elect' crucem infeci. ✠

Signum manus Wecca. ✠

Ego Tidbald abbas crucem infeci. ✠

Signum manus Ceduualla regis. ✠

Signum manus Wynberhti abbatis. ✠

Signum manus Cissi ministri. ✠

Ego Brihtuuoldus archiepiscopus crucem infeci. ✠

Ego Brihtmaerus episcopus consentiens subscripsi. ✠

Ego Waldhere episcopus consentiens subscripsi. ✠

Ego Eadmund elect' crucem infeci. ✠

Ego Cotta abbatis crucem infeci. ✠

TEXT

Westminster Abbey Muniments, Charter No. 1.

FACSIMILES

(1) OS Facs, Part II.

(2) J. G. Taylor, *Our Lady of Batersev,* 1925.

EDITIONS

(1) CS 82.

(2) J. G. Taylor, *op. cit.*

(3) ECBA pp. 20–1, omitting the bounds and endorsements.

(4) This edition is based on the Ordnance Survey facsimile. Bounds
and endorsements are omitted here, since they are fully edited in (2).
See below for the words in italic, and those supplied in square brackets.
Abbreviations are extended, and punctuation is introduced.

TRANSLATIONS

(1) J. G. Taylor, *op. cit.*

(2) ECBA p. 21.

ERASURES

In three places, indicated in this edition by square brackets, there are gaps in the text of the surviving version, and careful examination shows them to have been occupied by words which have since been erased. Now the charter itself is in a hand of the eleventh century, but there is a fifteenth-century endorsement which claims that the gaps were originally filled with the words *Agelricus*; *Petri Westm.* (i.e. Peter of Westminster); and *Agelricus Dorkes Eps.* (i.e. Agelricus, bishop of Dorchester) respectively.

The see of Dorchester was held by Agilbert from 650 to 660 and by Ætla in 679, and it is possible that an Agelricus could have held it in 693; there was in fact a Bishop Alricus of an unknown see who attended a Mercian witenagemot in that year (CS 85; ECWM no. 382. According to a list in Florence of Worcester, his see may have been *Dommoc* in East Anglia).

There is no difficulty, however, in proving the endorsement to be completely unfounded. The gaps in the succession following Agilbert and Ætla imply that the see of Dorchester was then in abeyance (Haddon and Stubbs, *Councils*, III, 129–30); probably it was abolished by Cedwalla (PN *Oxford*, p. xxi), and Surrey at the period of this charter was subject to Erkenwald's see of London (PN *Surrey*, p. xiv). There is no reliable evidence for the existence of Westminster Abbey in the seventh century. DB records that Battersea belonged to Harold, and it was given to Westminster Abbey by the Conqueror in 1067 (ECBA p. 22 n. 5). It was probably soon after this that the copy of the Battersea charter now in the abbey muniments was made. No advantage could accrue to Westminster from the erasures if the original names were those suggested by the endorsement; almost certainly they were other names, which challenged the abbey's ownership.

This impression is confirmed on closer inspection of the charter. The word *beatae* before the second erasure could only refer to a dedication to a female saint, and the only female saint to whom English churches were consecrated in the seventh century was St Mary (Levison pp. 259–65); the church of the monastery at Barking is one of the very few known examples. If the erased word had been "St Peter" it would have required the masculine adjective *beati*.

Turning now to the first and third erasures, the length of the gaps left by the erased words is too great for them to have been filled by the name *Agelricus*, although *Ercnuualdus* would occupy the spaces satisfactorily. Moreover, inspection under ultra-violet light[1] shows that the first letter of the erased word was in each case a capital E with a

[1] I am especially grateful to Mr Lawrence Tanner, Keeper of the Muniments, Westminster Abbey, for undertaking this examination personally at my request, and communicating to me the results.

E*

long bar at the top, such as occurs among the witnesses—"Ego Waldhere." The only English bishops of this period whose names begin with
E are Erkenwald of London and Ethelwin of Lindsey, and of these the
former is the only name which could reasonably be supposed to have
filled the spaces left by the first and third erasures.

We are therefore on fairly safe ground when we assert that the intention of these erasures and the fifteenth-century endorsement was
to destroy evidence which might challenge the right of Westminster
Abbey to the ownership of Battersea. Whoever made the endorsement
would no doubt have been acquainted with the legend of the foundation of the abbey by an Essex king early in the seventh century, but he
would not have known that this legend was spurious (cf. *Flete's History
of Westminster Abbey*, ed. J. Armitage Robinson, 1909). Nor could he
have realized that a record of William's gift of Battersea to Westminster was available among the abbey archives.

Sufficient evidence has now been presented to suggest very strongly
that the words in the first and third spaces were originally (in Latin)
"Erkenwald bishop of London," and that the second gap was filled with
the words "St Mary of Barking." If this is the case, then Erkenwald's
charter and the Battersea charter are substantially in agreement on the
details of this gift.[1]

WITNESSES

The bishops *Erkenwald*, *Wilfrid*, and *Haedde* appear as witnesses to
Hodilred's charter, together with Abbot *Hagona* and *Hooc*, who is still
only a priest at the time of the Battersea charter.

Caedwalla was king of Wessex 685 × 688.

Ethelred was king of Mercia 674 × 704.

Haedda was bishop of Lichfield 691 × 716–27.

Tirtil was bishop of Hereford 688 × 707–10.

Waldhere was bishop of London 693 × 707–16.

Brihtwald was archbishop of Canterbury 693 × 731.

Brihtmaer's see is unknown.

Wynberht was abbot of Nursling, near Southampton (Levison p. 228;
EHD I, p. 716).

Tidbald was not an uncommon name; our witness can hardly be
identical with the Abbot Tidbald who had charge of a West Saxon
monastery in 759 (EHD I, p. 443; ECW no. 557).

Cotta witnessed as an abbot CS 111, an East Saxon charter drawn up
during the Mercian supremacy, dated 704, and apparently authentic.

Wecca was possibly a Peterborough monk; cf. Stenton's *Medesham-*

---

[1] For earlier discussions, see A. Girand Browning and R. Kirk, 'The Early
History of Battersea,' *Surrey Archaeological Collections*, x, pp. 205–54, and
J. G. Taylor, *Our Lady of Batersey*, 1925.

stede, p. 316. An Abbot Wecta witnesses two Evesham charters (CS 116, 118; ECWM nos. 201, 8) which incorporate some extraneous material, but appear to have reliable witness lists.

Cissi was possibly the important West Saxon of that name, discussed in Stenton's *Abingdon*, p. 17, and B. Colgrave's *Life of St Guthlac*. Traditionally he was the founder of Abingdon Abbey. A man of this name was one of the three persons to whom King Caedwalla gave land at Farnham for a monastery (CS 72).

Eadberht also witnesses CS 72.

Eadmund and *Eadgar* remain unidentified.

Careful analysis shows that except for four persons otherwise unknown (Tidbald, Eadmund, Brihtmær, and Eadgar), all the witnesses can be placed in one of two groups, clearly defined by date and allegiance:

West Saxon supremacy (685–7)	*Mercian supremacy* (693 × 704)
King Caedwalla	King Ethelred
Bishop Erkenwald	Archbishop Brihtwald
Bishop Wilfrid[1]	Bishop Haedda
Bishop Haedde	Bishop Tirhtil
Abbot Hagona	Bishop Waldhere
Abbot Wynberht	Abbot Cotta
Hooc, priest	Wecca
Cissi	
Eadberht	

PLACE-NAMES

Batrices ege is Battersea, Surrey. *Watsingaham* is Washingham, a lost village lying just south of Battersea. *Hidaburna* is the River Wandle.

DATE

The internal date is 13 June 693 from the incarnation; the indiction is given as 6, which is correct for the date. The Mercian part of the witness list is compatible with this date.

DIPLOMATIC

However much tampering may have crept in during the transmission of the text, there is ample evidence that the basic formulas in this charter are characteristic of the late seventh century. The earliest appearance of the proem is in a West Saxon charter dated 670 × 676 (CS 107; EHD I, p. 442). It recurs later in charters of the Mercian supremacy, e.g. the Dengie charter dated 706 × 709 (*Early Charters of*

---

[1] Wilfrid's signature could also be assigned to the period of Mercian supremacy: it is possible that he witnessed both the original gift by Caedwalla and its later confirmation by Ethelred.

St Pauls, p. 5; ECEss No. 7), and one of King Ethelbald in William of Malmesbury's *Gesta Regum*, I, c. 4. On the word *cyrographis* in the proem, see Levison p. 232 n. 4. The phrase *absque meritorum precedentium prerogatiua* closely resembles passages in the letters of Boniface and Aldhelm (*ibid.*, p. 238 n. 7).

The anathema is particularly interesting. It is based partly on Matthew xiii, 39–42, and xxv, 31–4, on which see Levison pp. 228–9; but its authority is reinforced by reference to the hierarchy of the "nine orders of angels," the existence of which was asserted by the second council of Constantinople in 553. This sanction appears also in CS 108, King Ine's grant of privileges to the churches of Wessex, dated 704.

AUTHENTICITY

It is easy enough to conclude that the text of Erkenwald's transfer to Barking of Caedwalla's gift of Battersea, as preserved in the Westminster muniments, is corrupt and misleading. It would be easier still to dismiss it as a forgery, but such an attitude cannot be too strongly condemned. However corrupt the text may be, there are so many points at which the Battersea charter fits in with known facts obtained from independent and authentic sources that one cannot conceive the whole thing to be the manufacture of some half-literate medieval forger. It is far more likely that the charter is based on a succession of events which really did take place. As our *apparatus criticus* improves it should be possible to sort out with increasing certainty the hard core of reliable historical data from the accretions and distortions which have crept into the text since the original draft was made.

In our present state of knowledge it is convenient to postulate the following stages through which the text may have passed.—

1. The prototype was a charter by which Caedwalla gave Battersea to Erkenwald for the endowment of Barking Abbey. This supposed prototype, which may be called Caedwalla's charter, is now lost, but the text may be reconstructed almost entirely by deleting from the Battersea charter certain passages which are almost certainly interpolations, and which are therefore printed in italics in the above edition. It is very probable that Caedwalla's charter was drawn up by one of its witnesses, namely Wynberht, abbot of Nursling, for the proem occurs in CS 107 and part of the anathema in CS 100, both of which were composed by Wynberht (EHD I, p. 441). Caedwalla's gift would be dated 685 × March 687, before Erkenwald's charter, which confirms it.

2. During the period 688 × 693 Erkenwald died and Mercia regained ascendancy over Essex. A new charter was then drawn up, incorporating in the prototype a confirmation by King Æthelred of Mercia. It may be supposed that the occasion chosen was a Mercian witenagemot held in 693 (CS 85; ECWM No. 382), and that to the original list of West

Saxon signatories were added the names of the Mercian bishops present at the gemot—Wilfrid, Haedda, and Tirhtil, together with Archbishop Brihtwald of Canterbury, and Waldhere, Erkenwald's successor in the see of London.

3. Some time in the succeeding centuries—possibly during the Danish invasions—the estate passed out of the hands of Barking Abbey, and eventually into the possession of the Crown, whence it descended to Harold. The Conqueror gave it to Westminster Abbey. Soon afterwards, the Mercian charter postulated above was copied and placed in the Westminster archives. It is this copy, in a hand of the eleventh century, which we know as the Battersea charter. The bounds of Battersea with which it concludes must have been added at this stage. They are given in OE, and the detail is too great for them to have appeared in a seventh-century charter. These bounds are, in fact, closely related to another list of the bounds of Battersea which is endorsed on Westminster Abbey Charter No. III, dated 957 (CS 994, in a twelfth-century hand).

4. A fifteenth-century monk found the charter among the Westminster Abbey muniments. Believing this copy of a seventh-century charter constituted a challenge to the ownership of Battersea by Westminster, he erased the names of the donor and recipient, and added an endorsement suggesting alternative names, "proving" Westminster's ownership.

5. Finally, early in the present century these erasures were painted over with hydrosulphide or some similar chemical in an attempt to restore the writing, with the unfortunate result that the underlying letters are not now visible under ultra-violet light.

This is the condition of the Battersea charter as we know it today.

THE LAND GIFTS TO BARKING ABBEY

We are now in a position to discuss the individual gifts of land to Barking Abbey, dealing with them in rough chronological order. The numbers before the gifts refer to the order in which they are recited in Erkenwald's charter; the dates to which the gifts have been provisionally assigned appear in brackets after the descriptions of the gifts.

THE FOUNDATION ENDOWMENT

I. King Suidfrid gave 40 cassatae called Berecingas and Beddanhaam (c.666).

Hodilred's charter speaks of the "monastery called *Beddanhaam*," and this name recurs in the form *Budinhaam* later in the charter. In the recitation by Erkenwald the variant *Bydinhaam* is used. This seems to be the nearest approach to the original name, for Dr P. H. Reaney writes: "*Beddanhaam* and *Budinhaam* were obviously the same place. Variation between *e* and *u* rules out *Bedda*, if such a (personal) name ever existed,

and points to OE *y*. Variation between *dd* and *d* raises a further difficulty, and there is no safe etymology."[1]

Whatever its origin, it seems that this name fell out of use at an early
date, for writing in the first part of the next century Bede speaks of the
monastery "in the place called *in Berecingum*" from which the modern
name Barking is derived. Its significance has been explained by Dr
Reaney: "Such names as Barking, 'dwellers by the birch-trees' . . .
belong to a type similar to that of Essex, denoting first the inhabitants
and only later the place."[1] In other words, there was a group of people
known as the Berecingas, some of whom inhabited a place called
Beddanhaam. After the site was given to the monastery its name fell
into disuse, and the monastery came to be called after the folk living
in the district.

With this in mind, it is reasonable to assume that the first donation
recited by Erkenwald represents the foundation endowment.

King Suidfrid the donor is possibly to be identified with King Suebred the son of King Sebbi, although this identity is difficult to defend
on purely etymological grounds.

THE LONDON DONATIONS

VI. King Wulfhere gave one manens beside Lundonia (c.666 × 674).

*VII. Cwoengyth the wife of ......ald gave 10 manentes "super vicum Lun-
doniae"* (c.666 × March 687).

The first of these is dated before the death of Wulfhere in 674. He
became the overlord of London and confirmed the foundation endowment of Chertsey made by his subregulus Frithuwald,[3] so there are
good reasons for believing that this record represents an authentic
tradition. It seems very likely to me that Wulfhere's gift was really
of 50 hides, i.e. *L manentes* in the original, mistranscribed by Joscelyn
as *unius manentis*. The word *unius* is in any case unlikely to have appeared
in the original text, for the hidage was habitually recorded in roman
numerals in early charters, and we know (from his transcript of Hodilred's charter) that Joscelyn usually converted these to arabic. A single
hide, even near London, was too small a gift for a seventh-century
overlord. One is reminded of the 50 hides at Fulham given by Bishop
Tirhtil to St Paul's soon after 706.[4]

The second gift cannot be dated closely. Professor Bruce Dickins
says that there is no difficulty in the way of assuming that *Quoenguyda*
represents a Latinized version of OE *Cwoengyth*, a feminine personal
name.[5] A Cwoengyth, nun of Wimborne, occurs 729 × 744,[6] and it is

---

[1] Personal communication.

[2] *Essex Review*, LVIII, p. 10. Also PN *Essex*, p. 88.

[3] Stenton pp. 54–7; CS 34.   [4] *Early Charters of St Paul's*, pp. 3–4.

[5] Personal communication.   [6] CS 167.

possibly of some significance that Cuthburga, the abbess of Wimborne, had been a nun at Barking. But a more likely identification is with Kinigitha, the wife of Wihtred,[1] who became king of Kent in the autumn of 690. It appears from the lacuna in Joscelyn's transcript at this point that he could not read the name of Cwoengyth's husband in the text which lay before him; his representation of the last three letters of this name is possibly no more than a guess on his part.

This possibility that the donor of land *"super vicum Lundoniae"* to Barking Abbey was connected with the Kentish royal house should not lightly be set aside. One recalls that 24 hides "near the wall of the city of London" were said to have been given to St Paul's by its founder, King Ethelbert of Kent.[2] There is evidence that in 673–85 the kings of Kent possessed a hall in London,[3] and early in the following century the Kentish churches of Minster and Rochester secured remission of toll for their ships trading there.[4]

At the time of Edward the Confessor, Barking Abbey held twenty-eight houses and a half of a church within the city of London, which rendered 6s. 8d.[5] The church was certainly All Hallows, Barking-by-the-Tower, which paid a pension of 6s. 8d. to Barking Abbey in 1291.[6] The other half descended to Christ Church, Canterbury.[7] The parish formed part of a soke belonging to Barking Abbey,[8] which must have been of Saxon origin.[9] It was a common early custom for rural manors to possess town houses, but the considerable extent and value of this soke marks it out as something more than a convenient *pied à terre* for an out-town monastery,[10] and when one recalls that bombing during the last war laid open the foundations of a seventh-century church beneath the present church of All Hallows, the temptation to connect this eleventh-century soke with the seventh-century gifts of Cwoengyth and King Wulfhere becomes irresistible.

---

[1] CS 86.

[2] H. W. C. Davis, *Regesta Regum Anglo-Normannorum*, Oxford, 1913, Nos. 246 and 274 (pp. 65, 72); cf. *Early Charters of St Paul's*, p. xxiv.

[3] EHD I, p. 361.   [4] *Ibid.*, p. 451.   [5] DB; cf. VCH *Essex*, I, p. 449.

[6] *Taxation of Pope Nicholas*, Record Commission, 1802, p. 196.

[7] EHD II, pp. 954–5. It was rented to Gundulf, bishop of Rochester, who built the Tower of London.

[8] *The Hundred Rolls*, Record Commission, Vol. I, 1812, p. 405.

[9] For the site, see W. Page, *London, Its Origin and Early Development*, 1929, p. 133. The Tower occupied some of the territory of this soke, and it is significant that the Conqueror was staying at Barking Abbey at the time when the Tower was being built for his London residence; cf. Stenton, p. 590.

[10] D. Whitelock, *The Beginnings of English Society*, 1952, p. 128.

THE DONATIONS OF KING ÆTHELRED OF MERCIA

IV. King Ædilred gave 53 manentes called Gislheresuuyrth (674 × *March* 687).

VIII. King Ædilred gave 40 cassatae called Suanescamp and Earhyth (c.676).

Gislheresuuyrth has been located provisionally at Isleworth in Middlesex.[1] The site satisfies topographical and historical requirements as well as those of etymology; its position on the Thames bank is in conformity with the other sites given to Barking. Middlesex at this period was of course part of the East Saxon kingdom, and therefore subject to Æthelred's overlordship.

Suanescamp and *Earhyth* are undoubtedly Swanscombe[2] and Erith[3] in Kent. Ethelred invaded Kent in 676, and established a member of the East Saxon royal house as its joint king under his subjection.[4] It is probable that these gifts to Barking Abbey represented some of the spoils of Ethelred's invasion. Possibly the abbey lost possession of them upon the restoration of the Kentish royal line, for the lands did not survive as monastic property.[5]

THE CHARTER OF KING CEDWALLA OF ESSEX

V. King Cedwalla gave 70 manentes called Badoricesheah, beside Hydaburna (685 × *March* 687).

Joscelyn's version has *ab œduualla rege* in error for *a Cœduualla rege*, and it is fortunate that the Battersea charter survives to confirm this important correction.[6] Battersea lies at the junction of the Thames with its tributary the River Wandle, the *Hydaburna* of this charter. The Battersea charter gives the hidage as 68, and it is important to note that the figure is the same in DB.

THE DONATIONS OF HODILRED

II. Oedilred gave 75 manentes called Ricingahaam, Bydinhaam, Daeccanhaam, and Angenlabeshaam, with the open country called Uuidmundesfelth (*March* 687).

III. The same Oedilred gave 10 manentes called Celta (probably 687).

The first entry is clearly an abstract of Hodilred's charter (p. 127), the only discrepancy being the hidation. *Bydinhaam* and *Daeccanhaam* are Barking and Dagenham, and *Uuidmundesfelth* is the lost Wy-

---

[1] PN *Middlesex*, p. 27.   [2] Ekwall, p. 434.

[3] J. K. Wallenberg, *Kentish Place-Names*, 1931, p. 17, and *Place-Names of Kent*, 1934, pp. 26–7.

[4] See p. 120.

[5] In about 950 Erith was in the possession of Ælfheah, a Kentish landowner, son of Ælfstan, son of Heahstan: R XLI.

[6] See p. 140.

fields in Barking. *Angenlabeshaam* and *Ricingahaam* remain unidentified. The etymology of *Celta* is obscure,[1] but Dr Reaney has suggested that it was the name of a stream running through the parish of Childerditch in Essex, which forms part of the parish boundary.[2] DB shows that the manors of Warley and Bulphan belonged to Barking Abbey TRE, and as these both abutted on Childerditch there are topographical reasons for supporting Dr Reaney's identification. Moreover, it is possible that in the seventh century this name *Celta* was applied not only to the small stream running through Childerditch, but to the whole of the Mardyke, of which it is a tributary. This would account for the abbey's possession of Stifford, which is also on the river.[3]

Before leaving this matter of the early endowment of Barking Abbey, two important features need to be emphasized. The first is that all the seventh-century donations relate to land sited on the banks of the Thames or its tributaries.[4] Clearly it was intended that the abbey should maintain contact with its estates by water rather than by land, and it is not irrelevant to observe that by the time of DB Barking was a port with its own fishing fleet.

Secondly, it is significant that the estates in Essex and London, as well as the block of territory immediately adjacent to the abbey on the north and east, were all still in the abbey's possession at the time of Domesday. Whatever evils befell the monastery in the late ninth and early tenth centuries, some of its muniments survived the devastation, and the eclipse was sufficiently short-lived for the abbey to be able to retain or regain a substantial portion of its original endowment. The same generalization is true of Ely, of Peterborough, and of the Essex estates of the cathedral church of St Paul, and this needs to be borne in mind when assessing the impact of the Danish settlement in eastern England.

[1] PN *Oxfordshire*, I, p. 197; *Studia Neophilologica*, VI, 1934, pp. 91 ff.
[2] PN *Essex*, p. 124.   [3] ECEss II, pp. 25–7.
[4] ECBA, map facing p. 37.

CHAPTER IX

THE EARLY CHARTERS OF
THORNEY ABBEY

THORNEY was one of the great fenland abbeys founded in the eastern Danelaw during the monastic revival which swept all England in the second half of the tenth century. Like its neighbours at Peterborough and Ely, it was re-established by Bishop Æthelwold on the derelict site of an earlier monastery which had been sacked by the Danes; unlike them, however, it did not survive the Reformation as a cathedral church, and it is possibly due to this circumstance that there is no modern history of the house commensurate with its importance.

This edition comprises the ten pre-Conquest charters which appear in the Red Book of Thorney, a fourteenth-century cartulary now preserved in two volumes at Cambridge University Library, Add. MS. 3020–1.[1] Until the end of the nineteenth century it was in the possession of the earls of Westmorland,[2] and was not accessible to scholars. The only available source of the information it contained was a paper book of extracts from the Red Book, made in the reign of Elizabeth or James I by Strangeman and St George, and now in the British Museum, Add. MS. 5937; from this some details of the pre-Conquest charters were published by Nichols in his *Collectanea Topographica et Genealogica* early in the nineteenth century, an edition made use of by Kemble, Thorpe, and Birch in their compilations of the charters of the Old English period.

None of the ten charters, therefore, has been edited directly and completely from the Thorney text. In the case of Nos. IV, V, VI, X, and XI, the British Museum extracts consist of a brief précis of each charter, often omitting the bounds and witness

[1] Davis, no. 964.

[2] The Red Book of Thorney was Lot 1034 in the earl of Westmorland's sale at Sotheby's, 13–15 July 1887, when it was acquired by Messrs Quaritch. It was bought from Quaritch by Cambridge University Library on 22 Nov. 1890.

list. Nos. VIII, IX, and XIII are not included in the extracts, and
do not, therefore, appear in Kemble's *Codex*. Of these, No. XIII
is entirely unknown, and the whole text of No. VIII, with the
exception of the bounds, is here published for the first time.
No. IV, which relates to Water Newton, Hunts., has never before been correctly located, and No. XI, an almost unique charter of Edmund Ironside, has formerly been ascribed to King
Edmund who reigned in the previous century. In the case of
No. VII, which has been widely published from inferior sources,
an important early recension of the charter, differing consider-
ably from the only one so far known to scholars, is here edited
from the Red Book.

An edition of the Thorney charters does not, however, re-
quire such highlights for its justification. The charters of the late
Old English period have long been neglected by scholars,[1] and
these ten charters from a single house, concentrated within a
single century, form a convenient subject for an exercise in
charter criticism, employing a modern apparatus. At the same
time, this does not claim to be a definitive edition, for the commentary is not restricted to those topics upon which a final pro-
nouncement is possible. Instead, each charter is dealt with com-
prehensively, utilizing diplomatic, historical, etymological, and
topographical criteria for its elucidation. At the present stage
of charter criticism, much of the discussion must be of an ex-
ploratory nature. To ignore controversial matters would render
the edition sterile and impair its usefulness. Whenever statements appear which are tentative rather than definitive, an attempt has been made to introduce sufficient qualifying adjec-
tives to give the reader fair warning; however, it is tiresome to
be continually hedging the discussion about with "ifs" and "buts,"
and occasionally resort has been made to a more dogmatic approach, e.g. in dealing with the descent of Yaxley on pp. 162–3.

The charters are edited chronologically, an order different
from that in which they appear in the Red Book. The texts are
presented with abbreviations extended, and in places the punctuation is modernized. Occasional unimportant spelling ano-
malies are corrected silently, but place- and personal names are
always spelt as found. After some hesitation, I have retained the

[1] LC pp. 83–4.

archaic OE letters (except the *wen*) as they appear in the text, but it should be borne in mind that this fourteenth-century version of tenth- and eleventh-century charters shows no consistency in retaining the original alphabet.

The commentary on each charter concludes with a statement on authenticity, based on all the evidence which has been marshalled under the various sectional headings. The Thorney charters can be said to emerge favourably from the investigation. Two only (Nos. VII and XIII) show any signs of having been tampered with at an early date, and even these appear to be based on authentic material. Here, for once, we have a house which is absolved from the charges of forgery which so often have to be made. There is good reason to suppose that *all* the pre-Conquest charters surviving among the Thorney muniments in the fourteenth century were entered in the Red Book.[1] The copyist habitually abbreviated the witness lists, and in the case of one charter (No. XIII) he may have omitted the bounds, but apart from this he appears to have reproduced the full texts of all the charters which lay before him. He could read Old English, and his general accuracy is substantiated by comparison of his version of No. VIII with versions by other copyists.

Reviewing the charters as a whole, the first point to emerge is the existence of three charters, Nos. IV, V, and VI, of a date prior to Æthelwold's re-establishment of the monastery in 973. These all relate to Huntingdonshire estates which came into the abbey's possession before the Conquest, and their presence in the monastic archives may be accounted for by the fact that they establish the estates concerned as *bocland*, land held by royal charter. Possession of such title-deeds enabled the owners either to sell or to make outright gifts of the estates to monasteries, if they so desired, and it was to the advantage of a monastery to be able to produce such a charter in the event of a dispute. These three charters, therefore, probably came into the possession of the abbey at the same time as it acquired the estates themselves. The Twywell charter, No. X, although later in date, also falls within this category.

---

[1] No. XIII, which was entered much later in the cartulary than the rest of the pre-Conquest charters, nevertheless bore on its membrane a press-mark in roman numerals which was consecutive to those of the earlier entries.

Three further charters, VIII, IX, and XIII, relate to estates which had no known connection with Thorney, either pre- or post-Conquest. Many monasteries possessed charters of this type in their muniments, deposited by their lay owners for safe keeping. It may be in some cases that the king was staying at the monastery at the time the charter was drawn up; one of the three copies habitually made was often laid up close at hand.

Nos. XI and XII are the only two charters conveying lands specifically to Thorney. The former could hardly have remained effective for very long, and the latter was not, properly speaking, a charter at all, but rather an OE will.

No. VII, the great confirmation charter of King Edgar, is often described as the foundation charter of Thorney. Of all the pre-Conquest charters entered in the Red Book, this is the only one whose text suggests that it was compiled within the abbey scriptorium. Like most surviving foundation charters, it shows evidence of having been worked over extensively by later copyists, but in many ways it is the most useful historically of the surviving charters of Thorney. It is the only pre-Conquest charter entered in the Red Book which survives elsewhere in an earlier copy. The many late enrolments show that the supposed original remained in the monastic archives until the Dissolution. Probably all the others did, too, but the originals have all since disappeared without trace. We owe our knowledge of them today to the painstaking industry of the scribe of the Red Book of Thorney.

This brief review of the Thorney charters would be incomplete without some reference to the role of the royal chancery in the last century of the Anglo-Saxon state. A classical study by Drögereit established conclusively that from the time of King Athelstan to the accession of King Edgar, the issue of solemn diplomas in the name of the king was the prerogative of a royal chancery.[1] With the advent of the Benedictine reform, however, this generalization no longer holds good for all cases. Mr Eric John has shown that the royal foundation charters of the reformed monasteries of King Edgar's reign were the products of monastic scriptoria,[2] and Dr Harmer has pointed out that in succeeding reigns a custom was established for the king to order interested ecclesiastics to draw up landbooks for indivi-

[1] *Archiv für Urkundenforschung*, XIII, 1935, pp. 335–46.   [2] See p. 183.

dual estates newly acquired by the church.[1] At the same time, changes in the distribution and conditions of land tenure tended to diminish the demand for the issue of fresh landbooks by the royal chancery. It is probable that the persistent extension of monastic endowments led to a substantial reduction in the number of estates devolving by forfeiture and legacy upon the royal fisc; not only were fewer properties becoming available for redistribution to laymen, but it appears likely that kings copied increasingly the trend set by the monasteries, of putting out to lease and to farm those estates which did fall into their hands, rather than granting or selling the outright freehold.

Coupled with these developments was the ever-widening scope being found by the chancery for royal writs addressed to the shire courts. These were short letters of stereotyped form, written in the vernacular; they soon became a most economical and efficient means of making the king's will generally known to his subjects in a particular district, and no doubt in many cases they served in lieu of a direct title deed in settling a new owner upon an estate. For all this, a limited output of landbooks continued to be required, and there is ample internal evidence that the chancery maintained its privileged position as the *fons et origo* of royal diplomas issued to laymen.[2] No other explanation of the consistent format of Æthelred II's charters to lay recipients will suffice.[3]

IV

937. KING ATHELSTAN TO SIGULF: 5 HIDES AT WATER NEWTON, HUNTS.

IN nomine altithroni qui cuncta supra simul et in imis gubernat atque regit quique sua multimoda potentia omnibus ut uoluerit finem imponit iccirco ille diuitie cum mentis intentione diligende sunt que nunquam decipiunt habentem, nec in ipsa morte

---

[1] H p. 39.

[2] This fundamental difference between the origin of late Anglo-Saxon landbooks for ecclesiastical endowments, and those issued for lay persons, has been insufficiently stressed in the past. There is no evidence that the issue of *all* diplomas was withdrawn from the royal chancery to local scriptoria after 963.

[3] See p. 191 for a description of this format.

amittuntur set plus habundant dum cernitur quod amatur. Qua propter ego Æthelstanus diuina michi adridente gratia Rex anglorum et eque totius albeonis gubernator, Rogatus fui a meis fidelibus ministris ut aliquam partem terre in eternam hereditatem laxarem Sigulfe, eorumque precibus annuens pro eius amabili subiectione atque obedientia cum consensu obtimatum meorum terram .v. manentium ubi ab incolis nominatur, "Niwantun," iuxta diriuatiuis fluentium successibus ubi uulgares prisco usu moralique relatione nomen imposuerunt, "Use," quatinus ille bene perfruatur ac perpetualiter possideat et posteritatis sue successoribus cuicumque uoluerit heredi derelinquat ceu supradiximus in eternam hereditatem, cum omnibus ad se rite pertinentibus, pascuis, pratis, campis, siluis, siluorumque nemoribus. Sit autem predicta terra libera in omnibus mundialibus causis preter pontis et arcis constructione expeditionisque adiuuamine in cunctis successoribus. Hoc ius donationis augendo conseruantibus feliciter perueniant inter celibes celestium turmarum, et sine fine in eterna doxa letentur. Si quis autem, quod non optamus, infringere temptauerit hoc nostrum donum, sciat se in examine tremendi iudicii redditurum temeritatis audaciam perpessum esse, nisi pura emendatione et singulta lamentatione emendauerit. Istis terminibus predicta terra circumgirata esse uidetur:

Þis ben þe land mæro æt Niwantune. Ærest of stanwege andlang slædes on ða fulanrode. of þare fulanrode andlang slædes to dinneshangran ut þurh denegiðe graf. to þan hægeþorne. and þanne to þam hlæwe and þanne to þam ellene. and þanne on Use stæþe on ealferþes hlæwe and þanne on suðfeld and swa be wýrtwalam on þa efsan. and þanne on þone Wýþig. and swa be wýrtwalam on þone mereþorn on east halfe branteswýrðe and þanne on þone stanwege.

Acta est prefata donatio anno ab Incarnatione domini Jhesu Christi .dcccc. xxxvii. Indictione .x. Ego Æthelstan Rex totius britannie prefatam donationem cum tropheo agýe crucis confirmaui. Ego Wulfhelm Dorouernensis ecclesie archiepiscopus eiusdem Regis donationem cum tropheo agýe crucis consignaui. Ego Ælpheag wintanensis ecclesie episcopus triumphatem tropheum agýe crucis impressi. Ego Þeodred Lundonensis ecclesie episcopus consignaui. Et cetera.

TEXTS

A. The Red Book of Thorney, fo. 16ᵛ (old numbering, fo. v). See p. 146.

B. BM Add. MS. 5937, fo. 180, an abbreviated copy of A which omits the witness list and a large part of the text. See p. 146.

EDITIONS

(1) *Collect. Topogr.*, IV, p. 56, from B.

(2) K 1114, from B or (1).

(3) CS 712, from (2).

(4) This edition is from A. Abbreviations are extended, and in places the spelling and punctuation are modernized.

DATE

937, according to the charter. This is in agreement with the indiction given, and the witness list is compatible.

PERSONAL NAMES

The donor, King Athelstan, reigned 924–39. The recipient, Sigulf, has not been identified, unless he be the moneyer of that name who struck coins in Athelstan's reign. The name is a common one, but does not appear elsewhere in Athelstan's charters. The witnesses are: Wulfhelm, archbishop of Canterbury 926–42; Ælfheah, bishop of Winchester 934 × 951; and Theodred, bishop of London 926 × 951.

DIPLOMATIC

The elaborate and highly stylized formulas are reminiscent of Aldhelm's writing. In this they are in conformity with other charters of Athelstan. In particular, the introductory clause as far as ". . . imponit," and the whole of the middle section of the charter, from "Æthelstanus divina michi adridente . . ." as far as the OE bounds, is closely paralleled by CS 682, a charter dated 7 June–7 December 931, which is accepted as genuine by Stenton; cf. *Abingdon*, p. 39. The remainder of the introductory clause, from "iccirco . . ." to ". . . amatur," appears in CS 708, dated 935, which also repeats most of the body of the text. On the royal title adopted in Athelstan's charters, see Crawf p. 111, *Abingdon*, p. 40, Robinson p. 60, and Stenton pp. 348–9. The description of the bounds, "istis terminibus predicta terra circumgirata esse videtur," the dating clause, and the titles of the witnesses all appear in CS 709, dated 936, and in other charters of similar date. Later charters, from 938 onwards, show a change of formula, although individual phrases of earlier date recur. The witness list has no doubt been abbreviated by the scribe of the Red Book, as with other charters in the series.

HISTORY

Thorney Abbey possessed a five-hide estate at *Newetone* at the time of DB, identified as Water Newton beside the River Nene (DB fo. 205; VCH *Hunts.*, I, p. 345*b*). This is presumably the *Niwantun* of both versions of the Thorney foundation charter (VII), for the estate was beside a river large enough to take a fishing boat (R pp. 254, 503). It would seem reasonable to suppose that this is also the five hides at *Niwantun* of the charter under discussion, for the only version of this comes from the Thorney Red Book.

There is no record of the descent of the estate between Sigulf, who was given it by King Athelstan in 937, and Ælfric Cild, later ealdorman of Mercia, from whom it was bought by Bishop Æthelwold of Winchester in 963 × 973 for the endowment of Thorney (VII). Early in the following century it was tenanted of Thorney by Æthelferth (R p. 253; on the date see Ker pp. 126–7), but there are no other pre-Conquest references to the estate. See further, CAS LVI–LVII, 1962–3, pp. 86–7.

TOPOGRAPHY

Equation of the *Niwantun* of this charter with Water Newton carries with it the corollary that *Use* was the earlier name of the River Nene at this point. The name remains in the River Ise, the largest tributary of the Nene, and there is independent evidence (PN *Northants.*, p. 184) that the Nene itself was formerly called the Ise in the region of Islip, some distance south of the junction of the modern Ise with the Nene. All the other surviving place-name forms for the Nene are of a date later than our charter,[1] and it must not be overlooked that the River Nene, on its old course, was itself but a tributary of the River Ouse. It would appear that the river-name *Use* was originally applied not only to the parent river but also to all its tributaries—the Wissey, the Little Ouse, the Nene,[2] the Ise—the whole complex of rivers draining the uplands surrounding the southern fenlands, and originally entering the Wash below Wisbech.[3]

Although in the absence of intermediate forms no named point in the charter bounds can be traced unequivocally by direct etymological descent to a surviving place-name, the topography of the present parish boundary of Water Newton fits in sufficiently well to make it appear likely that the existing bounds are virtually the same as those of the tenth-century estate. The following analysis rests on this supposition.

---

[1] The earliest reference to the Nene is in CS 871, a text from the Peterborough Black Book dated 948 (No. 163).

[2] And hence in No. 5 *Wusan*=Nene, *Ofertune*=Orton, Hunts.

[3] For the early geography of this complex of rivers, see H. C. Darby, *The Mediaeval Fenland*, Camb., 1940, pp. 94–7, and map.

1. First at *stanwege*.

The bounds commence where the Billing Brook crossed Ermine Street (Grid reference 973119), about 100 yards N.W. of the wall of the Roman camp at Durobrivæ. They proceed in a clockwise direction.

2. Along the valley to *fulanrode*.

Moving southwards along the valley of the Billing Brook to a 'foul clearing' at the point where the brook is joined by a small unnamed tributary (967117). Here the parish boundary, still following the Billing Brook, turns sharply westwards.

3. Along the valley to Dynne's *hangra*.

Proceeding upstream, first westwards then southwards, to the wooded slope just N. of the Elton–Chesterton road, where the Water Newton boundary leaves the Billing Brook, turning sharply westwards (949118).

4. Through Denegyth's grove.

This personal name is not elsewhere recorded, but the elements are common enough; the second element shows that this is a woman's name. The grove is now called Hop Spinney, and marks another sharp turn in the bounds (949107).

5. To the hawthorn.

Probably near where the parish bounds cross the cart track from Elton to Water Newton Lodge (954101).

6. To the burial mound.

No visible remains survive. It cannot be far from Water Newton Gorse (965102).

7. Then to the elder tree.

Crossing the newly constructed section of the Great North Road (972098).

8. To *Use stæthe*.

The bank of the River Nene (978102). Just E. of this point the river forks to enclose a small island, to the N. of Water Newton church. The present boundary runs along the southern limb, but it seems probable that it once followed the northern limb of the river, which was originally the principal navigable channel.

9. To Ealhfrith's barrow.

The tumulus is shown on the 6-inch OS map, lying on the N. bank near where the two limbs of the river reunite (977113).

10. Then to South field, and so by the stump to the edge (the river bank).

The bounds appear to run northwards from the tumulus, to enclose part of Sutton field (an unrecorded local field name), returning to the Nene at about the point where it was crossed by Ermine Street (977116).

11. Then to the willow, and so by the stump to the boundary thorn.

Possibly these bounds enclose another portion of meadow to the north of the river. The boundary thorn may be the point where the present parish bounds leave the Nene (976120).

12. To the east side of Brand's enclosure, and so on to *stanwege*.

Back to Ermine Street, where the bounds began.

If the identification of the *Niwantun* of this charter with Water Newton be accepted—and it is difficult to see any alternative in view of the later history of the estate—then Ekwall's location of *dinneshangra(n)* in the charter bounds with Denshanger in Passenham (Northants.) can no longer be maintained. It follows that the further identifications (in PN *Northants.*, p. 101) of *stanwege* in the bounds with Watling Street, and *branteswyrthe* with Brownswood Cottage in Potterspury, should also be set aside.

AUTHENTICITY

There are no suspicious elements in this charter, which may be regarded as a good copy of a genuine charter of King Athelstan, with well-preserved place-name forms, lacking only part of the witness list. It is the earliest authentic Huntingdonshire charter.

V

951. KING EADRED TO THE THEGN ÆLFSIGE: 5 HIDES AT HADDON, HUNTS.

PROPHETICA primitus predicatio et apostolica deinceps disceptatio et quod precellentior est euangelica Jhesu Christi promulgatio cunctis indicat dogmata dicens: "Date et dabitur uobis." Ideoque Eadredus Rex Anglorum quos uult honorifice larga manu locupletat. Hoc potest ueraciter miles iste Ælfsige nunc cum ceteris intimare quem perhenni huius ruris "æt haddedune" usurpatione, preter urbis pontisque constructione et expeditionis obsequio beatizat, concedens ei eiusque heredibus

hanc tellurem magnis rebus ac modicis rite pertinentibus per-
fruendam, Eadred Rex albionis alma iam manu hanc munificentiam anno dominice incarnationis .Dcc°cc.lj. sexto quoque quo
scepta¹ regebat regalia annorum laterculo cum consensu sena-
torum quorum hic calculantur uocabula triumphali uidelicet
uexillo stabiliter roborauit. Odá archiepiscopus cum ceteris
suffraganeis. Kænwaldo. Æthelgario. Æthelmund dux. et Eadmund alhelm. Ælfsige miles. Wulric præses. Bertferð. Eadhelm
abbas atque Dunstan cum signo sancte Crucis hec carismata
caraxabant. Iam imperat rex prefatus obsecrando et obsecrat
imperando per clauem euangelicam quam Petro ipse Jhesus
Christus auctore apostolico contulit ligandi atque soluendi potestate tradita quatinus in posterum nullus diabolica fraude de-
ceptus preualeat huius largitatis libertatem delere. Set pocius
qui studeat adimplere eulogium largitoris, larga lucra coram
Christo integra caritate cum choris angelicis Jhesuali gýmnasio
sine fine inueniat amen in eternum.

Þis aren þe landmæres into Haddedune. Erest of erninge-
strete into Sumerlededic. and of þare dic into billingbroc; andlang broces, and of þan broce into þe mære. norð. of þan mære
andlong Weýes into aldandic. éast andlang dices into ellen stýb
and on þa stræte. and suð andlang stræte þat it comeð foren on
gean sumerlededic þer it ær bigan þat fiue hiða land mære.

TEXTS

    A. The Red Book of Thorney, ff. 17–17ᵛ (old numbering, ff. vi–viᵛ).
    B. BM Add. MS. 5937 f. 180, from A, omitting most of the text, the
bounds, and the witness list.

EDITIONS

    (1) *Collect. Topogr.*, IV, p. 57, from B.
    (2) K 1167, from B or (1).
    (3) CS 893, from (2).
    (4) This edition is from A. Abbreviations are extended, and in places
the spelling and punctuation are modernized.

DATE

    951, in the sixth year of Eadred, as stated in the charter. Eadred
succeeded on 26 May 946. The witness list is compatible with the date.

---

¹ *Sic*, for *sceptra*.

PERSONAL NAMES

The donor, King Eadred, reigned 946–55. The recipient, the thegn Ælfsige, is discussed on p. 162 below. This charter is the first to show a trend in Eadred's reign, in which the number of ealdormen and thegns witnessing becomes appreciably less than had formerly been the custom. The episcopal witnesses are Oda, archbishop of Canterbury 942 × 958; Cenwald, bishop of Worcester 929 × 958; and Æthelgar, bishop of Crediton 934 × 953. The next three witnesses are probably all ealdormen. Æthelmund witnesses as *dux* 940 × 965. His ealdordom was probably a Mercian one; see R p. 314. Eadmund is probably the *dux* of that name who witnesses in 949 × 963; he may have been ealdorman of Devon; cf. R p. 314. Alhelm may be identified with the Ealhhelm, another Mercian *dux*, who witnesses CS 763, 865, 888, and 891. Of the remainder, Ælfsige is too common a name for identification to be possible. A thegn named Wulfric regularly witnesses Eadred's charters. A thegn named Bertferth (or Beorhtfrith) witnesses CS 879, dated 949, and was probably made an ealdorman in 955 (W p. 104). An abbot Eadhelm witnesses a Kentish charter dated 949 (CS 880), and a Staffordshire charter dated 951 (CS 890). Possibly he is the Abbot Eadhelm who was killed at Thetford, Norfolk, in 952 (ASC D); alternatively, he is Eadhelm, abbot of St Augustine's, Canterbury, who occurs in CS 1010, dated 958 (cf. R p. 316). Dunstan was abbot of Glastonbury 940 × 955.

DIPLOMATIC

The arrangement of the various parts of this charter, with the witness list in the middle and the bounds at the end, is highly unusual. The chief interest, however, lies in the alliterative and poetical formulas, which are shared with a small group of charters of Eadred's reign (cf. EHD I, p. 340), being identical with those of a Burton charter, CS 890, as is the date and most of the witness list. As this charter and the Thorney one survive in two independent archives, it seems unlikely that either is a forgery utilizing the text of the other, or that they are forgeries based on a common source, unless indeed they be the product of a "peripatetic forger" (cf. LC p. 19). Very probably, however, these two charters were drawn up and witnessed on the same occasion. Some of the phraseology occurs, in an OE version, in No. 7, a charter by which King Eadred gave the adjacent estate of Alwalton to the thegn Ælfsige Hunlafing, who is not to be confused with the Ælfsige of the charter under discussion (see below).

HISTORY

This is the earliest reference to Haddon. Its subsequent fate can best be followed by reference to the pedigree which appears on p. 162. In the absence of direct evidence, it may be inferred that Haddon descended, like part of Yaxley, from Ælfsige to his son Wulfstan Uccea. Wulfstan entered into a transaction with Bishop Æthelwold by which this part of Yaxley was exchanged for another estate; Æthelwold then used it for the endowment of Thorney (No. 16). Haddon, however, did not become the property of Thorney until some time later. A late thirteenth-century source (*Rotuli Hundredorum*, Record Commission, II, p. 644) states that Thorney obtained Haddon from King Edgar in free and perpetual alms. If this is to be believed, the estate must have reverted to the Crown from Ælfsige or his descendants (e.g. by will or by forfeiture). Presumably Edgar's gift was made some time after the refoundation of Thorney, for the estate is not mentioned in either recension of Edgar's charter (No. 16).

TOPOGRAPHY

The boundaries of Haddon are remarkably easy to follow from the OE description. They are identical with the present parish bounds—a textbook example of continuity.

1. First from Ermine Street to Somerled's ditch.

Starting at the s.e. corner of the estate, where a small unnamed stream (Somerled's ditch) reaches the Great North Road (Ermine Street) (Grid reference 925153). The bounds proceed clockwise.

2. From the ditch to Billing Brook.

Westwards along the ditch until the cart track from Morborne to Haddon is reached; then continuing due west along field boundaries to the Billing Brook, the name of which is unchanged after a millennium (918120).

3. Northwards along the brook to the landmark.

The point where the boundary turns due eastwards away from the Billing Brook (935124).

4. Along the way to the old ditch.

The boundary follows a footpath along the edge of a field until it reaches Haddon Lodge (940132), where a ditch commences which now has no name, but which must be the "old ditch" of the OE bounds.

5. East along the ditch to the elder-tree stump, and on to the street.

Following the ditch eastwards until it reaches Ermine Street at the site of a disused brickworks (943140).

6. South along the street until you reach Somerled's ditch, where the landmarks to the five hides begin.

AUTHENTICITY

This may be accepted as a good and complete copy of a genuine charter of King Eadred, preserving reliable forms of personal and place-names, and with contemporary bounds. Fortunately the witness list occurs in the body of the charter, and has thus escaped abbreviation by the scribe of the Red Book.

VI

956. KING EADWIG TO HIS MINISTER AND THEGN ÆLFWINE: 10 HIDES AT YAXLEY, AND 5 HIDES AT FARCET, HUNTS.

REGNANTE ac gubernante domino nostro Jhesu Christo. Memoria igitur hominum cito elabitur, ideo studendum est omnibus perseuerantibus et manentibus in hoc presenti seculo ut certis litterarum apicibus notentur que deuotis mentibus notis ac fidelibus amicis ad corporéé necessitatis iuuamina largiuntur. Ideo ego Eadwin[1] Anglorum Rex ac totius britannice telluris gubernator et rector, cuidam meo fideli ministro ac militi, qui in sue uoluntatis ac deuotionis obsequio semper faciendo ac implendo paratus ac promptus fuit, qui ab incunabulis sue infantilitatis non fortuitu set uoluntate parentum nomen accepit "Ælfwine" dapsili deditione quandam partem ruris libenter dedi .xv. mansas duobus in locis, decem uidelicet illic ubi anglica apellatione dicitur "æt Geakeslea," quinque uero "æt fearresheafde." Habeat et possideat prefatam dapsilem donationem quamdiu uitalis flatus carnem mundana fragilitate corruptam aluerit. Cum igitur dies dissolucionis sue aduenerit, quo de corruptibili uita ad incorruptibilem beatitudinem migrauerit, cui sibi libet heredi sine ullo obstaculo derelinquat in eternam hereditatem, cum campis, pascuis, pratis, siluis, exceptis istis tribus, expeditione, pontis, arcuisue constructione.

Si quis igitur tetri demonis stimulatione instinctus hoc nostrum decretum infringere uoluerit, sit ipse sub stigei fluminis undam preceps in ima tartara trusus, nisi hic prius ad satisfactionem uenire maluerit. Istis terminibus predicta terra circumgirata esse uidetur.

Þis aren þe land mære to Geacesléa to þam ten hýden. Þanne lýð ægþeres landes mæres her togedere to dichýþe. of dichýþe

---

[1] *Sic* for *Eaduui*, i.e. Eadwig.

to suðhýthe. þonan to westfenne. of westfenne to trendelmere. þonan to wýllepole. of wýllepole to drægmere. of drægmere andlang meres to hemmingesbroke. þonan to holtwille. of holtwille to flýte and swa to þam dicum. And þis aren þe land mære þara .v. hýde to færresheafde. ærist hit scet to þan hæcce. of hæcce to stangrunde. þonan to briggegraue. of briggegraue to lampitte. þonan to færresheafde hýþe. þonan to norðhype. of norðhýþe est to dichýþe. and witlesmere þridden deal. and þes wateres and þes wudes þe þær to hýrð. þat is on ragrenholte þat þridde treow into fearresheafde.

Hec carta scripta est anno dominice Incarnationis .dcccc.lvj. Indictione .xiiii. Ego Eadwin[1] gratia dei totius britannice telluris rex meum donum proprio sigillo confirmaui. Ego Eadgar eiusdem regis frater celeriter consensi. Ego Odo Dorouernensis Ecclesie archipresul alme crucis signo roboraui. Ego Ælfsinus Wintoniensis ecclesie diuinus speculator proprium sigillum impressi. Et cetera.

TEXTS

A. The Red Book of Thorney, ff. 17ᵛ–18 (old numbering, ff. vi–viᵛ).
B. BM Add. MS. 5937, fo. 180ᵛ, from A, omitting most of the text and the bounds.

EDITIONS

(1) *Collect. Topogr.*, IV, p. 57, from B.
(2) K 1180, from B or (1).
(3) CS 940, from (2).
(4) This edition is from A. Abbreviations are extended, and in several places the punctuation is modernized.

DATE

956, as stated in the charter. The indiction is given as 14, which is correct. The witness list is compatible with the date.

PERSONAL NAMES

King Eadwig, the donor, succeeded on 23 November 955; he was then about 15. He died in 959. The recipient, the thegn Ælfwine, cannot be identified with certainty with the thegn of that name who appears in several of Eadwig's charters (CS 935, 1029, 1036, 1050, 1051). The witnesses commence with Eadgar, described as the king's brother. In 956 he was only 12 or 13; he succeeded to Mercia (includ-

---

[1] *Sic* for *Eaduui*, i.e. Eadwig.

ing the territory within which Yaxley and Farcet lay) the following
year, and to the rest of England in 959. The only other witnesses
mentioned are Oda, archbishop of Canterbury 942 × 958; and Ælfsige
I, bishop of Winchester 951 × 958.

DIPLOMATIC

The charters of Eadwig show considerable variations in formulas, and
a text bearing close resemblance to the Yaxley and Farcet charter has
not been found. It commences with an invocation found in CS 974,
which is of the same date. The proem cannot be paralleled exactly in
form, but its content consists of the usual reference to the desirability
of committing land gifts to writing. The title of the king, which follows, is the same as that of CS 960, which is also dated 956, and CS
988, dated 957. The unusual description of the recipient is identical
with that used in CS 888, a charter of King Eadred dated 946 × 951 by
Stevenson: ". . . cuidam meo fideli ministro ac militi, qui ab incunabulis suæ infantilitatis, non fortuitu sed voluntate parentum, nomen
accepit. (Ælfgar)." The words "dapsili deditione," which come next,
are found in CS 925 and CS 1004, dated 956 and 957 respectively.
After a description of the land gift comes a statement that Ælfwine is
free to dispose of it to his heirs as he wishes; the phrase "derelinquat
in eternam hereditatem" occurs also in CS 974. The description of the
perquisites and obligations of the estate, from "cum campis . . ." to
". . . arcisve constructione," is the same in CS 982, another charter of
956. The phrase "sub stigei fluminis undam" in the anathema was used
in translation in vernacular charters of the following century, see p.
89. The bounds are introduced by the sentence "istis terminibus predicta terra circumgirata esse videtur," which is characteristic of contemporary charters, as is the dating clause. Finally, the witness list
(which is incomplete), with the descriptive phrases following each
name, is identical with those in CS 981 and CS 963, charters of the
same year and probably witnessed on the same occasion.

HISTORY

There are more pre-Conquest records of Yaxley and Farcet than of
any other estate in Huntingdonshire. Unfortunately, in spite of the
abundance of sources—or possibly because of it—there remains much
that is obscure concerning the descent of the estate during the last
century of the OE period. Most of the difficulties arise from apparently contradictory statements given in the two versions of the Thorney foundation charter (No. VII); although these are undoubtedly
muddled, they cannot be ignored. The account which follows is presented in dogmatic form to save space and tedious explanations, but it
is tentative rather than definitive.

The estate at Yaxley was originally a twenty-hide property divided

F

into two separate holdings, each assessed to the geld at 10 hides. One of these holdings comprised the village itself, the other the adjacent fenland. To avoid confusion they are called Yaxley I and Yaxley II respectively. Farcet was originally a five-hide property, including both upland and fenland within its bounds.

The earliest reference to Yaxley I occurs in a record of a series of legal transactions which were set in motion towards the end of the reign of King Eadred (946–55) when, to quote the text: "the beginning of this case was that a woman was stolen at *Ieceslea* (Yaxley) from Ælfsige, Brihtsige's son. The woman's name was Thurwife. Then Ælfsige vouched the woman in the possession of Wulfstan, Wulfgar's father . . ." (R XLIV).

This Ælfsige is identical with the Ælfsige who received part of Ailsworth in Northants. from King Eadred in 948 (CS 871). He also obtained Haddon from Eadred in 951 (No. v above) and Kettering in Northants. from King Eadwig in 956 (CS 943). He is to be distinguished from the Ælfsige Hunlafing who obtained Alwalton in Huntingdonshire from King Eadred in 955 (No. 7). Ælfsige Hunlafing must have been the son of Hunlaf. A thegn of this name witnesses CS 665 and CS 689, dated 929 and 932 respectively. But the Ælfsige who held Yaxley I is referred to as the son of Brihtsige in the document quoted above, which had evidently escaped Professor Whitelock's attention when she suggested that the two Ælfsiges were identical (W p. 130). Ælfsige was a very common name; no fewer than four thegns named Ælfsige witness a charter dated 956 (CS 963).

Ailsworth descended from Ælfsige to his son Wulfstan Uccea, who must be the Wulfstan, Wulfgar's father, of the document quoted above. Wulfstan Uccea exchanged Yaxley I and Ailsworth[1] with Bishop Æthelwold for an estate of 24 hides at Washington in Sussex (No. 12). The date of this transaction is uncertain, but it must lie between 963, when Æthelwold became bishop of Winchester and also received the estate of 24 hides at Washington from King Edgar (CS 1125), and 975, the date of King Edgar's death. An inventory of Yaxley I at the time of its acquisition by Æthelwold has been preserved (R XXXIX).[2] He used the estate to endow Thorney Abbey (No. VII below), and apart from a temporary alienation, it remained thereafter in the abbey's possession. It is interesting that Ælfsige's estate at Kettering also came into the hands of Æthelwold, who used it to endow Peterborough Abbey (CS 1128; R XXXIX); it appears likely that he obtained this

[1] The whole of Ailsworth was rated at 9 hides (divided into 2 portions, of 3 hides and 6 hides respectively) at the time of DB. See my forthcoming "Hidation of Northamptonshire."

[2] R XXXIX is a composite document. Part of it relates to Yaxley I (R p. 74, ll. 17–23), and another part to Yaxley II and Farcet (*ibid.*, p. 74, ll. 24–8).

from Wulfstan Uccea. To complete this account of what is known of Wulfstan, it is necessary to mention that he was left the estate of God-stone in Surrey in the will of his relatives Brihtric and his wife Ælfswith (W xi). He may be the thegn Wulfstan who was granted 9 hides at Conington, Hunts., by King Eadwig in 957 (No. 9; see notes to No. xii below).

The history of Yaxley II, the fenland estate, is rather more obscure. It first appears in the charter under discussion, by which King Eadwig gave it, together with Farcet, to the thegn Ælfwine. Later these two estates descended to Æthelstan and Ælfwold (their alliterative names suggest that they were related to Ælfwine—perhaps his sons), who also held an estate at Peterborough. They sold all three of these estates to Earl Æthelwine of East Anglia and Abbot Ealdulf of Peterborough some time between 963 and 973.[1] Evidently the purchase money had been provided by Bishop Æthelwold.

At this stage, while Yaxley I, Yaxley II, and Farcet were all in Æthel-wold's hands, he redistributed the hidage assessment between the estates. Yaxley I and II were combined to form an estate of 17 hides, and given to Thorney Abbey; Farcet was reassessed at 8 hides, and given to Peterborough Abbey.[2] After the death of King Edgar the anti-monastic reaction produced a tenurial upheaval among the many estates acquired by Æthelwold for the endowment of his fenland foundations, during which those which had come to him from Wulfstan Uccea were temporarily alienated. Kettering was recovered for Peterborough only after a dramatic intervention by Earl Æthelwine and his brother Ælf-wold (LE pp. xii–xiii, 84–5); Yaxley was bought back for 40 pounds, which Æthelwold had to pay Ælfric Cild,[3] who was possibly the son[4] and certainly the successor of Ealdorman Ælfhere of Mercia, the leader of the anti-monastic faction. It will be recalled that Ælfric Cild also challenged Æthelwold's purchase of Water Newton at this period.[5]

It seems probable that after Æthelwold's settlement of the claims of the anti-monastic faction an agreement was transacted between Thorney and its neighbour at Peterborough, by which Wittering, Ox-ney, and Thorpe were transferred to Peterborough Abbey in return for Farcet. The estate at Farcet extended into Whittlesey Mere (as we know from the bounds of the present charter, discussed below), and the "A" recension of the Thorney foundation charter records a further agreement drawn up between the two abbeys, by which Peter-borough's fishing rights in the mere were protected, in spite of its

---

[1] R xxxix (p. 74, ll. 24–7) and R xl (p. 78, ll. 20–4).

[2] No. vii below (B recension). Farcet kept this assessment until the time of DB, but Yaxley's assessment was subsequently reduced to 15 hides.

[3] Ibid. (A recension).   [4] According to Florence of Worcester.

[5] No. vii (A recension).

surrender of Farcet to Thorney. This agreement was repeated in the time of the Confessor, and was still in force in 1086.[1]

TOPOGRAPHY

Both sets of bounds are very vague, as one would expect in fenland districts. The bounds of the ten hides of Yaxley comprise the fenland part of the present parish. They run clockwise, embracing the two fens now known as Yaxley Fen and Hod Fen. *dichythe* appears to represent the bank of what is now Pig's Water; the landing-place itself is identified from later medieval deeds in the Thorney Red Book as lying opposite the present Duck and Drake public house. The area is still called Water End by the villagers. *suðhythe* is less easy to locate, but it is probably the south bank of the stretch of Pig's Water from Cow Bridge to Conquest Lode (see below, under Farcet bounds). It may be difficult to imagine this stream ever having been large enough to take fishing boats and other water traffic, but it is essential to remember that the topography of the whole district has been vastly altered by the drainage of Whittlesey Mere and its dependent lakes a century ago.

Next in the bounds comes *westfenne*, so called because it lay to the west of Whittlesey Mere; its modern name is Yaxley Fen. Then comes a chain of three small lakes extending westwards from the N.W. border of Whittlesey Mere (the border is now represented by the river called Black Ham). From east to west these were *trendelmere*, *wyllepole*, and *drægmere*; they appear on eighteenth-century maps as Trundle Mere, Wellpool, and Dray Mere. They disappeared when Whittlesey Mere was drained, but the exact bounds of Trundle Mere are still easily visible on air photographs. *hemminges broke*, which occurs again as *Heninges* in No. 32, an eleventh-century description of Whittlesey Mere and the surrounding fenland, is probably now represented by Stilton Dyke. *holtwille* is presumably the small stream which ran from the site of Heyes's Farm (6-inch OS map—now vanished owing to the excavations at Norman Cross brickworks) through fields formerly wooded, to join *flyte*, which is now Yard's End Dyke. *tham dicum* probably refers to Yaxley Lode, which joins Yard's End Dyke near the old *dichythe*.

The text describing the bounds of the 5 hides at Farcet falls into two distinct portions. The first section, from "*than hæcce* . . ." to ". . . *dichythe*," comprises the whole of the modern parish of Stanground, together with that part of Farcet lying to the N.W. of the old course of the River Nene. The bounds, which run clockwise, are so vague that they are impossible to follow in detail, but *than hæcce* probably refers to a floodgate at the junction of Pig's Water and the old course of the River Nene, about half a mile south of Farcet village. *stangrunde* is the

[1] See p. 183.

modern Stanground, and as the region is not at all stony I can only suggest that the reference is to the thickly scattered Roman remains in the neighbourhood, which was an important pottery area in Roman times. Farcet was not separated administratively from Stanground until the nineteenth century. *briggegrave* was either a claypit or a small wood, near Horsey bridge. *lampitte* is an unidentified claypit (the whole area is on thick clay). *færresheafde hythe* must have been a landing-place on the old River Nene to the east of Farcet village. *norðhythe* obtains its prefix from the need to distinguish it from the *suðhythe* in the bounds of Yaxley; it appears to me probable that they refer to the north and south banks of Pig's Water, to the east of Cow Bridge. *dichythe* has been described already under the Yaxley bounds; evidently this part of the Farcet boundary stretched rather nearer to Yaxley a millennium ago than it does at present.

The second section of the text describing Farcet, from "and witles-mere . . ." to ". . . into fearresheafde," deals with the fenland portion of the estate. It comprises a third share of *witlesmere*[1]—the earliest recorded reference to Whittlesey Mere—and "every third tree"[2] in *ragrenholte* or heron's wood, a lost place-name located between Whittlesey Mere and Cnut's Dyke (PN *Hunts.*, p. 186). The wood has vanished, but herons still abound in the locality.

AUTHENTICITY

This may be accepted as a reliable copy of a genuine charter of Eadwig, lacking only a part of the witness list. Whoever transcribed it into the Thorney Red Book misread *Eaduui* (for Eadwig) as *Eaduin*, and wrote it as *Eadwin*. For the most part, however, the place- and personal names appear reliable. The bounds are rather vague, as one would expect in the fenland region, but there is no reason to doubt that they are contemporary with the charter.

VII

973. KING EADGAR TO THORNEY ABBEY:
CONFIRMATION OF ESTATES AND PRIVILEGES

UNIVERSIS *sophie studium intento mentis conanime sedulo riman-tibus liquido patescit, quod instabilis huius miserrime ac caduce uite curriculus cum marcido inanis glorie flosculo tabescendo lugubriter*

---

[1] A century later, Thorney still possessed one-third of Whittlesey Mere, the remaining two-thirds being possessed by Ramsey. Thorney and Ramsey then shared Heron's Wood equally; cf. No. 44.

[2] The phrase recalls similar partitions of woodland listed in H p. 498. A further example occurs in W xxix.

deficit, et friuola eius gloria numquam in eodem statu permanens, velud
fumus rotatu celerrimo evanescit. Attamen annuente Christi mundi
creatoris ac redemptoris gratia tam recidiuis presentis uite munusculis
futuram eterne uite beatitudinem centuplicato questu adquirere lucrando
fide uigente catholica prudentissime ualemus.

Quam ob rem ego Eadgar totius Britannie basileus, quoddam mona-
1 sterium beate dei genitrici semperque uirgini Marie ad laudem
et honorem eiusdem domini nostri Jhesu Christi mundi saluatoris dedicatum, in loco qui quondam Ancraig, nunc uero usitato Þornig nuncupatur uocabulo, et rura prefato monasterio
subiecta, cum omnibus utensilibus, pratis uidelicet, pascuis,
siluis, piscuariis, capturis, gronnis, atque culparum emendationem que reatu aliquo in ipsis peraguntur ruribus, domino
nostro Jhesu Christo eiusque genitrici semperque uirgini Marie
octauodecimo mei terreni imperii anno, attamen primo mee
regie dedicationis, *Aþeluuoldo michi* episcoporum dilectissimo
20 cum omni subiectionis humilitate impetrante, *eterna largitus sum*
hereditate, ea semper interposita conditione, ut nullius altioris
uel inferioris gradus hominis reatu a *domino nostro Jhesu Christo*,
sanctoque loco quod tam a me quam a predicto episcopo uel a
ceteris catholicis concessum uel concedendum est, ulla occa-
sione diabolo instigante *priuetur. Si uero crimen quod uenie non sit*
dignum suadente diabolo quod absit loci procurator commiserit, agatur
rationabiliter de eo quod de regis agitur preposito, ut uidelicet reo rite
decuriato ac iusto ordine depulso, illi qui dignus sit Christi designetur
uti regis solet prepositura, a nullo secularium Christi possessione
30 *uiolata.* Nam in ipso prefato loco anachoretice uite aptissimo,
duo quondam precipue sanctitatis germani antistites, Than-
credius uidelicet et Torthredus, celestis uite beatitudinem,
alter martyrio, alter confessionis gloria obtinentes cum gloriosa
ægregii triumphali palma migrauerunt ad Christum. Toua uero
eorum soror, non solum carnalis propinquitatis federe compagi-
nata, set etiam imitatione uirtutum et caritatis repagulo conexa,
in ultima huius insule parte anachoreticam uitam ducens, ago-
nem sancte conuersacionis decentissime complens, ac putidam
huius fragilitatis mortem deserens, membrum tripudians per-
40 rexit ad capud quod Christus est humani generis redemptor, qui
cum coeterno patre et spiritu sancto utriusque sexus milites

infiniti tripudii gloria beatificando coronat. Hic namque tante
et tam secrete quietis ac uenustatis locus, peccatis promeren-
tibus prius *a paganis uastatus* et diu postea miserabiliter a secu-
laribus possessus, sine dei seruicio et spiritalium conversacione
extiterat. Tali igitur tanteque miserie prefatus presul compassus,
et insulam unius uidelicet manse quantitatem a quadam muliere,
que noto Æthelfled uocitabatur onomate, cum quadraginta auri
mancusis emendo obtinuit et edificia monachorum habitationi
50 conuenientia inibi construens, ecclesiam ad laudem trinitatis
que in coeterne deitatis unitate consistit, in unitate tripartitam
construens ad sanctitatis memoriam trium sanctorum quorum
suffragiis precipue confidebat, dei scilicet genitrici semperque
uirgini Marie orientale altaris presbiterium dedicans, occiden-
talem uero cleri ac populi eiusdem ecclesie partem beato petro
regni celorum clauigero, nec non aquilonalem ipsius basilice
porticum beato Benedicto omnium monachorum patrono con-
secrauit, multisque et diuersis telluris portiunculis locupletans
ac diuerso ecclesiastici iuris supellectili ornans decorauit. Uite
60 igitur regularis monachos inibi constituens, ipse abbatis uice
fungens abbatem sancte monachorum congregationi preferre
post obitum suum instituit ut ita deinceps abbatum electio
secundum regule preceptum ex eadem congregatione usu tenea-
tur perpetuo, id est ut ex eadem congregatione qui ordinandus
est, et aliunde nequaquam nisi peccatis quod absit promeren-
tibus uel impediente imperitia, talis qui dignus sit in ea reperiri
nequiuerit, cum regis consilio eligatur. Rex autem non ad
tyrannidem sed ad loci munimen et augmentum uti mos est
super pastorem et Christi gregem dominium sollerti uigilantia
70 misericorditer custodiat. Secularium uero nec episcoporum
quispiam ne ad magni detrimenti ruinam deueniat ut dominium
loci teneat, excepto rege nunquam eligatur. Sunt etenim rura
hec que a prefato rege et diuine seruitutis obsequio cum magna
humilitate obtinuit, et auro argentoque non solum a rege, sed
etiam a diuersis hominum personis comparauit, et in exordio
domino nostro Jhesu Christo eiusque genitrici semperque uirgini Marie nec non beato Petro apostolorum principi ad usus
monachorum inibi sub regula patroni nostri beati Benedicti
degentium eterno concessit donario. Id est:

A

80 Witlesig, niwantun, wȳdestun,
geakeslea, et oþer geakeslea,
fearresheafod, bearuwe,
teafolscet.

Duas mansas
iuxta Huntandune.
Et monasteriolum
Sancte Marie extra oppidum
dedicatum supradictum.

90 Nam supradictam insulam
que Witlesig nuncupatur totam
prudentissime adquirens eius
mediam partem ab Leofsige filio[1]
Ælfsiges cum quadraginta meri
argenti libris, et cum sex
mansis æt Bigrafan emendo
obtinuit. Duas uero partes
alterius medietatis, cum .xx.
libris a leofwine filii Aþulfi[2]

100 comparando adquisiuit. Tertiam
uero partem eiusdem medietatis,
et duas partes illius stagni quod
Witlesmare[3] nominatur, emit ab
Ufan et ab eius uterinis[4] fratribus
cum triginta argenti libris
purissimi. Has autem triginta
libras prefatus miles dedit
Henrico et sibi ab eo rus quod
Drægtun nuncupatur cum ipsa

110 argenti pecunia quam illi
episcopus subueniendo ne de-
populationaretur dederat, multis
coram testibus comparauit,
rursumque cum illi im-
mutare uellent hanc
commutacionem idem
episcopus illis uiginti
libras appendit.

B

Witlesig, Wiðringaig et
Oxanig, Þorp, Niwantun,
Ticanmersc, Wydestun,
geaceslea, beruwe. in Holande,
Giddanig, Hludantun,
Angarhala, Tid. Duas mansas
iuxta Huntandune et terciam
æt Broctune, et monasteriolum Sancte Marie extra oppidum
dedicatum supradictum.

Nam supradictam insulam
que Witlesig nuncupatur totam
prudentissime adquirens eius
mediam partem ab Leofsige filii[1]
Ælfsiges cum .xxv. meri
argenti libris

emendo
obtinuit. Duas uero partes
alterius medietatis, cum .xx.
libris a leofwine filii adulfi[2]
comparando adquisiuit. Tertiam
uero partem eiusdem medietatis,
et duas partes illius stagni quod
Witlesmere[3] nominatur, emit ab
Ufan et ab eius uterinus[4] fratribus
cum .xxx. argenti libris
purissimi. Has autem .xxx.
libras prefatus miles [dedit]
Henrico et sibi ab eo rus quod
Drægtun nuncupatur cum ipsa
argenti pecunia quam illi
episcopus subueniendo ne de-
populationaretur dederat, multis
coram testibus comparauit.

---

[1] A filio; B filii. [2] A Aþulfi; B adulfi.
[3] A Witlesmare; B Witlesmere. [4] A uterinis; B uterinus.

A | B

A

120

Niwantun a quodam milite
qui Ælfric cild uocitatur[1]
130 deuotissime primo cum uiginti
libris, ac deinde cum prefatus miles hoc inmutare
disponeret, predictus
episcopus illi duas mansas
æt ræsnan duasque æt
ẏranceaster, unam quoque
æt ticceanmersce, insuper
et tresdecim libras pro
pecunia appendit et sic
140 altera uice niwantun
mercando adquisiuit. Leofstan
quidam miles ob patrocinium
sui muniminis episcopo mansam
ac dimidiam in Ticcanmersce[2]
gratuite dedit. Dimidiam uero
mansam a quadam uidua comparauit. Unam autem mansam
quam fur quidam ante posse-
derat, a rege cum triginta auri
150 mancusis emit.
Wẏdestun[3] prefatus presul a
rege mutauit, dans uillam in[4]
peninctun in commutatione,
quam episcopo[5] superstiti
Ælfsige post obitum eius con-
dixerat.

B

Wiðringaig quoque et
Oxanig ab Gearweardo et
a Wulfnoðo et a diuersis
et paupertinis hominum
personis cum .xv. argenti
libris comparauit. In ðorp,
tres mansas a Sigeferðo
cum .xvi. libris emendo
comparauit.
Niwantun a quodam milite
qui Ælfric cild uocitata[1]
deuotissime cum .xx.
libris

mercando adquisiuit. Leofstan
quidam miles ob patrocinium
sui muniminis episcopo mansam
ac dimidiam in Ticanmersce[2]
gratuite dedit, dimidiam uero
mansam a quadam uidua comparauit. Unam autem mansam
quam fur quidam ante posse-
derat, a rege cum .xxx.
mancusis auri emit.
Wudestun[3] prefatus presul a
rege mutauit, dans uillam[4]
Peninctun in commutatione,
quam episcopus[5] superstiti
Ælfsige post obitum eius con-
dixerat.

---

[1] A uocitatur; B uocitata.   [2] A Ticcanmersce; B Ticanmersce.
[3] A Wẏdestun; B Wudestun.   [4] A uillam in; B uillam.
[5] A episcopo; B episcopus.

F*

A

Uigintiquinque mansas que
Geakeslea nominatur quas dedit
Sancte dei genitrici semperque
160 uirgini Marie æt Thornige

mutauit a Wulfstano[1] primo
cum uigintiquatuor mansis in
Wassengatune[2] in Suðsexon,[3]
rursumque cum ille totum
hoc in aliud transferre
170 moliretur, episcopus
alteram comparationem
innouans cum quadraginta
purissimi libris argenti ab
ælfrico supranominato
predictas uigintiquinque
mansas æt twam geakeslean
et æt fearresheafod com-
parauit.
    Nam uillam que *bearuwe*[4] in
180 lindisige[5] nominatur, idem
episcopus a rege prefato cum
quadraginta meri argenti libris
emendo comparauit, *et* insuper
munera sibi *multo* hac *pecunia*
cariora pro eadem addidit tellure.

190

B

xvii mansas que
Geakeslea nominatur quas dedit
Sancte dei genitrici semperque
uirgini Marie æt Þornige,
et viii in Fearresheafde
quas idem episcopus beato
Petro apostolorum principi
ad Medeshamstede con-
cesserat, mutauit a Wulstano[1]
cum .xxiiii. mansis in
Wassengtone[2] in Suðseaxon.[3]

    Nam uillam que Beruwe[4] in
Lindesige[5] nominatur, idem
episcopus a rege prefato cum
.xl. meri argenti libris
emendo comparauit, *et* in super
munera sibi *multo* [h]ac *pecunia*
cariora pro eadem addidit tellure.
    Rura vero prefata in
Holande supernominatus
presul emit ab æðelwine
duce cum .xx. limpidissimi
argenti libris et ducentis
bene examinati auri man-
cusis, et insuper cum .xv.
fecunde telluris mansis in
Grantandene hoc merci-
monium corroborando
confirmauit. Regi uero

---

[1] A Wulfstano; B Wulstano.   [2] A Wassengatune; B Wassengtone.
[3] A Suðsexon; B Suðseaxon.   [4] A bearuwe; B Beruwe.
[5] A lindisige; B Lindesige.

A

B

pro consensu et eiusdem
mercimonii licentia ac pro
reatus emendatione quam
200   Dani socne usitato nomi-
nant uocabulo, centum
dedit splendidissimi auri
mancusas.

Ecclesiam autem in Huntan-   Ecclesiam autem in Huntandune cum cimiterio et[1] tribus   dune cum cimiterio a[1] tribus
agellulis[2] mansis, Rex prefatus   agelluli[2] mansis rex prefatus
supradicto monasterio ob eterne   supradicto monasterio ob eterne
beatitudinis premium gratula-   beatitudinis premium gratula-
bundus eterna largitus est   bundus eterna largitus est
210   hereditate. Hoc excepto, supra-   hereditate. Hoc excepto, supra-
nominata rura omnia mutauit   nominata rura omnia mutauit
uel emit a rege uel possessoribus   uel emit a rege uel possessoribus
maiori minori ue pretio.   maiori minori ue pretio.

Piscuaria uero in circuitu
uillularum, Wyllan scilicet
et elm prefatus emit epi-
scopus cum uiginti libris
ac una in quibus per
singulos annos xvj milia
220   anguillarum capiuntur.
Cuius medietatem capture
octo scilicet milia ad
Thornig, similiter et octo
milia ad burh annuatim
distribui idem concessit
episcopus. Quartam partem
quoque stagni quod solito
Witlesmere nominatur,
ac duo piscuaria, decem-
230   que mutuata sunt iugera
[de Þornig uidelicet][3] ad
Burh [pro commutacione
centum uiginti porcorum
pascualium, ac pro do-
morum, sepium, et
stabulorum emendatione].[3]

---

[1] A et; B a.   [2] A agellulis; B agelluli.
[3] Words in square brackets erased in text of A: supplied from C.

Sint igitur donanti domino nostro Jhesu Christo eiusque genitrici semperquue uirgini Marie a predicto rege et episcopo perpetualiter representata, *omni terrene seruitutis iugo libera, tribus*
240 *exceptis, rata uidelicet expeditione, pontis, arcisue restauratione.*[1] *Si-*
quis igitur hanc nostram donationem in aliud quam constituimus trans-
ferre uoluerit, priuatus consortio sancte dei ecclesie, eternis baratri in-
cendiis lugubri cum Juda Christi proditore eiusque complicibus puni-
tur, si non satisfactione emendauerit congrua quod contra nostrum deli-
quit decretum. Anno dominice incarnationis .Dcccc.lxxiii. scriptum
est hoc priuilegium primo mee regie dedicationis anno. *Hiis*
testibus concordantibus *quorum infra caraxantur* uocabula :

✠ *Ego Edgar totius albionis basileus, hoc priuilegium* tanta robo-
ratum auctoritate *crucis* taumate *confirmaui.*

250   ✠ *Ego Dunstan Dorouernensis ecclesie Archiepiscopus hoc idem cum*
tropheo agie crucis corroboraui.

✠ *Ego Oswold Eboracensis ecclesie Archiepiscopus subscripsi.*

✠ Ego Adelwold episcopus *consignaui.*[2]
✠ Ego Ælfstan antistes assensi.
✠ Ego Alfstan presul faui.
✠ Ego Aþulf pontifex concessi.
✠ Ego Aescwig abbas non rennui.
✠ Ego Osgar abbas inpressi.
✠ Ego Æþelgar abbas consensi.
260 ✠ *Ego Ælfhere dux.*
✠ *Ego Æþelwine dux.*
✠ Ego beorhtnod dux.
✠ *Ego oslac dux.*
✠ *Ego Æþelward disc'.*[5]
✠ *Ego Eanulf disc'.*
✠ *Ego Ælfsige disc'.*

✠ *Ego Æþelward disc'* Sigeferið.
Wulfstan.
✠ *Ego friþegist.* trumw.[3]
frÿþegist.
✠ *Ego Þoreð. ulf. hringulf.*
✠ Ego Þurefrð. Þurefereð.
ælfstan.
✠ *Ego Alfhelm. ulf. æþelsige.*
✠ Ego *freana. Wulfri. leofsige.*
✠ Ego Ulf. *osferð.* Wulfgeat.[4]

---

[1] B *interpolates here:* Insulis tamen quibusque loco supradicto subiectis de-
gentes, duo tantum modo dum oportunum fuerit exerceant .i. pontis arcis
ue recuperationem; tercium uero nequaquam, id est, expeditionem, set quod
oportunum et necessarium sancti loci procuratori misericorditer uisum fuerit
insula pro expeditione deuotissime adhibeant.

[2] In c the list ended here originally: the remaining names were added later
by the same scribe. The list is the same as in A, except for repetitions; but one
name, ADELMUND, is added.

[3] Probably for "trumweald." Kemble has "truniþ" mistakenly.

[4] A mistaken copy of "Wulfeah" in CS 1270.

[5] Probably for "discþegn."

TEXTS

A. Peterborough Cathedral Library, MS. 1, ff. 124ᵛ–126 (old folia-tion). This MS., known as the Register of Robert of Swaffham, was compiled about 1250. It is described in Davis (No. 757) and by W. T. Mellows, *Henry of Pytchley's Book of Fees*, Northants. Record Soc., II, 1924, p. xxviii. Swaffham's version is the oldest and most reliable surviving text of the final recension of the charter, with good early forms of personal and place-names. He usually transcribes roman numerals into words, but apart from this his version is probably a faithful copy of the lost original.

B. Red Book of Thorney, ff. 13ᵛ–15 (old numbering, ff. iiᵛ–iv), see p. 146. This version is a copy of an earlier recension of the charter, described on p. 185.

C. Red Book of Thorney, ff. 12–13ᵛ (old numbering, ff. i–iiᵛ). A copy of the final recension; personal and place-name forms are inferior to A, but it supplies a passage erased in A.

D. BM MS. Cotton Aug. II, 12. A fourteenth-century charter of inspeximus; personal and place-name forms are inferior to A.

E. Many late copies of the final recension exist; these will be listed in Mr P. H. Sawyer's forthcoming hand-list. They do not supply any fresh information.

EDITIONS

(1) Dugdale II, pp. 598–9, from C, with many errors among the proper names.

(2) K 579, from D.

(3) CS 1297, from D.

(4) This edition is from A, except that ll. 230–5, which are erased in A, have been supplied from C. An interpolation from B is added as a footnote. In the section of the charter relating to the estate trans-actions, the texts of A and B are given in parallel, with portions unique to each in spaced lettering. Minor differences are listed in the foot-notes. The portions of the charter printed in italic are derived from CS 1270 (see p. 175).

DATE

According to the charter, A.D. 973, the year of King Edgar's con-secration. This took place on Whit Sunday (ASC Ā, *s.a.*). The witness list is compatible. But see under AUTHENTICITY below.

PERSONAL NAMES

Æthelfled, the owner of the monastic site, remains unidentified. The names of persons involved in Bishop Æthelwold's estate trans-actions are dealt with elsewhere (see pp. 177–83). The major wit-nesses are as follows.—

Dunstan, archbishop of Canterbury 960–88.

Oswald, archbishop of York 972–92.

Æthelwold, bishop of Winchester 963–84.

Ælfstan, bishop of London 961–84.

Ælfstan, bishop of Rochester 964–95.

Æthelwulf, bishop of Hereford 955–1012.

Æscwig, abbot of Bath c.963–c.977.

Osgar, abbot of Abingdon 963–84.

Æthelgar, abbot of New Minster, Winchester c.964–80.

Ælfhere, ealdorman of Mercia 956–83.

Æthelwine, ealdorman of East Anglia 962–92.

Brihtnoth, ealdorman of Essex 956–91.

Oslac, earl of York 963–73.

Æthelweard, *minister*, witnesses CS 1260; K 611, 642, 673. Possibly the Æthelweard who was ealdorman of the Western Shires 975–98.

Eanulf, *minister*, witnesses CS 1036, 1042, 1056, 1292; temp. 958–73.

Ælfsige, *minister*—too common a name for identification.

Ælfweard, *minister*, witnesses CS 1316, dated 975.

The names of the remaining witnesses form an interesting group. It will be shown (p. 175) that the whole witness list originates in a Peterborough charter, and it cannot be mere coincidence that the names of these minor witnesses, many of them Scandinavian in origin and uncommon in English documents, are to be found in the late tenth-century records of Peterborough and adjacent houses.

Thus Sigefrið, Ulf, Fræna, Osferð, Frithegist, Æthelsige, Thureferð, and Leofsige all appear in the list of sureties for estates bought by Æthelwold for Peterborough (No. 164). Some, if not all of them, must be among the thegns who witnessed the exemplar upon which the Thorney charter was based. Very many of these thegns also witness No. 55, Edgar's charter of privileges to Ely, and some of them—in particular Thureferð, Wulfstan, Ælfhelm, and Hringulf—figure prominently in the *Liber Eliensis*. Fræna and Frithegist are among the donors to Peterborough listed in Hugh Candidus; the Peterborough version of the Anglo-Saxon Chronicle records that men bearing these names fled from a battle against the Vikings in 993.

DIPLOMATIC

The text under discussion falls into the class labelled as "panchartæ" by W. H. Stevenson (EHR xxvii, xxix, 1912, 1914), but within this large category the foundation charters of the tenth-century Benedictine reform constitute a self-contained group.[1] The Thorney charter,

---

[1] Discussed with authority by E. John, 'Some Latin Charters of the Tenth Century Reformation in England', in *Revue Bénédictine*, LXX, 1960, pp. 333–59.

as will be seen, is concerned with the same range of topics as other members of this group; it has indeed some passages in common with them, but it cannot be described as a characteristic example.

Its general structure is modelled upon the (probably genuine) grant of Barrow-upon-Humber by King Edgar to Bishop Æthelwold, which the latter may have intended as an endowment for Thorney (p. 177), but eventually assigned to the newly founded monastery at Peterborough in 971 (No. 150). Nearly all the text of this charter is repeated in the Thorney pancharta, as is the witness list, even to the various forms of attestation used by the witnesses. The same witness list is used in the spurious charter of the second foundation of Peterborough Abbey (No. 15). Ultimately, certain of the formulas in the Barrow charter can be traced to other charters of Edgar, particularly those connected with Æthelwold. For instance, the proem first appears in a grant by Edgar to Æthelwold of land at Washington in Sussex, dated 963 (CS 1125); this estate is also mentioned in the Thorney pancharta (l. 148). Much of the body of the text is contained in Edgar's charter granting Stoke near Ipswich to Æthelwold's foundation at Ely, dated 970 (No. 77).

Into the text of the Barrow exemplar, the compiler of the Thorney pancharta interpolated various clauses derived from a number of different sources. In the first of these, a long passage commencing at l. 9 ". . . basileus, quoddam monasterium . . ." and ending at l. 25 "diabolo instigante," King Edgar is made to confirm to Æthelwold the monastic site. The passage contains phrases characteristic of charters of the period, e.g. ll. 21–2 "nullus altioris uel inferioris gradus hominis" is paralleled in CS 1302, dated 963 × 970,[1] ". . . altioris uel inferioris ordinis homo"; also in K 640, dated 983, ". . . nec aliquis hominum altioris uel inferioris gradus . . . ," and again in K 688, dated 995, "ut nulla . . . altior inferiorue . . . persona." The passage contains a dating clause, partly repeated later (l. 245) just before the witness list, in which the phrase "primo [anno] mee regiee dedicationis" occurs. This appears also in CS 1307, dated 973–4, and tallies with the statement concerning King Edgar's consecration in ASC A, s.a. 973.

The second interpolation of this group, ll. 30–59, commencing "Nam in ipso prefato loco" and ending "ornans decorauit," consists of a recital of the early history of the monastery. Much of this information is unique, and suggests that the compiler had available a *Fundationis Historia*, now lost. After a brief account of the saints of the first foundation (presumably in the seventh or eighth century), namely the anchorites Tancred, martyr, and Torhtred, confessor, and their sister Tova, this interpolation states that Bishop Æthelwold bought the island site, comprising one hide of land, from the matron Æthelflæd for 40

[1] On the date, see ECW no. 101.

gold mancuses, and built the monastery there. Three altars were consecrated, the eastern one being dedicated to St Mary, the western to
St Peter, and one in the north porch to St Benedict, "the patron of all
monks."

The account then runs straight into a third interpolation, ll. 59–72,
commencing "Uite igitur" and ending "nunquam eligatur," which deals
with the election of the abbot; this was to proceed according to the
Rule of St Benedict, as interpreted in the *Regularis Concordia*, Proem
c. IX.[1] This section is repeated almost verbatim in King Ethelred's
great foundation charter to the monastery of Eynsham, dated 1005.[2]
Mr Eric John has pointed out, however,[3] that the reference in the
Thorney passage to the exclusion of episcopal authority (ll. 70–2,
commencing "Secularium uero" and ending "nunquam eligatur") appears in neither the Eynsham charter nor the *Concordia*.

However, the parallel between these two charters does not end
here, for each proceeds at this point to list the early endowments
which the founder has obtained *ad usus monachorum* of the respective
house. The lists are introduced by identical passages in the two charters, commencing "Sunt etenim" and ending "concessit donario" (ll.
72–9 in the Thorney text). Besides referring to the king as "(a) prefato rege"—an obvious incongruity in a royal charter constructed in
the first person—these passages are noteworthy for containing the
phrase "patroni nostri beati Benedicti"; the mention of "our patron"
suggests that this clause (and indeed the bulk of the Thorney *pancharta*) was originally drafted by a Thorney monk, or even possibly by
Æthelwold himself. The same phrase occurs in the genuine Tavistock
foundation charter[4] dated 981, and is important supporting evidence
for the suggestion that the whole group of these reform charters was
drafted in the scriptoria of the respective houses.

THE FOUNDATION ENDOWMENT

In common with the other reform charters in this group, the Thorney text includes an account of the estates which are said to have
formed the foundation endowment. The account is available in two
recensions, A and B, which are presented side by side in the above
edition. Bishop Æthelwold had embarked upon a long series of trans-

---

[1] *Regularis Concordia*, ed. Dom T. Symons, London, 1953, p. 6.

[2] K 714; better edited by H. E. Salter, *Cartulary of the Abbey of Eynsham*,
Oxford Hist. Soc., I, 1906–7, pp. 19–28. Probably the compiler of the Eynsham charter made use of the Thorney text as his exemplar for this and subsequent sections. See the comments to No. VIII below for a further connexion
between the Thorney and Eynsham muniments.

[3] *Op. cit.*, p. 358 n. 1.

[4] K 629; better edited by H. P. R. Finberg, *Tavistock Abbey*, Cambridge,
1951, pp. 278–83.

actions in order to build up an endowment for his four fenland foundations, and there seems to have been some form of composite record,
written in OE, of his activities, which has unfortunately since been
lost. Various Peterborough documents (Nos. 13, 164) draw upon this
lost record. So too does the Ely *Libellus* (p. 213). The compilers of
both recensions of the Thorney *pancharta* also make use of it. There is
little doubt that Æthelwold sometimes acquired individual estates (or
groups of estates) before deciding which of his fenland foundations was
to receive them as an endowment; it will be seen that of the ten groups
of estates for which transactions are entered in the A and B versions of
the Thorney charter, two were eventually given to Peterborough and
two more did not become Thorney property. These ten transactions
will now be discussed in turn.

THE ISLE AND MERE OF WHITTLESEY

A and B: "Half the aforesaid island called *Witlesig* [Whittlesey,
Cambs.] he [i.e. Bishop Æthelwold] bought from Leofsige the son of
Ælfsige, for 40 silver pounds, and for an estate of 6 hides *æt Bigrafan*
[Bygrave, Herts.].[1] Two thirds of the other half he bought for 20
pounds from Leofwine the son of Athulf. The remaining third (of the
half of the Isle of Whittlesey), together with two thirds of the lake
called *Witlesmere* [Whittlesey Mere, Hunts.], he bought from Ufi and
from his uterine brothers, for 30 silver pounds. These 30 pounds the
aforesaid Ufi gave to Henric, and before many witnesses bought from
him [i.e. Henric] the estate called *Drægtun*, with the sum of money
which the bishop had given him [i.e. Ufi] to help lest it should have
been denuded of inhabitants. Later, when they wished to question this
exchange, the bishop gave them a further 20 pounds."[2]

This account reads like a précis of a longer and more detailed text
(see above) which has been shortened so much that in places it is
difficult to follow. Ælfsige and Ufi may be identified with the persons
of those names from whom Bishop Æthelwold bought fenland at Upwell and Outwell for the endowment of Peterborough and Thorney
(R p. 73). For Bygrave, see W p. 173. Leofwine the son of Athulf was
a benefactor to Ely who was sometimes employed on that abbey's
business (LE p. 109). He witnessed a Ramsey land agreement in 987
(No. 22), and attended a council held in London c.990 (R pp. 376–7).
According to the *Liber Eliensis* (pp. 131–2) he quarrelled with his
mother, and beat her to death. In expiation he made a pilgrimage to
Rome, where he was instructed by the Pope that as part of his penance
he should give his lands to the church. His land gifts to Ely (No. 65)
are dated 1002 ×c.1016, and he made gifts in kind also (LE p. 294 *bis*).

---

[1] B has 25 pounds, and omits the estate at Bygrave.
[2] B omits this last sentence.

Since his mother survived into the eleventh century, it may be assumed
that Leofwine was quite a young man at the time of his dealings with
Bishop Æthelwold. Henric is evidently the Henric of *Waneting* (Wantage, Berks., a royal estate) who sold Gransden to Bishop Æthelwold
(No. 11). He may be the *minister* Heanric who appears in charters of
the period, some of them relating to Ely (CS 1266, 1269, 1286; cf.
Freeman, NC I, p. 656). The name is uncommon. *Drægtun* is too
common a place-name for certain identification, but it may be one of
the Cambridgeshire Draytons. See later (p. 183) for a further passage
in the Thorney *pancharta* relating to Whittlesey Mere.

WITTERING, OXNEY, AND THORPE

B: "He [i.e. Bishop Æthelwold] bought *Withringaig* and *Oxanig*
[Wittering and Oxney, Soke of Peterborough] from Gerweard and
Wulfnoth and divers poor persons for 15 silver pounds. In *Thorp*
[Thorpe Hall, Peterborough] he bought three hides from Sigeferð for
16 pounds."

This information is undoubtedly drawn from the same source as
No. 164, the list of sureties for Peterborough estates. Even the spellings of the place- and personal names are identical. The estates were
given by Æthelwold to Peterborough, probably in exchange for Farcet
(see p. 163).

WATER NEWTON[1]

A and B: "And he [i.e. Bishop Æthelwold] bought *Niwantun* [Water
Newton, Hunts.] for 20 pounds from a certain very devoted thegn
called Ælfric Cild. And when the said thegn sought to deny the validity
of this transaction, the bishop gave him a further 13 pounds, together
with 2 hides *æt Ræsnan* [? Market Rasen, Lincs.], 2 at *Yranceaster*
[Irchester, Northants.], and one at *ticceanmersce* [Titchmarsh, Northants.], so buying Newton for a second time. A certain thegn called
Leofstan freely gave 1½ hides at Titchmarsh to the bishop, for his protection [i.e. commendation]. And he [the bishop] acquired ½ hide
there from a certain widow. And he [the bishop] bought from the
king, for 30 mancuses, another hide there which a certain thegn had
formerly held."

Niwantun is wrongly identified as Newton in Wisbech hundred,
Cambs., in PN *Cambs.*, p. 274; for its correct location, see the notes
to No. IV above. Ælfric Cild, who became earl of Mercia in 983, also
sold part of Yaxley to Thorney. See R pp. 369–70 for his biography.

It is clear that the information in the last three sentences of this
account, relating to land at Titchmarsh over and above that which was
traded to Ælfric in part exchange for Water Newton, is quite irrele-

[1] B omits part of the Water Newton transaction, and includes Titchmarsh
among the summary list of estates which heads this section of the charter.

vant to the needs of the compiler of the Thorney charter; this illus-
trates further the thesis that the compiler was drawing upon a more
comprehensive record of Æthelwold's estate transactions. It is significant that Peterborough was holding 3¼ hides at Titchmarsh TRE (DB
fo. 222); almost certainly this was by gift of Æthelwold.

WOODSTON

A and B: "The aforesaid bishop i.e. [Æthelwold] obtained Woodston
[Hunts.] from the king, giving him in exchange for it *Pæninctun* [Pen-
nington, or Penton Grafton or Weyhill, Hants.], which had been
granted to the above mentioned bishop [i.e. Æthelwold] by Ælfsige,
by a gift in reversion after his [i.e. Ælfsige's] death."

Woodston became a Thorney property. Ælfsige has too common a
name for his identification with other contemporaries of that name.

YAXLEY, THE OTHER YAXLEY, AND FARCET

A: "Twenty-five[1] hides called *Geakeslea* [Yaxley, Hunts.] which he
[i.e. Bishop Æthelwold] gave to St Mary of Thorney, he obtained first
from Wulfstan in exchange for 24 hides in *Wassingatune* [Washington]
in Sussex. Then later, when Wulfstan was trying to undo the transaction, the bishop began another purchase of the estate, giving to the
aforesaid Ælfric [i.e. Ælfric Cild] for it 40 pounds of the purest silver,
and so obtaining the 25 hides *æt twam geakeslean* and *æt farresheafde* [at
the two Yaxleys, and at Farcet, Hunts.]."

B: "17 hides called Yaxley which [the bishop] gave to Thorney, and
8 [hides] at Farcet which he gave to *Medeshamstede* [Peterborough], he
obtained from Wulfstan in exchange for 24 hides at Washington in
Sussex."

From other records discussed above (pp. 25, 159) it appears that
both A and B recensions oversimplify this transaction.

BARROW

A and B: "The said bishop [i.e. Æthelwold] bought the village called
Beruwe [Barrow-upon-Humber] in Lindsey from the aforesaid king for
40 pounds of the purest silver, and in addition he gave [the king] many
costly presents for the land."

Mention has been made already of King Edgar's grant of Barrow, an
early monastic site, to Æthelwold (No. 150), by a charter the text of
which was used as a formulary for the Thorney *pancharta* now under
discussion. The dependence of the Thorney text upon the Barrow
charter is further illustrated by the account each gives of this transaction:

Barrow charter: ". . . dedit prefatus episcopus regi prædicto .xl.

---

[1] A has 20, but C has 25, which is to be preferred.

meri argenti libras et unam auream crucem ei multo cariorem pecunia predicta."

Thorney *pancharta*: ". . . idem episcopus a rege prefato cum .xl. meri argenti libris emendo comparauit, et insuper munera sibi multo hac pecunia cariora pro eadem addidit tellure."

Barrow was given by Æthelwold to Peterborough, and there is no evidence that Thorney ever possessed the estate. It was lost by Peterborough during the period 1013 × 1016 (HC p. 64 and ASC E *s.a.* 1013).

TEAFOLSCET

This appears in the A list only, without any description of the transaction. It must be the *Tæafersceat* which Ælfgifu left by will to Bishop Æthelwold (W p. 120). The site is unidentified, but there is a *Telferscot Road* in Tooting Bec, Surrey, a possible location, for the bulk of Ælfgifu's possessions were in the Buckinghamshire–Berkshire–Oxfordshire region. It is a clue worth following up. The form in the Red Book of Thorney does not appear in the discussion of this name in PN *Elements*, II, p. 177.

GEDNEY, LUTTON, ANGARHALA, AND TYDD

B: "The aforesaid estates in *Holande* [Holland, Lincs.] were bought by the aforesaid bishop from Ealdorman Æthelwine [of East Anglia] for 20 pounds of purest silver, and 200 well-tested mancuses of purest gold, and in addition [the bishop gave] 15 hides of fertile land in *Grantandene* [Gransden in Hunts. and Cambs.]; and the king consented and gave his licence for this purchase, and for the right of jurisdiction which the Danes call *socne*, he [the bishop] gave [? the king or the ealdorman] 100 most splendid mancuses of gold."

The names concerned are given (in B only) in the list which introduces the estate transactions: *Giddanig*, *Hludantun*, *Angarhala*, *Tid* (Gedney, Lutton, *Angarhala*, and Tydd St Mary, all in Holland, Lincs.). The three estates of Gedney, Lutton, and Tydd St Mary lie in a compact group (forming TRE a double hundred of twenty-four carucates) to the north-east of Thorney. They did not remain in the possession of any of Æthelwold's foundations, for TRE they were all in the hands of Earl Ælfgar, who probably inherited them as part of the East Anglian earldom which he held until his banishment in 1055. *Angarhala* must have been near by—possibly it was an early name for the manor of Fleet, which was also held TRE by Earl Ælfgar. It could hardly be the lost *Angerhale* in Bottisham, Cambs. (PN *Cambs.*, p. 131), of the *Gesta Herewardi*, where Abbot Thurstan took refuge with the Ely treasures in the siege of 1070–1 (cf. LE p. 189 n.).

As H. E. Hallam pointed out (*The New Lands of Elloe*, Leicester University Dept. of English Local History, Occasional Paper No. 6, 1954,

p. 8), "there are few documentary sources for the history of the ninth, tenth, and eleventh centuries in Holland," and this record is important for the historical geography of the Lincolnshire fenland. The reference to *Holande* ("the high land") is unlikely to be a late interpolation, and carries the name as a subdivision of Lincolnshire to a century before DB, at which period Tydd, Gedney, and Lutton formed part of the eastern seaboard. The mention of the purchase of soke is noteworthy; this is the only pre-Conquest record known to me in which the value of an estate can be compared with the value of the soke over it, which appears to me to be astonishingly high. Moreover, we have in this passage important confirmation of a point made by Professor Finberg, that when Æthelwold acquired an estate he tried to obtain the profits of justice over it: an approach rightly described by Professor Finberg as "a landmark in the history of seignorial jurisdiction" (ECW p. 229).

Grantandene must have comprised Great Gransden (Hunts.) and Little Gransden (Cambs.). In DB the former is assessed at 8 hides, the latter at 5. The estate seems to have been divided after Æthelwine acquired it, and it appears likely that Æthelwine himself was responsible for the division, for Little Gransden descended to Ely, to which house Æthelwine is known to have been a benefactor. An account survives (LE p. 115) of the agreement by which Æthelwold purchased Gransden: "Bishop Æthelwold bought *Grantedene* for 200 [mancuses] of gold, from Henric of *Waneting*, and there were present as witnesses King Edgar, Ealdorman Ælfhere [of Mercia], Æthelwine [ealdorman of East Anglia], Brihtnoth [ealdorman of Essex], Ælfric Cild [who succeeded Ælfhere as ealdorman or earl of Mercia in 983], Ringulf, Thurferth, and other counsellors. And the agreement was made in their presence, that if anyone in later times should attempt to obtain the land falsely, Henric and his heirs should return to the bishop the 200 mancuses, and should themselves rebut the falsehood."

THE CHURCH OF ST MARY, HUNTINGDON

A and B: "Two hides near to *Huntandune* [Huntingdon], and a third *æt Broctune* [Broughton, Hunts.],[1] and the *monasteriolum* dedicated to St Mary lying outside the aforesaid town. . . With commendable liberality the above-mentioned king [i.e. Edgar], for the reward of eternal happiness, gave to the monastery [of Thorney] the [aforesaid] church in Huntingdon, with its cemetery and a small estate of 3 hides, as a perpetual inheritance.

"With this exception, for all of the above mentioned places which he exchanged with or bought from the king, he [the bishop] gave the appropriate sum of money, be it great or small."

The one hide at Broughton did not remain in the possession of

---

[1] The reference to the hide at Broughton occurs in B only.

Thorney, but was given by Æthelwold to Ramsey in exchange for land which he used to endow his foundation at Ely (No. 317). For a detailed commentary on the remainder of the passage, see C. Hart, 'The Church of St Mary, Huntingdon', CAS LIX, forthcoming.

FISHERIES AT UPWELL, OUTWELL, AND ELM

A: "Fisheries surrounding the villages of *Wyllan* and *Eolum* [Upwell, Outwell, and Elm, Cambs. and Norfolk] were bought by the aforesaid bishop [i.e. Æthelwold] for 21 pounds. And 16,000 eels were captured there each year, of which the bishop decreed that 8,000 should go annually to Thorney, and 8,000 to *Burh* [Peterborough]."

A Peterborough document refers to the "many fens at *Wellan*" which Æthelwold bought from Ælfsige and Ufi for 13 ores, and gave to Peterborough (No. 13). The confirmation charter of King Edgar to Æthelwold's foundation of Ely includes an annual grant of 10,000 eels from the estate *æt Wyllan* (No. 55),[1] and subsequent Ely records show that parts of Upwell and Outwell became Ely property (VCH *Cambs.*, IV, p. 209). Æthelstan Mannessune, the Ramsey benefactor who died in 986, owned a fishery at *Welles* (Chron Rams p. 60), and Ealdorman Æthelwine gave to Ramsey 20 fishermen at *Welles*, together with 60,000 eels each year, a gift confirmed in the spurious foundation charter of King Edgar to Ramsey Abbey (No. 18). These figures appear unduly large; they may be an approximation in round numbers derived from the DB record of 17 fishermen at Wisbech (who probably came from Upwell) who produced 59,260 eels annually. Of these, the annual share allotted to Ramsey at the time of DB was only 5,260 eels, rendered by 8 fishermen (VCH *Cambs.*, I, p. 371; IV, p. 208 n. 17). Early in the following century, however, Ramsey extended still further its Upwell holding, by the acquisition of two more fisheries there (Chron Rams pp. 240, 242).

It is remarkable that four of the five great fenland monasteries (no pre-Conquest records survive for Crowland) should possess muniments claiming an interest in this estate, dating from the early years of their refoundation. Even more remarkable is the steady spread of the interest to other monasteries. By the time of DB, both Crowland and Bury St Edmunds were obtaining eels there (VCH *Cambs.*, IV, p. 243); and two centuries later, no fewer than sixteen religious houses held lands, rents, and fisheries at Upwell (*ibid.*, IV, p. 210). The Benedictine rule forbade meat in the diet, and eels must have been a staple food of the monks in the fenland abbeys, but the numbers of eels rendered to some of the houses were far in excess of what could be consumed on the premises, and point to their use by the abbeys for

---

[1] Besides these, Ely was receiving at least another 26,275 eels annually, from Fordham (Cambs.) and Hilgay (Norfolk) (No. 27).

trade.[1] One recalls Bede's statement that Ely got its name (OE *el-ge*, 'eel district') from the great number of eels caught in the fens there. It seems to me that the form *eolum* for Elm in the Thorney *pancharta* points to a dative plural of OE *æl*, 'eel', and this is the true origin of the place-name, rather than the usually accepted OE *elm*, 'elm tree'. See further RE pp. 249–51.

WHITTLESEY MERE

A: "A quarter of the lake called *Wytlesmere* [Whittlesey Mere, Hunts.], and 2 fisheries and 10 acres of land, were loaned from Thorney to Peterborough, in return for 120 feeding swine, and for enclosing the houses, and repairing the stables."

It will be recalled that Whittlesey Mere already occurs earlier in the Thorney account of Æthelwold's estate transactions (p. 177) and this agreement evidently records a later phase in the arrangements for the exploitation of the holding. It must be compared with a DB entry (fo. 205) which runs: "In Whittlesey Mere the abbot of Ramsey has one boat, the abbot of Peterborough one boat, and the abbot of Thorney two boats. One of these two boats, and 2 fisheries, 2 fishermen, and one virgate of land, are held of the abbot of Thorney by the abbot of Peterborough, and in return for these he provides sufficient pasture for 120 pigs, and if pasture fails, he feeds and fattens 60 pigs with corn. Moreover, he finds timber for one house of 60 ft, and poles for the enclosure (*curia*) round the house. He also repairs the house and enclosure when they are decayed. This agreement was made between them in King Edward's time."

Either the agreement TRE repeated an earlier agreement of the time of Bishop Æthelwold recorded in the Thorney *pancharta*, or else this passage in the Thorney text is a late interpolation based on some written record of the agreement made TRE and since lost, or possibly on the DB entry itself.

AUTHENTICITY

Our approach to this extremely complex problem must start from the proposition advanced by Mr Eric John,[2] that the confirmation charters of Æthelwold's new foundations, though issued in the name of the king, were in fact internal documents, drafted (under Æthel-

---

[1] D. Whitelock, *The Beginnings of English Society*, 1952, p. 118. It does not necessarily follow, however, that trading was done outside the sphere of their own estates. Eels from fenland estates such as Upwell might be exchanged for corn and other agricultural products from upland estates such as Haddon, but such an economy could well be an enclosed one, restricted to dealings between the monastic properties.

[2] *Op. cit.*, p. 358.

wold's direction) within the scriptoria of the houses themselves. To the extent that they claim to be royal diplomas they are, strictly speaking, *all* spurious; nevertheless it is clear that they were drawn up with royal approval, and the essential task of the historian is to test the genuineness of the land endowments and liberties which they claim, rather than to quibble overmuch about their diplomatic form. Orthodox criteria of authenticity are therefore of little value as analytical tools for investigating this group of texts, for the compilers were bound by no rigid rules of protocol; on the contrary the monks, working without the aid of both the formularies and the clerical *expertise* of the royal proto-chancery, must have been forced to experiment, creating entirely new types of instrument to embody their objectives.

The objectives themselves were, of course, common to all the houses. For each foundation the privileges, both lay and spiritual, of the community had to be enumerated; and each charter had to incorporate a comprehensive list of the territories forming the foundation endowment of the house concerned. Because of the universal nature of these requirements, we may postulate that every house had to meet them; i.e. for each and every new monastery there was drawn up within its precincts a charter of confirmation in the name of the king.[1] In such circumstances it was only to be expected that some measure of collaboration should evolve between the scriptoria of the individual houses. The propagandists of this as of any other reform movement soon developed a common *expertise* employing a common vocabulary, so that not only do the charters of the group share words, phrases, and even passages in common; in some degree their whole lay-out follows a characteristic pattern.

Within this pattern, the extent to which each compiler succeeded in producing a lucid and convincing charter varied widely from house to house. The Thorney charter ranks low on the list, for its creator unwisely chose to drape his fabric about the framework of a straightforward royal donation charter dealing with a single estate, which he borrowed from the archives of a neighbouring monastery.[2] The formulas of this simple charter were not designed to convey the sort of information required to be embodied in an elaborate confirmation diploma, and the more the Thorney scribe struggled to adapt the text of his exemplar to incorporate this complicated new material, the more muddled and distorted the resultant diploma became. Some of the more obvious incongruities arising from this ill-conceived plan have been discussed already (p. 176), and the situation is not eased by

[1] Winchester was probably an exception to this rule, cf. ECW p. 240, and E. John, 'The Church of Winchester and the Tenth-Century Reformation', in *Bulletin of the John Rylands Library*, XLVII, 1965, pp. 404–29.

[2] See p. 175.

the fact that the original text of the Thorney confirmation charter passed through at least one later recension, not to mention the further damage it suffered unwittingly at the hands of various transcribers. So clumsily worded is the final product, that Mr Eric John himself has fallen into the trap of describing it as being "of very doubtful reputation."[1]

But when we come to study the charter in detail, it is seen to be reputable enough; its clumsiness of drafting in no way dilutes the authenticity of its contents. This essential authenticity emerges more clearly upon closer inspection of the substantial differences between the two surviving versions of the charter, which soon lead one to the important conclusion that the B recension antedates the better known A version.

It is possible to arrive at a fairly close date for both recensions by careful comparison of their contents. The B text was probably compiled between the refoundation of the monastery in 973 and King Edgar's death in 975, for unlike the A text, it omits all reference to the large sums of money which Æthelwold had to pay out to secure the abbey's possession of Whittlesey, Water Newton, and Yaxley during the anti-monastic reaction which followed the death of King Edgar. The A text may be dated 975×984, between the deaths of Edgar and Æthelwold.[2] It is noteworthy that this final recension no longer claims the great estate at Tydd, Gedney, and Lutton in Holland as part of the abbey's possessions; nor does it maintain the abbey's claim to partial exemption from *fyrd* service, which is recorded in the B version only. These losses too may have resulted from activity by the anti-monastic party.

It seems probable that at some date between the two recensions a transaction took place between Thorney and its neighbour at Peterborough, by which Wittering, Oxney, and Thorpe were transferred to Peterborough Abbey in return for Farcet. The estate at Farcet extended into Whittlesey Mere, and the A version also records an agreement drawn up between the two abbeys, by which Peterborough's fishing rights in the mere were protected, in spite of its surrender of Farcet to Thorney.

There is nothing in the estate transactions, then, to raise doubts about the charter's authenticity. The same holds good for the privileges claimed within the charter. Mr Eric John has, indeed, queried the clause purporting to free the monks, when choosing their abbot, from interference by any bishop. "Disputes about episcopal authority

[1] *Rev. Bénédictine*, LXX, p. 358 n. 1.

[2] Note that the A version still repeats B's statement (drawn from Peterborough material) on Æthelwold's acquisition of Barrow in Lincs. This estate was lost by Peterborough before 1016, and the A recension must antedate this.

over monasteries," he claims, "did not arise in England until after 1066."[1] Without wishing to challenge this in any way, it is pertinent to observe that Oswald himself was apprehensive of interference in the affairs of his small foundation at Westbury-on-Trym by his successors in the see of Worcester.[2] Thorney was similarly vulnerable, for it lived under the shadow of its overwhelmingly more powerful neighbour at Peterborough, whose first abbot, Ealdulf, was highly connected and eventually received the archbishopric of York. Moreover, within a stone's throw lay Crowland, whose abbot, Thurcytel, was probably a kinsman of Oscytel, the diocesan bishop (as well as archbishop of York) until his death in 971.[3] Rivalry between these three neighbours long antedated the Norman Conquest. The clause queried by Mr Eric John appears in both recensions of the Thorney foundation charter, so that if it was a post-Conquest interpolation (as he appears to imply), the interpolator took unusual pains to insert identical passages in both versions of the charter, when one of these versions had ceased to have any evidential value a century previously. This does not appeal to me as a likely hypothesis; it imposes much less of a strain upon one's credulity to assume that the passage in question is not an interpolation at all, but an integral part of the original text, reflecting the special circumstances obtaining at Thorney at the time of its refoundation.

To summarize, the B recension represents a clumsy but basically authentic text compiled very soon after the abbey's refoundation. The activities of the anti-monastic party in the years immediately following Edgar's death made necessary a substantial restatement of the abbey's land endowment, and also its public obligations, which is embodied in the A recension. This came to be adopted as the final text of the charter, and was used by the abbey as its chief title-deed right through until the Dissolution.

VIII

KING ÆTHELRED II TO HIS MINISTER ÆTHELMÆR: 9 HIDES AT THAMES DITTON, SURREY

VARIANTE cosmi statu tam uolubili quid aliud ammonentur graciosi nisi anhelando festinare quo perfruitur insatiabili contemplatione trinitatis unice, et quasi in apertione regni celestis aditus mercuri conceditur eterna caducis dono super-

[1] *Rev. Bénédictine*, LXX, p. 358 n. 1.

[2] *Vita S. Oswaldi auct. anon.*, in *Historians of the Church of York*, London, 1879, I, pp. 424–5.

[3] D. Whitelock, in *The Anglo-Saxons*, p. 75: and *Saga-Book of the Viking Society*, XII, 1937–45, pp. 174–5.

uenientis gracie dei que operari in nobis et uelle et posse benigne non cessat. Cooperemur igitur bonum ad omnes dum sole superstite uiam oportunitatis patescit faciendo maxime uidelicet ad fideles nostre deuotionis. Qua propter ego Æthelred monarchiam totius Albionis sollempniter regens dono suffragante septiformis spiritus, cuidam ministro michi oppido fideli qui ab huius patrie gnosticis nobili Æthelmær appellatur uocabulo, quandam telluris portionem. nouem uidelicet cassatos in loco qui celebri æt Dittune uocitatur onomate eterna largitus sum hereditate, ut uita comite uoti compos possideat, ac post obitum suum heredi cuicumque uoluerit immunem derelinquat. Nunc igitur hoc donum solutum omni regali sarcina luceat salua expeditione pontis et arcis munimine sicut condecet usquequaque climatis mundi. Ammouere autem hoc decretum quis audeat nisi deo contra ire non timeat a quo liberaliter conceditur aucta potestas. Siquis hoc nostrum donum amouerit, eternis baratri incendiis iugiter reus puniatur.

Þis synd þa land gemæra into dittune. of cranmeresþorne to blacan græfan. of þere blacan græfan. on þa seofan æceras eastewearde of þam seofan æceran. on emenan andlang emenan be healfan streame innan cýtanforð. of cýtanforða to tatan broke. of tatan broke on cwicelmeswýrþe eastewerde. Þis is se wude on þes agan ende to býrlegate. fram býrlagate to wiðan gate. fram wiðangate. to cnuceshirste and to egænlea. fram ecganlæa to þam haran wýðie.

Acta est hec libertas autem agelli anno Dominice incarnacionis .Dcccc.lxxxiii. indictione .xi. hiis testibus quorum nomina inferius caraxantur consentientibus. Ego Æthelred rex Anglorum triumpho sancte crucis hoc donum immobile corroboraui. ✠Ego Dunstan archiepiscopus consensi. Ego Oswold archiepiscopus adfirmaui. ✠Ego Æþelwold episcopus confeci. ✠Ego ælfstan episcopus annui. ✠Et cetera.

TEXT

The Red Book of Thorney, ff. 15ᵛ–16 (old numbering, ff. ivᵛ–v).

EDITIONS

(1) *The Place-Names of Surrey*, p. 90 (bounds only).
(2) In this edition abbreviations are extended and punctuation is modernized.

DATE

A.D. 983 in the eleventh indiction, as stated in the charter. The indiction is correct for the year given, and the witness list is compatible.

PERSONAL NAMES

The abbreviated witness list includes the names of archbishops Dunstan of Canterbury and Oswald of York, and bishops Æthelwold of Winchester and Ælfstan of London. For Æthelmær, the recipient, see below.

DIPLOMATIC

In general structure this charter is characteristic of the period.[1] A pious proem is followed by a statement that Æthelred grants his faithful *minister* Æthelmær nine hides at Ditton, to hold freely and leave to whom he pleases. Next comes a clause granting exemption from all except the three common burdens, then an anathema. The OE bounds follow, then a dating clause and list of witnesses.

Some of the phrases appear regularly in contemporary texts; for instance, "status cosmi" and "æterna caducis mercari" occur in the proems of K 692 and K 932 respectively, and the king's title "totius Albionis monarchiam" in K 709. The description of Æthelmær can be paralleled in K 621, "cuidam mihi oppido fideli ... qui a gnosticis noto nuncupatur uocabulo," and the description of the estate, and the way in which it is to be held, is similar to that of K 622 and K 624: "quandam ruris particulam .v. videlicet cassatos, in loco qui celebri ... perpetua largitus sum hereditate," this last phrase being repeated in K 932 and other charters, which contain also the phrase "eternis barathri incendiis lugubris iugiter" in the anathema. In the dispository clause, the phrase "ut uita comite uoti compos possideat" occurs (with minor variations) in K 633, 640, and 655; "uoti compos" appears also in K 629, 672, and 688, and "uita comite ... possideat" in a series of Bishop Oswald's leases (K 613–17, 623, 625, etc.), as well as the royal charters K 621, 623, 647–8, 652, 654, etc. The dating clause is similar to those in K 629, 633, and 932, and the order in which the witnesses appear is the correct one for the period; e.g. K 621.

In spite of all these parallels, many passages in this charter appear to be unique. The proem is cast in a form which is not to be found elsewhere except for a few isolated phrases, and I have been unable to find another charter with "sollempniter regens dono suffragante septiformis spiritus" following the king's title. Other apparently unique phrases include "nunc igitur hoc donum solutum omni regali sarcina luceat," "sicut condecet usquequaque climatis mundi," and "ammouere autem

[1] See p. 191.

hoc decretum quis audeat nisi deo contra ire non timeat a quo liberaliter conceditur aucta potestas," although all these passages are loosely paraphrased in contemporary charters, and there is nothing suspicious about their style or vocabulary.

Within a general and easily recognizable framework, the royal charters of Æthelred exhibit considerable variations of phraseology (cf. EHD i, p. 345), of which these unique passages in the Ditton charter form a characteristic example.

HISTORY

Æthelmær became ealdorman of the Western Shires, and founded a monastery at Eynsham, Oxfordshire, in 1005, using Thames Ditton for part of the foundation endowment (K 714; better edited by H. E. Salter, *Cartulary of the Abbey of Eynsham*, Oxford Hist. Soc., i, 1906–7, pp. 19–28).

TOPOGRAPHY

The bounds are identical with those given for the estate in the Eynsham foundation charter referred to above. As far as possible, they have been worked out in Salter's edition and in *The Place-Names of Surrey*.

AUTHENTICITY

There is nothing to arouse suspicion in this charter, which fits in well with the known history of the estate. At some stage in the charter's transmission the hidage of the estate has probably been changed from roman numerals to the word *nouem*, and in common with most of the charters in the Red Book, the witness list has been abbreviated, otherwise the text appears to be complete and untampered with. The estate had no known connection with Thorney, and it is not known why this charter came to be placed in the Thorney muniments. Possibly the king was in the vicinity of Thorney when the charter was drawn up—copies of charters were often stored in nearby religious houses. As yet there is no satisfactory itinerary of Æthelred's reign. There can be little doubt, however, that this charter is a product of the royal chancery, or a local monastic compilation using a chancery charter as its exemplar.

IX

1006 × 1011   KING ÆTHELRED II TO A DANE NAMED
TOTI: ONE HIDE AT BECKLEY, AND 5 HIDES AT
HORTON, OXON.

QUICQUID mundanarum rerum in hoc adquiritur cosmo. muniri debetur litterarum attramento ne forte iniuste iniquorum perdatur consilio, quod iuste cum bonorum uirorum adquiritur testimonio. Unde ego Æthelredus Anglorum Rex piissimus, meis notum uolo adesse fidelibus, quod quidam Danus nomine toti, cum consilio sui propinqui uidelicet Celi, dedit mihi in adiutorium unius libre argenti appensionem de auro purissimo ad reddendum tributum, et ego eidem pro premio reddidi sex terrarum mansos, unum in uilla que dicitur Beccalege, quinque in alia que¹ uilla que nominatur Hortun, tali scilicet tenore, ut cuicumque uoluerit post suam mortem derelinquat heredi. Hec eadem terra hiis limitibus circumgirata esse uidetur.

Þis sýnd þe land mæro to beccalege. of scipwege into meoslege. of meoslege into Westlege. of Westlege into holowege. of holowege into mærbroce. of mærbroce in to francansló. of francansló into miclandic. of mýclandic into þere ealden éa. up of þere ealdan éa in to ottanmere. of ottanmere þuýrs ouer bugenroda. of bugeroda into mærmer. of mærmere on merþorn. of mærþorn to eadlaues óc. of eadlaues ác to luhanþirne. of luhanþýrne on þone ealdan mærweg into wude. andlang þes ealdan mereweges into hildesdene. of hildes dene into Wýueles hó to roces æcere. of roces æcre to þolege. of þolege to gold willan. of gold wýllan to grenewe into scipwege.

Predictum igitur tellus regali precepto permaneat liberum exceptis tribus, populari expedicione, pontis restauracione, regie arcis constructione. Si quis autem cupidus hoc infringere temptauerit donum, sit anathema, hoc est alienatio a consortio Christianorum. Et ut hoc scriptum inuiolabilem semper obtineat firmitatem, ego primus Rex propria manu confirmo, aliisque testibus adfirmandum trado. Ego Ælfgiva collateranea regis

¹ Underlined with dots in MS. to indicate an erasure.

testificor. Ego Ælfhegus Dorouernensis Archiepiscopus uolo. Ego brihtwaldus episcopus consentio. Et cetera.

TEXT

The Red Book of Thorney, fo. 16 (old numbering, fo. v).

EDITIONS

(1) PN *Oxfordshire*, I, p. xxv (most of the body of the text, with translation), and II, p. 484 (bounds). The clauses following the bounds are omitted (they include the exemption clause, the anathema, and the witness list).

(2) This edition of the text has modern punctuation, and abbreviations are extended.

DATE

The charter contains no dating clause, but it is witnessed by Ælfheah, archbishop of Canterbury 1006–12, who was a prisoner of the Danes from 29 September 1011 until his martyrdom on 19 April 1012 (ASC E). The remaining witnesses are compatible with these dates.

PERSONAL NAMES

For the position of Queen Ælfgifu in the witness lists of King Æthelred's charters, see *Encomium Emmæ*, p. 65. Brihtwald was bishop of Ramsbury.

DIPLOMATIC

Although Stenton described this as "a characteristic charter of Æthelred II" (LC p. 84), its structure is in fact abnormal. The texts of characteristic chancery charters of Æthelred II follow a fixed and recognizable plan. Sometimes they begin with an invocation of the type "In nomine domini nostri Jhesu Christi." Most (but not all) of them have a proem, which follows the invocation (when present) and comprises either a reflection of a pious nature or a comment that it is safest to record land gifts in writing. Next comes the name and title of the king, speaking in the first person singular, often introduced by a conjunction such as *quamombrem*, *quapropter*, or *unde*. The name and description of the grantee follows, then the hidage and name of the estate which is being transferred. Sometimes the purchase price is mentioned. A phrase usually follows stating that the recipient is to hold the estate freely, with full powers of alienation, and granting exemption from all except the three common dues. The more elaborate charters then proceed to recite the history of the estate concerned. There follow the anathema, bounds, dating clause, and witness list (the witnesses appear in a fixed order of precedence), in that order.

The great majority of Æthelred's charters follow this sequence. Individual clauses may be omitted, but the order in which the clauses appear is rarely disturbed. Within this framework there is scope for considerable variation in phraseology, but in the case of the invocation, the king's title, the description of the estate, the phrases granting freedom of alienation and exemption from all but the common dues, the dating clause, and the clause introducing the witness list—in all these certain formulas (many of them current in the charters of Æthelred's predecessors) recur regularly, although in any particular charter a unique phrase may be utilized for any of these passages. The greatest variation occurs in the proem, which is often unique to a particular charter. I have found only one case in which the complete formula of a charter of Æthelred II is repeated in another charter.[1] It is the structure of Æthelred's charters—the order in which the phrases appear—rather than any particular formula used, which is characteristic. Otherwise typical charters often omit individual clauses such as the invocation or proem (rarely both), and the clause reciting the history of the estate, but certain other clauses such as the description of the king's title, and the dating clause, are nearly always present.

The structure of the charter under discussion varies from the norm in that the exemption clause and anathema follow the bounds, instead of preceding them; the dating clause is omitted, and the witness list is introduced by the unique sentence "Et ut hoc scriptum inuiolabilem semper obtineat firmitatem, ego primus Rex propria manu confirmo, aliisque testibus adfirmandum trado," in which the name of the king is not given.

As far as the formulas themselves are concerned, the proem appears to be unique, although individual phrases occur in similar form elsewhere, e.g. K 1305, "emendare conamur firmissimo litterarum libro munire debemus," and K 1289, "litterarum firmiter munire debetur." The king's title "Æthelredus Anglorum rex" is that commonly used in charters of this period (e.g. K 688, 691–2, 698, 700, 706, 710, 718, 723, and 1303), and the epithet *piisimus* which follows occurs in K 715, the spurious confirmation charter of Æthelred to Christ Church, Canterbury, dated 1006 (cf. ECEss (Saxon) p. 22). The next phrase can be paralleled in K 1289, "cunctis meis uolo notum adesse fidelibus," and in K 1305, "notum uolo adesse omnibus meo subiectis imperio quod quidem miles Ælfgarus nomine." The terms of the grant are discussed further below. The clause granting power of alienation is similar to those in K 1283, "cuicumque uoluerit hæredi derelinquat," in K 1299, "et cuicumque uoluerit heredi post se," and in K 1303, "et de reliquo cuicumque uoluerit hæredi in perpetuum derelinquat haereditatem." The introduction to the boundary clause is one occurring commonly in charters of the period, but the phraseology of the passage granting exemption from the common dues is rather unusual. The

---

[1] K 648 and K 650, two apparently reliable charters from the *Codex Wintoniensis* with identical witness lists.

anathema recalls that of K 1294, "sit anathema marantata, hoc est, alienatio a consortio Christianorum." In the witness list, the unusual subscription of Æthelred has been mentioned above; his wife's title is paralleled in K 1303 and K 1305, "Ælfgifu eiusdem regis conlaterana." The subscriptions of Archbishop Ælfheah and Bishop Brihtwold are of normal form.

HISTORY

The chief interest of this charter lies in the statement "a certain Dane called Toti, on the advice of his kinsman Celi, has assisted me (King Æthelred) by paying me one pound in pure gold, for the purpose of paying the tribute. And in return I granted him six hides." For comments on this passage, see Stenton p. 376 n. 1, and PN *Oxon.*, I, p. xxv.

TOPOGRAPHY

The bounds are worked out in PN *Oxon.*, pp. 166–7, 179, 208, 241–2.

AUTHENTICITY

Although the charter has a highly unusual structure, it should not be condemned on this account. One might cite K 705, a charter of Æthelred II granting Long Itchington in Warwickshire to his thegn Clofig, as a case in point. In this charter the dating clause precedes the bounds and the anathema follows the witness list, but its authenticity is certain, for it is preserved in the original (cf. LC p. 74 and n. 3). The formulas used in the Beckley and Horton charter do not exhibit any suspicious features, and one can conceive no reason why it should have been forged. It seems safe to accept the charter as a genuine text, which has suffered to a minor extent in transmission; besides omitting part of the witness list, the Thorney copyist is probably responsible for entering *ottanmore* as *ottanmere*, and *Ælgifu* as *Ælfgiva*. The second element of *bugenrode* is also possibly post-Conquest, but for the most part the OE names are rendered faithfully. The estate had no known connection with Thorney, and it is not known how this charter came to be entered in the Thorney Red Book.

X

1013. KING ÆTHELRED II TO THE THEGN NORTHMAN:
3½ HIDES AT TWYWELL, NORTHANTS.

OMNIS theorice contemplationis sagacitas, uel practice conuersationis simplicitas diuinis constat dogmatibus mancipanda. Qua propter proculdubio gratia dei suffragante nostri antecessores censerunt ob memoriam posteritatis uentura regnorum moderamina litteris luce clarius illustrare. Nos quoque

G

secundum posse eorum subsequi uestigia satagimus indicantes quod Æthelred Rex anglosaxonie atque Norðhẏmbrensis gubernator monarchie, paganorumque propugnator, ac Brettonum ceterarumque prouinciarum imperator, plura praestat suis carismata clientibus, hoc dumtaxat Norðman miles ore veridico potest propalare, de tribus cassatis atque [dimidie usurpatione][1] in loco qui Twiwelle nominatur. Denique hanc tellurem idem Rex perpetuo iure prefato principi, preter arcem atque pontem agonisque obsequium subrogauit, certis tramitibus terminatam hoc modo:

Þis synd þa land gemæro innto Twiwelle ꝥ is andlang nafrys broce upto ðrawoldeswelle and swa andlang ðæs sclædes up to þam garan and of ðam garan up to þam mere and of ðam mere innto eallesherestrete.

Anno Dominice Incarnationis .M°.xiii. scripta hec cartula hiis testibus consentientibus quorum inferius nomina caraxantur.

✠Ego Æthelred Rex triumphali tropheo uiuifice crucis cum archiepiscopis ceterisque præsulibus hoc uexillum stabiliter sigillabo. ✠Ego Æthelstan clito testimonium adhibui. ✠Ego Eadmund clito assensum dedi. ✠Ego Eadward clito consolidaui. ✠Ego Ælfred clyto plaudens consensi. ✠Ego Eadwig clito non negaui. ✠Ego Wulstan Eboracensis Archiepiscopus configi. ✠Ego Lẏuing episcopus fauens benedixi. ✠Ego Adulf episcopus fauorem dedi. ✠Ego Brihtwold episcopus consensi. ✠Ego Eadnoð episcopus hanc scedulam dictitans. Rege suisque præcipientibus perscribere iussi. ✠Ego Ælfsige episcopus consignaui. ✠Ego Germanus abbas. ✠Ego Brihtred abbas. ✠Ego Godeman abbas. ✠Ego Ælfsige abbas. ✠Ego Brihtmer abbas. ✠Ego Wulgar abbas. ✠Ego Eadric Dux. ✠Ego Leofwine dux. ✠Ego Uhtred dux. ✠Ego Ælfric dux. ✠Ego Ulfcẏtel minister. ✠Ego Morcare minister. ✠Ego Sigeuerd minister. ✠Ego Æthelric minister. ✠Ego Godwine miles. ✠Ego Leofwine miles. ✠Ego Leofsige miles. ✠Ego eadwine miles. ✠Ego æthelwine miles.

TEXTS

A. Red Book of Thorney, ff. 15–15ᵛ (old numbering, ff. iiii–iiiiᵛ); see p. 146.

1 The words within the brackets are a later insertion, space having been left for them in the MS.

B. BM Add. MS. 5937, fo. 180, an abbreviated version, omitting the proem, mis-spelling some of the place-names, introducing a minor error into the dating clause, and abbreviating the forms of subscription in the witness list.

EDITIONS

(1) *Collect. Topogr.*, IV, p. 57, from B.
(2) K 1308, from B or (1).
(3) This edition is from A. Abbreviations are extended and punctuation is modernized.

DATE

1013, according to the charter. The very long witness list is compatible with this date, with one possible exception (see below, where it is shown that the charter was probably drawn up before September 1013).

PERSONAL NAMES

Professor Whitelock (*The Anglo-Saxons*, ed. P. Clemoes, 1959, p. 82 n. 1) suggests that Norðman, the recipient of Twywell, is to be identified with the son of Earl Leofwine who was killed in 1017 (ASC). Leofwine, who witnesses this charter, was earl first of the Hwicce and later of Mercia, in which earldom he was succeeded by his son Leofric, who was presumably Norðman's younger brother (Freeman, NC, 1, 737 ff.).

The charter ends with a long and notable witness list, which if genuine is important as the last recorded meeting of the witan to be held before Swein's invasion and Æthelred's flight to Normandy. The Northumbrian witnesses could hardly have attended at a date later than August 1013, when Swein's campaign began (ASC E, *s.a.*). The list is headed by Æthelred II, the donor, and five of his sons. The æthelings are Æthelstan, born c.986, died 1015 after a long illness—the Twywell charter is the last he witnesses; Edmund, born c.993, became king in April 1016 (see p. 200); Edward, born c.993, crowned 1043, later known as the Confessor; Alfred, killed by Cnut 5 February 1036 and buried at Ely (ASC C); and Eadwig, who was banished, and possibly killed, by Cnut in 1017 (ASC C). Of these Æthelred sent Edward and Alfred to Normandy before Christmas 1013, some time before he himself left Greenwich for the Isle of Wight, where he spent Christmas and then sailed for Normandy. The bishops are headed by Wulfstan (archbishop of York 1002–28 May 1023) who must have witnessed before Swein reached the Humber in the late summer, and Lyfing, who had been made archbishop of Canterbury early that year (ASC E). Then comes Adulf, who was possibly Æthelwulf, bishop of Hereford. A difficulty arises here, because his successor Æthelstan first witnesses as bishop in K 1307, an apparently authentic charter dated July 1012. The chronology of the bishoprics is, however, as yet insufficiently well established for this period to condemn the Twywell charter on this account. The remaining bishops are Brihtwold, bishop of Ramsbury 1005 × 1045; Eadnoth I, bishop of Dorchester 1006 × 1016; and Ælfsige II, bishop of Winchester c. 1012 × 1032, whose subscription to the Twywell charter is the first of a long series (H p. 268 n. 1). The abbots are Germanus of Cholsey (cf. R p. 374); Brihtred of Glastonbury; Godeman, the first abbot of Thorney, who must have been an old man: this is the last charter he witnesses (he witnesses also K 1307, dated July 1012, and a number of earlier charters); Ælfsige of Ely; Brihtmær of Newminster; and Wulfgar, abbot of Abingdon 990 × 1016 (ASC C). The four earls are headed by Eadric Streona, earl of Mercia 1007× 1017; next comes Leofwine, probably the recipient's father, and earl of the Hwicce in 997 (K 698), who probably succeeded to Eadric's earldom on the latter's death (R p. 396); Uhtred, earl of Northumbria, who submitted to Swein in the late summer of 1013 (ASC E), and who was killed by Cnut in 1016; and Ælfric, earl of Hampshire, slain at *Assandun* in 1016 (cf. R pp. 373–4). An unusual feature of the Twywell charter is that it distinguishes between two classes of thegns, who witness as *minister* and *miles* respectively.[1] I have not found this elsewhere in contemporary charters. Of the first group, Ulfkytel is probably the thegn of that name slain at *Assandun*, and Siferth and Morcar are probably the important thegns of the Northern Danelaw killed by Eadric Streona at Oxford in 1015 (p. 200); Æthelric is otherwise unknown. Of the *milites*, Godwine is probably the thegn who witnesses K 719, 1296, 1307, and 1309; the remaining names occur too frequently for them to be identified with any degree of certainty.

Reviewing the witness list, the preponderance of Wessex names suggests that Æthelred was somewhere in that region when the charter was drawn up.

DIPLOMATIC

This is an unusual charter, and it is profitable to begin the study of its diplomatic with an investigation of the extraordinary title given to the king, "Rex anglosaxonie atque Northymbrensis gubernator monarchie, paganorumque propugnator, ac Brettonum ceterarumque prouinciarum imperator." This is not to be found elsewhere among Æthelred's charters, and we have to search back to the time of Edgar before finding a similar formula. It occurs in a Wilton charter dated 968

---

[1] In the Red Book, the former have their title abbreviated as $\overline{m}$: the latter have their title given in full as *miles*. This distinction could of course have been a whim of the transcriber.

(Dugdale ii, pp. 323–4; cf. ECW No. 108), where Edgar is called "Rex Anglorum cum Northymbra regimine ac progenie Paganorum Brettonumque prosapia sublimiter roboratus." Stenton, discussing this, called the style "unique," and suspected that the charter might have been drafted privately in the abbey (LC p. 3 n. 1). There is no need, however, to credit such an invention to a Wilton clerk (or nun), for the title had a much earlier and more significant origin. It is found in a charter of Eadwig dated 956 (CS 937), "Eadwi(g) rex, nutu dei Angulsæxna et Northanhumbrorum imperator, paganorum gubernator, Bretonumque propugnator";[1] again in a charter of Eadred dated 949 (CS 883), "in rege Anglorum . . . Eadredo, quem Norðhymbra paganorumque seu caeterarum sceptro prouincianum rex regum omnipotens sublimauit"; and finally in the earliest known charter of Eadred (CS 815; ◆EHD i, No. 105), a remarkable text dated soon after his accession in 946, "post obitum Eadmundi regis, qui regimina regnorum Angulsaxna et Norðhymbra, Paganorum, Brettonumque septem annorum inter uallo regaliter gubernat." Later in this charter Eadred is made to adopt the same title as that given to his brother Edmund. The object is clearly to commemorate a series of actions recorded in the ASC under the years 942–6, whereby Edmund and Eadred recovered first the Northern Danelaw, then Northumbria, and finally conquered Strathclyde. The "Brettonum" in the charter are the Scots, and the "pagans" are the Norsemen from Dublin who occupied the Northern Danelaw, and who are called "pagans" in the poem in ASC A, D, s.a. 942 (cf. EHD i, p. 508; A. Mawer, 'The Redemption of the Five Boroughs', EHR xxviii, pp. 551–7; A. Campbell, 'The End of the Kingdom of Northumbria', EHR lvii, pp. 91–7). It is extraordinarily interesting that such a formula should have been repeated from time to time in later charters right up to the time of Æthelred.

So much for the king's title; but the Twywell charter derives a good deal more of its formulary than this from charters current in Eadred's reign. CS 815, the charter in which the king's style originates, contains also the formula "praeter arcem atque pontem agonisque obsequium (usurpatam)," which is repeated word for word in the Twywell grant; other identical phrases are "certis tramitibus . . . terminatum" and, following the king's subscription, "triumphali tropheo." Moreover, CS 815 contains the prototype of the dating clause: "Anno dominicae incarnationis (Dcccc. xliv) . . . his testibus quorum nomina (subsequuntur conscribentibus)." The final form of this clause in the Twywell charter first appears in CS 895, dated 952; it is commonly used in the reign of Edgar, but not often thereafter.

A feature of the Twywell charter which has not yet been mentioned

---

[1] This version is similar to that found in a doubtful charter in the Burton cartulary, CS 746.

is the alliterative and poetical style adopted, particularly in the first sentence. This, too, is not met with in other charters of the time of Æthelred; it occurs only in a small group of Eadred's charters, a discovery first made by W. de Gray Birch (CS III, note following preface) and further discussed by Professor Whitelock (EHD I, p. 340).

It seems very probable, therefore, that whoever drew up the Twywell charter was using a charter or formulary of Eadred's reign for his exemplar. It appears from the witness list that Eadnoth, the diocesan bishop, was entrusted by Æthelred with the preparation of this charter. Eadnoth had been abbot of the neighbouring monastery of Ramsey. The Twywell charter is therefore not a product of the royal chancery, but an example of a diploma drawn up by an interested ecclesiastic (cf. H p. 39). Evidently Norðman acquired the estate with the intention of endowing Thorney.

HISTORY

For the descent of Twywell, see the notes to No. XII below, p. 205.

TOPOGRAPHY

The bounds are worked out in PN *Northants.*, p. 188. They follow the line of the modern parish boundary. In the entry in the Red Book, a space was left for the bounds, which were entered afterwards in a different hand.

AUTHENTICITY

This appears to be a well-preserved text of a genuine charter of Æthelred II.

XI

1015–16. EDMUND IRONSIDE TO THORNEY ABBEY:
5 HIDES AT LAKENHEATH, SUFFOLK

ALTITHRONI moderatoris imperio triuiatim instruimur, ut illi oppido subiecti subpeditantes famulemur, qui totius mundi fabricam mira ineffabilie disponens serie microcosmum, adam uidelicet, tandem quadriformi plasmatum materia almo ad similitudinem sui instinctum spiramine, uniuersis que in infimis formauerat uno probandi causa excepto uetitoque, preficiens paradisiace amenitatis iocunditate collaterana, eua scilicet, comitante decentissime collocauit, laruarica prochdolor seductus cauillatione uersipellis suasibilisque tergiuersatione uiraginis pellectus, anathematis alogia ambro pomum mo-

mordit uetitum, et sibi ac posteris in hoc erumpnoso deiectus seculo letum promeruit sempiternum. Intacta igitur redolente Christi diuinitate, passaque ipsius humanitate libertas addictis clementer seruulis contigit. Hinc ego Eadmund altithroni adminiculante gratia, anglorum ceterarumque gentium incircuitu triuiatim persistentium basilei filius, ut huius dapsilitatis altithroni moderatoris clementia merear obtinere consortium, quandam telluris particulam mansas uidelicet .v. qui ab huiusce patrie gnosticis nobili appellatur onomate "æt lacingahiðe" perpetua largitus sum hereditate ad monasterium quod dicitur Þornig, in honorem domini nostri ihesu Christi et sancte Marie perpetue uirginis et sancti Botulfi abbatis atque confessoris pro redemptione anime mee atque coniugi[1] mee et pro presentis uite sospitate. Si quis igitur hanc nostram donationem in aliud quam constituimus transferre uoluerit, priuatus a consortio sancte ecclesie eternis barathri incendiis lugubris iugiter cum Iuda Christi proditor eiusque complicibus puniatur, si non satisfactione emendauerit congrua quod contra nostrum deliquit decretum inique. Hiis igitur metis prefatum Rus hinc inde giratur. Ærist of mutforða into pæscforða æt te dic. of þere dic into crenegate. of crenegate into eriswýlles sceamelas. of eriswylles sceamelon into þes fennes heafdon.

TEXTS

A. Red Book of Thorney, ff. 16v–17 (old numbering, ff. v–vi). See p. 146.

B. BM Add. MS. 5937, fo. 180, a few lines containing bare details of the grant, obtained from A. Most of the text, and the whole of the bounds, are omitted.

EDITIONS

(1) *Collect. Topogr.*, IV, p. 57, from B.
(2) K 1153, from B or (1).
(3) CS 809, from (2).
(4) This edition is from A. Abbreviations are extended, and the punctuation is modernized.

DATE

c.8 September 1015 × 23 April 1016, between the marriage of Edmund to Siferth's widow, and the death of Edmund's father, Æthelred

---

[1] *Sic*, for "coniugis."

II, and probably early in this period. For the reasons advanced for this dating, see below.

HISTORY

By this charter Edmund "the king's son"[1] grants 5 hides at Laken-heath, Suffolk, to Thorney Abbey, "for the redemption of my soul and that of my wife." It must be considered together with K 726, a similar grant preserved in a cartulary of the neighbouring house of Peter-borough, by which "Edmund Ætheling, rex"[2] gives $1\frac{1}{2}$ hides at Peakirk and 3 virgates of land at Walton, both in the Soke of Peterborough, to the New Minster (at Winchester), "for the redemption of my soul and that of my wife, and for the soul of Siferth," the New Minster to hold them just as they had been held formerly by Siferth.

Setting aside for the moment all questions of diplomatic and authen-ticity, it is helpful to view these two texts in the light of the swift succession of events recorded in the Anglo-Saxon Chronicle for the last few months preceding the death of Æthelred II. The entry for the year 1015 opens with an account of a great council at Oxford, at which Eadric Streona, earl of Mercia, treacherously murdered Siferth and Morcar, the chief thegns of the confederation of East Midland town-ships known as the Seven Boroughs. Thereupon, to quote, "the king confiscated all their [i.e. the thegns'] property, and ordered Siferth's widow to be seized and brought to Malmesbury. Then, after a short time, prince Edmund came and abducted the woman against the king's will, and made her his wife. Then, before the Nativity of St Mary (8 September), the prince proceeded from the west and went north to the Five Boroughs,[3] and thereupon seized all the property of Siferth and Morcar, and the people all submitted to him. At the same time king Cnut came to Sandwich, and straightway sailed round Kent into Wessex, until he came to the mouth of the Frome, and harried in Dorset and Wiltshire and Somerset."[4] The account then describes the expeditions of the various English and Danish hosts until the death of Æthelred II on 28 April 1016, whereupon Edmund succeeded to the kingdom.

The charters under discussion fit well into this larger picture. With

---

[1] The Thorney charter was mistakenly attributed to King Edmund (939 × 946) by Kemble and Birch, who did not have the full text available. The diplo-matic, however, appears to be of later date, and Thorney was not refounded until 969 at the earliest.

[2] The rex is anomalous and may be the insertion of a late copyist.

[3] The Danish boroughs of Lincoln, Stamford, Leicester, Nottingham, and Derby.

[4] The Anglo-Saxon Chronicle, trans. G. N. Garmonsway, London, 2nd edn, 1955, pp. 145–6.

the king lying ill and the Danes constantly harrying, the state of the country was bordering on anarchy, and one may suppose that Edmund, arriving in the Peterborough area[1] in the autumn of 1015, sought to strengthen his hand by granting Siferth's estates to those who might be of most use to him. Thus, local loyalty was encouraged by the gift to Thorney of the Suffolk estate of Lakenheath, with its valuable interests in an eel fishery (see below). Further afield, the support of Winchester was solicited at a time when the Danish host was ravaging the neighbourhood. It seems likely that the remainder of Siferth's estates were disposed of in similar bargaining manœuvres; if so, subsequent events soon rendered the transactions inoperative, and the charters recording them have not survived.

This charter is the earliest recorded reference to Lakenheath. It is unlikely that Edmund's gift to Thorney remained effective for any length of time. The estate next occurs in a charter of Cnut to Bury St Edmunds (K 735), which describes it as the place where the annual count was made of eels taken from the fishery at *Welle*, probably to be identified with Eriswell, rather than the *Wўllan* of No. VII above. By the time of the Confessor, Lakenheath belonged to Ely (K 907 and DB).

DIPLOMATIC

Edmund's charter to Thorney, while not claiming for him the title of king, is nevertheless couched in the phraseology of a solemn royal diploma. It is of the greatest interest that the first half of the text is taken verbatim from the formula employed for the "Orthodoxorum" group of charters, which come from the first generation of the tenth-century Benedictine reform. The authenticity of these charters has been established beyond all doubt by Mr Eric John in a classical paper which has already been referred to,[2] and the formula copied in the Thorney text had been fully developed at Abingdon by 958–9 (CS 1046, 1047).

The text of our charter follows the "Orthodoxorum" formula very closely right down to "obtinere consortium," except that it omits the most verbose part of the proem; also, for the king's title "Edgar altithrono . . . basileus" it makes the extraordinary substitution "Eadmund altithroni . . . basilei filius."

The *verba dispositiva* which follow, commencing at "quandam telluris particulam" and ending at "pro presentis uite sospitate," resemble the

---

[1] F. M. Stenton, *Anglo-Saxon England*, p. 383 n. 1, suggested that the Seven Boroughs comprised the Five Boroughs plus Torksey (Lincs.) and York. The content of the two charters under discussion suggests to me that Peterborough, rather than York, was the seventh member.

[2] See p. 174 n. 1.

G*

formula used in Edmund's charter to New Minster, K 726. In each case the gift is to a monastery, whose patron saints are mentioned, those of Thorney being the Virgin Mary and St Botulf, abbot and confessor. In the Thorney text the phrase "pro redemptione anime mee atque coniugis mee" follows, to be compared with "pro redemptione animae meae et coniugis meae et pro anima Siuerði" in the New Minster grant. The formulas of these two charters, while similar to each other, are not modelled at this point on any other text that I can discover.

In the New Minster charter a clause follows granting the usual exemption from all dues except work on bridges and fortresses, and service in the host. It may be significant that this clause is omitted from the Thorney charter.

Next in the Thorney text comes the anathema, together with a short clause introducing the bounds. These are of standard form for the early years of Edgar. Admittedly, they both occur in an isolated charter of King Athelstan dated 931 (CS 683), but this is an Abingdon text which is open to suspicion.[1] With this exception, the anathema does not occur until 960, in CS 1054. Immediately it becomes the normal form, appearing in no less than sixteen charters dated 961–3. Then there is a gap, but the series resumes abruptly in 966, and from then until 970 the clause appears in a further twenty charters. After this it occurs rather more sporadically, being found in seven more charters up to 978, then on odd occasions in 982, 987 (twice), 988, 996, 1004, 1008, 1033, 1046 (twice), and 1052–3.[2]

The text concludes with the bounds, which could be of any date from the ninth to the eleventh centuries. The word *sceamelas* which appears in the bounds is the best surviving example of its use in the sense 'bank of a river'.

One would expect the bounds to be followed by a dating clause and witness list, but these are not present in our text; whether or not they appeared in the charter which lay before the Thorney copyist, it is hard to say, but he reproduced the dating clauses and abbreviated the witness lists of all the other pre-Conquest charters, except No. XIII. Moreover, in the charter of Edmund to New Minster, the witness list and dating clause are also omitted. It is particularly to be regretted that no witness lists appear in these two texts, for it would be most interesting to discover how influential were the personages, both lay and clerical, who supported Edmund at this stage in his career, when he was acting in open defiance of the king.

[1] Drögerit, p. 419 n. 3. Two other Abingdon charters, CS 680 and CS 676, have the same date and witness list.

[2] The charters here quoted are all to be found in Kemble. Some may be spurious, but the great majority are authentic.

TOPOGRAPHY

The identification of *Iacingahyðe* with Lakenheath in Suffolk rests on place-name evidence.[1] Its bounds, which are less detailed than those in most charters of the period, commence at an unidentified muddy ford, and proceed in a clockwise direction to *pæscforða*, now represented by Pashford Wood; arriving at a *dic* which is possibly Smeeth Ditch, the bounds proceed to *crenegate*, evidently a floodgate, perhaps at the junction of Smeeth Ditch and Eriswell. The bounds now turn to follow *eriswylles sceamelas*, the bank of the river at Eriswell, and so to *þes fennæs heafdon*, probably Sedge Fen, although as Dr Reaney points out, such names are difficult to fix definitely in fen country.

AUTHENTICITY

While it is of interest that the charter is based on archaic formulas, this fact does not in itself give rise to suspicion. Such 'throwbacks' occur in other charters of the period; moreover, the charter was issued in abnormal circumstances, for the facilities of the king's writing office could not have been at the donor's disposal. The "Orthodoxorum" formula utilized in Edmund's diploma was one of those commonly employed in the scriptoria of Bishop Æthelwold's foundations, and it is not surprising that whoever drew up the Lakenheath text should find among the archives of a local house such as Peterborough or Thorney a specimen of this formula to act as his exemplar.

The dramatic chain of events leading to the Lakenheath grant is reflected also in the text of its companion piece in the Peterborough cartulary (K 726), which employs formulas that appear to be unique. Indeed, it is impossible to discuss the Thorney charter in isolation from the one at Peterborough, for these two charters of Edmund, preserved in the archives of adjacent houses, mutually support each other's authenticity. On viewing them against the background of the history of the times, there seems no reason to doubt their genuineness. Whether or not they were effective instruments is another matter; one doubts whether titles derived from grants issued on such uncertain authority would have been taken very seriously after the death of Edmund. For this reason alone, any idea that they are forgeries may be discounted, for no possible advantage could accrue to Thorney or Peterborough from the possession of such documents. A monk setting out to forge a charter purporting to give Lakenheath to Thorney would surely claim it as being the gift of an established monarch, rather than a pretender.

---

[1] I am indebted to Dr P. H. Reaney, who is editing *The Place-Names of Suffolk*, for advice on these identifications.

XII

1017 × 1035. THE WILL OF MANTAT THE ANCHORITE:
LAND AT TWYWELL, NORTHANTS.,
AND CONINGTON, HUNTS.

MANTAT ancer godes wræcca gretet[1] Cnut king[2] and Emma þe læfdie[3] swiþe[4] bliþelike mid godes blisse. and ic cýðe þat[5] ic habbe ure almesse criste betaht and hise allen halgan ure saule[6] to froure[7] and to blisse þær[8] it lengest wunian sculen. þæt is ærest þæt land at Twýwelle[9] into Þornige þær ure ban resteð. and þat[10] land at[11] Cunintun. prestes and diaknes þa þe hit at[11] me earnodan[12] on mine liue.[13] and hi habbeð[14] god behaten and me on hand[15] eseald[16] þat[5] hi sculen elke éár[17] don for us twa hundred messen and twa hundred sauters. and þerto eaken fele holýe beden. nu bidde ic inc for godes luue[18] and for ure wreccan bene þat þis non[19] man ne awende. þat wat god þat[5] inc ne was[20] non[21] bescoran man nýccere[22] þænne. and þat inc sceal ben cuð[23] on þan towarden liue. Gehealde inc here on liue heofan engle kinge. and ge lede[24] inc on his lihte mid him þer ýt wiþuten[25] sorhge euere[26] wunian. amen.

Collation with W xxiii: [1] greteð [2] cing [3] hlæfdie [4] swiðe
[5] þ̄ [6] sawle [7] frofre [8] þære [9] æt Twiwell [10] þæt
[11] æt [12] earnodon [13] life [14] habbað [15] hande [16] gesealde
[17] geare [18] lufe [19] none [20] wæs [21] nen [22] nytter [23] cuðe
[24] geleade [25] wiðuten [26] euer.

TEXTS

A. The Red Book of Thorney, fo. 18 (old numbering, fo. vii). See p. 146.

B. BM Add. MS. 5937, fo. 133b, a copy of A in which the spelling has been normalized; otherwise it is a complete and accurate rendering of the text.

EDITIONS

(1) ♦Collect. Topogr., IV, p. 58, from B, with an English translation.

(2) ♦Warner, History of Thorney Abbey, p. 51, from (1), translation only.

(3) K 1329, from (1).

(4) T p. 555, from B.

(5) ♦W XXIII, from B, with translation and notes.

(6) This edition is from A with collation from (5). There are no abbreviations, and the punctuation is unchanged.

DATE

The will is addressed to Cnut and his wife Emma; hence 1017 × 1035, and probably late in the reign (see HISTORY below).

DIPLOMATIC

Discussed in W XXIII. On the writ protocol of this will, see H p. 24 n. 2.

HISTORY

Conington was given by King Eadwig to his thegn Wulfstan in 957 (No. 9). The original charter is still preserved in Winchester Cathedral; this suggests that the Wulfstan of the grant was in fact Wulfstan Uccea, who had dealings with Bishop Æthelwold of Winchester (see the notes to No. VI). It may be, therefore, that the estate had already come into the possession of Thorney Abbey by the early eleventh century, and was leased by the abbey to Mantat the Anchorite for his lifetime. At a later period it was leased for life, with reversion to the abbey, to Thurkil of Harringworth, Northants. (DB fo. 206b; see VCH *Hunts.*, I, pp. 351a, 355b).

Twywell was given by King Æthelred II to his thegn Norðman in 1013, by a charter the text of which is preserved in the Red Book of Thorney (No. x). If this is the Norðman who was killed in 1017 (ASC), he may have willed Twywell to Thorney. It seems probable that Thorney then leased the estate to Mantat for his lifetime.

It would be in keeping for Thorney, once a foundation for anchorites, to use estates to endow the living of a hermit in some way. If this assumption is correct, the will is to be read as a confirmation of the reversion of these two estates to Thorney.

AUTHENTICITY

I am in agreement with Professor Whitelock's conclusion (W p. 177): "There is nothing improbable in the transaction, and it is possible that we ought to regard the will as the result of the tampering of later copyists with a genuine original."

XIII

1028. KING CNUT TO HIS THEGN GODWINE:
5 HIDES AT LYTLACOTAN[1]

FLUCTIUAGI presentis seculi fallax gloria per quam infausti deoque ingrati illiciuntur diatim noctuatimque ueluti fragilis stipula arescit et nutatur quia in est ei stabilitas nulla. Superni regis uerumptamen decor perpetim uiget quo frui omnis habet qui Christi oblitus est baptismatis unctione et memor est mandatorum eius sicut agyographa infit ad faciendum ea. Suis idem dominus mathitibus singulariter sub persona in se fidentium omnium "date" inquit "et dabitur uobis." Scilicet transitoria et caduca in eis[2] expendite qui minus uobis possident quatinus uice donacionis percipiatis inmarcessabilia[3] serta in celesti gloria. Qua intercedente gratia, ego Æthelred[4] rex cuidam militoni meo qui mihi adherendo suis bonis obsequiis graciosus est nomine Godwine—quandam terre particulam, idest mansas .v. do in loco illo qui dicitur lytlacotan—iugi possessione, ut heredem sibi efficiat quemcumque animo placuerit suo, siue ante seu post deposito corporis sarcina. Tali modo etiam liberum sit iugiter ab omnibus mundialibus seruiciis predictum solum cum omnibus ad se rite attinentibus ueluti cuncta quodque aliis a[5] meis institutum[6] decessoribus in hoc perstabit deo propiciante uitaque mihi comitante. Si autem quis hanc fuerit nisus addere donaticulam, augeatur ei temporalis uita et future felicitatis amenitate fruatur et quisquis instinctus stimulacione uersuti hostis fuerit qui omnis extat inuidus boni ut hoc decretum infringere temptauerit, sciat se participium sumpturum cum truculento proditore suppremi patris unici in eterna dampnacione cuius emulus extitit cupiditate, si non anticipauerit et anticipando emendauerit quod nequiter mente nefanda excogi-

---

[1] A has a rubric: "Carta regis Ethelredi filii regis Edgari de quadam terre particula data cuidam militoni nomine Godwine, anno domini millesimo xxviij. Capitulum xj.," and prefaces the text with the common chrismon: ☧

B has a rubric: "Carta regis Cnuti de terra data Godwino. Capitulum xij.," and a chrismon, which appears to be unique: ☨

[2] A *in eis* duplicated.   [3] B *in marcessibilia*.   [4] B *Cnut*.   [5] B *a* omitted.
[6] B *est* inserted.

tauit[1] Exemplum. Anno autem dominice incarnacionis millesimo xxviij. karax[a]ta et corroborata huius cyrographi cartula
sub adstipulacione uirorum illustrium quorum onoma hic infra
taxantur:

Scripta hec cartula anno dominice incarnacionis nostri Ihesu
Christi millessimo xxviij, hiis testibus consentientibus quorum
inferius nomina karaxantur:

Hec autem anno dominice incarnacionis dcccc paginola litteris decorata et sancita est testimoniis illustrium quam plurimorum uirorum quorum condita hic nomina sunt infra:

✠ Ego æthelred rex cum signo sancte crucis propriis digi-
tulis consignaui atque dono dedi.

✠ Ego cnut rex anglorum indeclinabiliter concessi.

✠ Ego æthelnoð archiepiscopus regie roborator donacionis
agye triumphale crucis signaculum depinxi.

✠ Ego cnut' regio sublimatus honore consensi et subscripsi.

✠ Ego ælfric archipraesul ciuitatis eburace hanc regiam
stabilitans donacionem signo prepollenti prefixi.

✠ Ego ælfgifu regina indeclinabiliter concessi.

✠ Ego æthric episcopus dorcācensis ecclesie hanc cartulam
dictitans rege suisque precipientibus prescribere iussi.

✠ Ego Hardecnut clyto eiusdem regis filius et regine plaudens
hilariter stabiliui.

✠ Ego ælfsige episcopus Wintoniensis ecclesie prepunxi.

✠ Ego[2] æthelnodus archipontificii podere prelatus consensi
et subscripsi.

✠ Ego brihtwolt episcopus prenotaui.

✠ Ego ælfwig episcopus lundoniensis ecclesie annotaui.

✠ Ego athelstan episcopus concessi.

✠ Ego brihtmer episcopus lichfeldensis ecclesie consignaui.

TEXTS

A. Red Book of Thorney, ff. 33ᵛ–34 (old numbering, ff. xxiiᵛ–
xxiii).

B. Red Book of Thorney, ff. 34–34ᵛ (old numbering, ff. xxiii–
xxiiiᵛ).

[1] B ends here.
[2] This entry is made at the foot of the folio, with a caret mark in the text.

EDITION

This edition is from A, collated with B.

DATE

There are three dating clauses, two of them for the year 1028. The witness list (with the exception of King Æthelred) is compatible with this date.

PERSONAL NAMES

There is no means of identifying Godwine, the recipient, who bore a very common name. The witness list includes Queen Ælfgifu and her son Hardecnut, and the following bishops:

Æthelnoð, archbishop of Canterbury 1020 × 1038.
Ælfric, archbishop of York 1023 × 1041.
Æthelric, bishop of Dorchester 1016 × 1034.
Ælfsige II, bishop of Winchester 1012–14 × 1032.
Brihtwold, bishop of Ramsbury 995 × 1045
Ælfwig, bishop of London 1014 × c.1035.
Æthelstan, bishop of Hereford 1012 × 1056.
Brihtmær, bishop of Lichfield 1020–6 × 1039.

HISTORY

Littlecote is a common place-name, and in the absence of a boundary clause we have no means of locating it. There is no evidence that an estate of this name was ever in the possession of Thorney.

DIPLOMATIC

As yet, little can be said on this topic, pending a more general investigation of the diplomatic of Cnut's charters; the Littlecote charter appears to follow the normal form for the period.

AUTHENTICITY

Each of the pre-Conquest charters transcribed into the Red Book of Thorney evidently bore a press-mark in roman numerals on the original membrane, and this was duly recorded by the copyist in the rubric introducing his entry of each charter. From these rubrics it appears that two versions of the Littlecote charter lay as separate parchments before the copyist, one (numbered xj) in the name of King Æthelred which I have labelled A, and the other (numbered xij) in the name of King Cnut, which I have called B. The Thorney copyist did not encounter these two texts until he had finished entering all the other pre-Conquest texts, and worked his way chronologically through the Norman royal charters and those of the Angevins down to Edward I. Then, when he did find these two versions of the Littlecote charter, he did not attempt to edit them, but simply entered them faithfully in successive folios of his cartulary, without any comment other than that contained in the rubrics.[1] It appears probable, however, that he did not transcribe the whole text of B, but stopped when he reached the OE bounds, and thus omitted also the dating clause and witness list.

If we accept this as the most likely hypothesis, then it is evident that B was an authentic charter of Cnut dated 1028, and A was no more than the clumsy early draft of a forgery, utilizing B for its exemplar, in which the name of King Æthelred was substituted as donor in the place of King Cnut, and Æthelred's name was also added to the witness list. The forger blundered badly in dealing with the dating clause; he made out three different drafts, of which the second probably appeared in the original charter. The forger's motive in attempting to back-date Cnut's charter in this fashion will never be known.

[1] He took the same line with the two versions which he found of the Thorney Foundation Charter (No. VII).

PART III

CHAPTER X

LAND TRANSACTIONS IN THE ELY
LIBELLUS

THE *Libellus quorundam insignium operum beati Æthelwoldi episcopi* is a work surviving in two twelfth-century manuscripts whose texts are almost identical.[1] They record the land transactions entered into by Bishop Æthelwold in building up the endowment of Ely Abbey. In some cases a brief abstract of title is given for the estates concerned, and often subsequent land pleas concerning the estates are recorded. The original was written in OE towards the end of the tenth century; it was translated into Latin between 1109 and 1131, and the surviving versions are copies of this translation.

One suspects that the great majority of these transactions were recorded at the time by charter, written will, law memorandum, or some other similar instrument; indeed in a few cases we know for certain that such written records existed,[2] but for the remainder no evidence survives for the existence of any such independent records. The account given in the *Libellus* is no doubt biased in favour of the monastery's title, but there is good reason to believe that for the most part it gives an accurate version of what took place.

The *Libellus* was incorporated piecemeal into the *Liber Eliensis*, Book II, and in the epitome which follows the chapter number of each entry in the LE is given. Where possible, a date is supplied for each entry; most of the remaining undated transactions took place some time between the refoundation of Ely and the death of Bishop Æthelwold, i.e. 970 × 984. For completeness, all land transactions entered in the *Libellus* are recorded in the epitome, even those for which it is known that a separate charter was issued. Two small transactions which do not appear in the

---

[1] BM MS. Cotton Vesp. A xix, ff. 2–27*b*; Trinity College Camb. MS. o.2.41, pp. 1–64*b*; see LE p. xxxiv.

[2] E.g. Nos. 193, 240, 275.

Libellus, but for which accounts were incorporated in this section of the LE, are also included.

Most of the material appearing in LE concerning additions to the abbey endowment made between the time of Æthelwold and the Norman Conquest is known to have been derived from charters, wills, and other similar sources now lost. In only two entries is there some doubt whether or not such original records ever existed. Chapter 74 records a grant to Ely made by the parents of Leofsige when he entered the monastery; the estates comprised Shelford and Snailwell in Cambridgeshire, Glemsford, Hartest, and Barking in Suffolk, and Feltwell in Norfolk. Leofsige became abbot in 1029, and as this grant was made while he was still a boy, it may be dated c.990. The next chapter records a grant to Ely made c.1016 by Ælfwine, bishop of Elmham, of estates including Wisbech "which is a quarter part of the hundred of the Isle [of Ely]," Walpole in Norfolk, and Debenham, Brightwell, and Woodbridge in Suffolk.

LAND TRANSACTIONS IN THE ELY 'LIBELLUS'

No.[1]	Chapter[1]	Estate	Size etc.	Old Owner(s)	New Owner(s)	Nature of Transaction	Date
		CAMBRIDGESHIRE					
168	8(a)	Linden End	12 h.[2]	Leofric of Brandon (Sf)	Ely	sale for 100 gold (mancuses)	after 970
169	10(a)	Stretham	8 h.	Æthelflæd and Æthelgifu	,,	sale for 30 silver pds	c.971
170	(b)	,,	1 h. + 2 pools	Ælfwold of Mardleybury (Hrt)	,,	sale for 20 gold (mancuses)+ (later) 2 os.	c.971
171	(c)	,,	24 a.	not known	Wulfstan f. of Wulflæd	not known (inherited)	925 × 939
172	(d)	,,	,,	Wulfstan f. of Wulflæd	Wulflæd	will	
173	(e)	,,	,,	Wulflæd wid. of Siferth	Ely	sale	c.971 (after No. 172)

[1] In this epitome, the numbers in the first column represent the position of the transaction in the hand-list: the chapter numbers are those of the chapters in *Liber Eliensis*, bk II, in which the entries appear.

[2] Abbreviations: a=acre(s), h=hide(s).

No.	Chapter	Estate	Size etc.	Old Owner(s)	New Owner(s)	Nature of Transaction	Date
174	11(a)	Downham	2 h.	Leofsige and w. Siflæd	Ely	sale for 15 pds, later altered to exchange for No. 175	before No. 173
175	(b)	Clayhithe	5 h.	Ely	Leofsige and w. Siflæd	exchange for No. 179 + a goblet worth 20s.	as No. 176
176	(c)	Downham	2 h.	Siferth of Downham	Ely	will	
177	(d)	Wilburton	„	„	d. of Siferth	„	
178	(e)	Downham	„	Leofwine s. of Count Hereric	Aluric his elder b.	exchange for his share of No. 179	
179	(f)	Chippenham	3 h.	m. of Aluric and Leofwine	Aluric and Leofwine	will	before No. 178
180	(g)	Downham	2 h.	Aluric	Ely	exchange for No. 181	
181	(h)	Chippenham	another 3 h.	Ely	Aluric, as in No. 178	exchange for No. 180 + 6 pds	
182	11a(a)	„	80 a. + 3 farm houses	Leofsige of Freckenham (Sf)	Ely	sale for 100s.	

183	(b)	Chippenham	10 a.+1 alodium	Ælfric of Wickham (Ca)	Ely	sale for 20s.
184	(c)	,,	10 a.	Wulfhelm b. of Wulfwine	,,	,, ,, 10s.
185	(d)	,,	another 3 h.	First h. of w. of Ælfwold	w. of Ælfwold the Fat	will (? same estate as No. 179)
186	(e)	,,	,,	Ælfwold the Fat and his w.	Ely	sale for 15 pds
187	(f)	Milton	2 h.	Ely	Ulf	exchange for No. 188
188	(g)	Fordham	2 h.+37 a.	Ulf	Ely	exchange for No. 187; 37 a. owing, cf. No. 233
189	12(a)	Witchford	100 a.	Sumerled	,,	sale for 11 pds+ (later) 30s.
190	(b)	,,	16 a.	Osmund the Hunchback	,,	exchange for No. 191 and its reversion
191	(c)	Cambridge	,,	Ely	Osmund the Hunchback	exchange for No. 190
192	(d)	Witchford	7 a.	Ælfnoth	Ely	sale at Wilburton (Ca)
193	13	Wold nr Witchford	100 a.	Æthelstan s. of Manne	,,	will, cf. Chron c.986 Rams pp. 59–61

No.	Chapter	Estate	Size etc.	Old Owner(s)	New Owner(s)	Nature of Transaction	Date
194	14	Witcham	1 a.	Æðelweard and Brihtferth	Ely	not known	
195	15	Sutton	3 h.	Wulfsige, his w. Mawa, and their s. Ælfsige	,,	gift for admission to confraternity (not recorded in the *Libellus*)	
196	16(a)	Hill+Haddenham	farm+70 a.	Wulfgar of Hill	,,	sale for 70s.	
197	(b)	Hill+Haddenham	"almost the whole of his land there"	Ælfsige	,,	sale	
198	(c)	Hill+Haddenham	many a.	numerous poor peasants	,,	sales	
199	(d)	Haddenham	farm+76 a.	Æðulf and w. Burgflæd	,,	sale at Thetford (Nf)	
200	(e)	,,	No. 199+20 a.	Ely	Grim s. of Wine	lease, for his service	
201	17(a)	Wilburton	2 h.+32 a. arable and meadow+5 *predia*	Ælfwine and w. Siflæd	Ely	sale for 90 gold (mancuses)	

No.		Place	Amount	From	To	Transaction	Date
202	(b)	Wilburton	70 a.	*Oppele* (?)	Ely	sale	
203	(c)	"	80 a.	Ælfric of Sutton (Ca)	"	exchange for No. 204	
204	(d)	Witcham	land	Ely	Ælfric of Sutton (Ca)	exchange for No. 203	
205	(e)	Wilburton	70 a.	Æding	Ely	sale	
206	(f)	"	many a.	names not recorded	"	sales	
207	18(a)	Stonea	the whole estate + a fishery	Æscwen of Stonea, a wid.	Wulfstan of Dalham (Ca)	gift, but see No. 228	c.955
208	(b)	"	"	Wulfstan of Dalham	Ely	gift	"
209	(c)	Cambridge	1 h.	Ogga of Mildenhall (Sf)	"	gift, first in reversion, then outright	"
210	19	Cambridge + Dullingham	40 a. land, a farm, + ½ of a wood	Oslac	"	gift, in return for assistance—value assessed at 26 gold (man-cuses)	before July 975
211	20(a)	Witcham	toft + part of 70 a.	Burchelm	"	sale	

No.	Chapter	Estate	Size etc.	Old Owner(s)	New Owner(s)	Nature of Transaction	Date
212	(b)	Witcham	toft + part of 70 a.	Ely	Brihtlaf	exchange for No. 213	
213	(c)	Cambridge	farmhouse + 30 a. arable and meadow	Brihtlaf	Ely	exchange for No. 212	
214	(d)	,,	7 a.	s. of Bp. Æthelmær	,,	sale at 16d. per a.	
215	(e)	,,	,,	Siflæd	,,	,,	
216	(f)	,,	5 a.	Hungifu, a wid.	,,	sale	
217	(g)	,,	10 a. + a fishpool	,,	,,	gift, in return for a pension	
218	21(a)	Doddington + Wimblington	60 a. + a fishery rendering 1,000 eels p.a.	Gunulf	,,	sale for 100s.	
219	(b)	,,	,,	Ely	Wine, s. of Osmund	exchange for No. 222	
220	(c)	Cambridge	part of 53 a. + a fishery rendering 1,000 eels p.a.	Eanflæd	,,	will, cf. No. 224	

No.		Place	Extent	relatives		Transaction	
221	(d)	Cambridge	the other part of No. 220		Wine, s. of Osmund	sale	
222	(e)	Hill	8 a. +No. 220 +No. 221	Wine, s. of Osmund	Ely	exchange for No. 219	
223	(f)	,,	5 a.	s. of Ælfstan	,,	sale	
224	(g)	not known	,,	Eanflæd	,,	will, see No. 220	
225	22(a)	Doddington +Weremere	1 h. +½ the mere+all the marshes belonging to it	Thurcytel, abbot of Bedford	,,	exchange for No. 305	
226	(b)	,,	,,	Ely	Wine, see No. 219	gift for his clothing	
227	23	Wimblington	10 a. +2 fisheries	Ramsey Abbey	Ely	sale for 20s.	
228	24(a)	Stonea	marsh	Ely	relative of the wid. Æscwen	lease for 2,000 eels p.a., see No. 207	955
229	(b)	,,	,,	,,	Begmund of Holland (Ess)	"theft"; restored after by grand placitum July 975 at Cambridge	
230	26(a)	Toft	10 h. +all the stock, living and dead	Wulfnoth (as in No. 274)	Bp Æthelwold	sale for 60 pds	same as No. 274

No.	Chapter	Estate	Size etc.	Old Owner(s)	New Owner(s)	Nature of Transaction	Date
231	(b)	Toft	1 h.	the monk Goding	Ely	will	
232	27(a)	Hauxton + Newton	4½ h. + 3 h.	Eadric Long of Essex	King Edgar	,,	975
233	31(a)	Fordham	2 h. (each of 120 a.) + 37 a.	Grim s. of Osulf	Ely	sale for 9 pds; see No. 188	
234	(b)	Milton	4½ h.	Thurcytel, formerly abbot of Bedford	St Paul's, London	gift, in return for a place in the *familia*	
235	(c)	,,	,,	St Paul's	Thurcytel	lease at 2 od. p.a.	after No. 234
236	(d)	,,	,,	,,	Ely	exchange for No. 271	
237	32(a)	Eye + Horningsea	2 h. + 5 h.	newly baptized "heathen"	monastery at Horningsea	gift	ante 870
238	(b)	Eye, *recte* Horningsea	2 h.	monastery at Horningsea	Wulfric, *prepositus* of the monastery	"theft"	c.870
239	(c)	,,	,,	Wulfric, *prepositus*	the priest Leofstan, *nepos* of Wulfric	will	

240	(d)	Eye, *recte* Horningsea	2 h.	the priest Leofstan	Wulfstan (of Dalham)	gift by charter, in forfeiture for a crime
241	(e)	"	"	Wulfstan of Dalham	Æthelstan *chusin*	gift by charter
242	(f)	"	"	Ethelstan *chusin*	Bp Æthelwold	sale for 8 pds, see No. 261
243	(g)	Eye + Horningsea	2 h. + 3 h.	King Edgar	"	sale for 50 pds
244	33(a)	Eye	2 h.	—	priest Æthelstan	claim to ownership by descent, after July 975
245	(b)	Horningsea	"	Ely	Leofstan and a s. of Wulfric	"
246	(c)	Eye	"	priest Æthelstan	Ely	exchange for Nos. 248 and 250 +4 pds and 18d.
247	(d)	Snailwell	1 toft + 1 h. of 240 a.	Wedwin s. of Aldstan	"	sale for 6 pds
248	(e)	"	"	Ely	priest Æthelstan	part exchange for No. 246
249	(f)	? Snailwell	1 toft + 75 a.	Hugo and Ælfric	Ely	sale
250	(g)	"	"	Ely	priest Æthelstan	part exchange for No. 246

No.	Chapter	Estate	Size etc.	Old Owner(s)	New Owner(s)	Nature of Transaction	Date
251	(h)	? Horningsea	1 h.	Leofsige and b. Ælfstan and their s. Wulfgar and Oslac	Ealdorman Brihtnoth	forfeiture	
252	(i)	,,	,,	Ealdorman Brihtnoth	Ely	sale for 4 pds	
253	(k)	,,	another 1 h. + 1 *campum*	priest Leofstan	priest Leofsige	sale for 100s.	
254	(l)	,,	,,	priest Leofsige	Ealdorman Brihtnoth	forfeiture	
255	(m)	,,	,,	Ealdorman Brihtnoth	Ely	gift	
256	34(a)	Swaffham	2 h.	Wynsige *cognatus* of Wulfric	Wulfstan (? of Dalham) *prepositus*	sale for 8 pds	
257	(b)	,,	,,	Wulfstan *prepositus*	Æthelwine, s. of Æðelward of Sussex	not known	
258	(c)	Swaffham + ?Barley, Hrt	2h. + estate	Æthelwine, s. of Æðelward of Sussex	King Edgar	sale for 80 gold (mancuses)	

259 H	(d)	Swaffham +?Barley, Hrt	2 h. + estate	King Edgar	Bp Æthelwold	sale for 80 gold (mancuses)
260	(e)	,,	,,	Bp Æthelwold	Wulfstan *præpositus*	forfeiture
261	45	Horningsea	2 h.	Æthelstan, b. of Æthelward	Bp Æthelwold	sale for 8 pds (subsequently lost), see No. 242
262	46	Gransden	estate	Henric of Wantage (Brk)	,,	sale for 200 gold 963 × 975 (mancuses)
263	49b	Armingford	1½ h.	Ely	unknown	"obtained by crime"
HERTFORDSHIRE						
264	7(a)	Hatfield	40 h.	Orðmaer and w. Ealde	King Edgar	will
265	(b)	,,	,,	King Edgar	Ely	grant
266	(c)	,,	,,	Ely	Ealdorman Æthelwine and bros.	"acquisition by force"
267	(d)	,,	,,	Ealdorman Æthelwine and bros.	Ely	exchange for Nos. 272 and 273

No.	Chapter	Estate	Size etc.	Old Owner(s)	New Owner(s)	Nature of Transaction	Date
				ESSEX			
268	31(e)	Holland	5 h.	Sprowe	Eadgifu, 3rd w. of King Edward the Elder	sale for 20 pds	c.919 × c.961
269	(f)	,,	,,	Eadgifu	Ælftred, w. of King Edgar	will	961 × 964
270	(g)	,,	,,	Ælftred	Ely	gift	after No. 269
271	(h)	,,	,,	Ely	St Paul's	exchange for No. 236	after No. 270
				HUNTINGDONSHIRE			
272	(e)	Wennington and Hemingford Abbots	6 h. and 30 h.	Wulfstan of Dalham (Ca)	Ely	will	
273	(f)	Yelling	5 h.	Wulfwine Cocus and w.	,,	forfeiture by crime	
274	25(a)	Bluntisham	estate	Wulfnoth	Bp Æthelwold	sale by charter for 30 pds	
275	(b)	,,	stock of men, property, and corn on No. 274	,,	,,	sale for 7 pds	

SUFFOLK

No.	Ref	Place	Hides			Transaction	Date
276	27(b)	Wangford	3 h.	Ely	Ealdorman Æthelwine	gift, in return for promise of help	years after 975
277	35(a)	Brandon+Livermere	5 h.	Ælfgar of Moulton (Sf)	Wulfstan of Dalham	will	
278	(b)	"	"	Wulfstan of Dalham	his relative Wihtgar	gift	
279	(c)	"	"	Wihtgar	Ely	sale for 20 pds+(later) 10 gold (mancuses)	
280	(d)	"	"	Ely	Ingulf	"theft"	
281	(e)	"	"	Ingulf	his w.+sons	descent	
282	(f)	"	"	Ingulf's w.+sons	Siferth b. of Ingulf	descent	less than 1 year after No. 281
283	(g)	"	"	Siferth b. of Ingulf	Ely	gift	
284	36	Brandon+Livermere	every 8th acre +3 h.	Count Scule	Ælfgar of Moulton	sale for 2 riding horses, 2 wall coverings, and 59 gold (mancuses)	931 × 949

No.	Chapter	Estate	Size etc.	Old Owner(s)	New Owner(s)	Nature of Transaction	Date
285	37	Sudbourn	estate	King Edgar and his w. Ælfthryth	Ely	gift, with its charter, in return for a translation of the Rule of St Benedict	
286	38	Woodbridge	3 h.	Wulfstan (of Dalham)	,,	sale for 15 pds	
287	39	Stoke	10 h. + 2 mills	King Edgar	,,	sale by charter for 100 gold (mancuses)	970
288	41	Sudbourn, Stoke, Wood-bridge + the 6 hundreds	estates + soke	Ely	Ealdorman Æthelwine	lease for 10 pds p.a.	
				NORFOLK			
289	40	East Dereham	estate	King Edgar	Ely	sale (not in *Libellus*)	
290	42(b)	Northwold	12 h.	,,	,,	part of exchange for No. 306	970

291	(c)	Northwold	12 h.	Ely	Thurferth	"theft," cf. No. 298	c.980
292	43(a)	Northwold+ Pulham	12 h.+ estate	Waldgist	King Edmund	forfeiture for a crime	
293	(b)	,,	,,	King Edmund	King Eadred	descent	946
294	(c)	,,	,,	King Eadred	Eadgifu, his m.	gift	946 × 955
295	(d)	,,	,,	Eadgifu	King Edgar	descent	after 961
296	(e)	,,	,,	King Edgar	Wulfstan of Dalham	presumably a lease	after 961
297	(f)	Pulham	estate	,,	Bp Æthelwold	sale for 40 pds	
298	(g)	,,	,,	Ely	Thurferth	"theft," cf. No. 291	c.980
299	44	Weeting	3 h.	Æthelward	Bp Æthelwold	sale for 6 pds (subsequently lost)	
300	48	Kelling	estate	Ædric the Dane	,,	sale of the land for 20 pds and the goods for 11 pds	before No. 301
301	49(a)	,,	,,	Bp Æthelwold	Ealdorman Æthelwine	sale	975 × 979

No.	Chapter	Estate	Size etc.	Old Owner(s)	New Owner(s)	Nature of Transaction	Date
302	(b)	Kelling	estate	Ealdorman Æthelwine	Ringulf	sale	975×979
				OTHER COUNTIES			
303	8(b)	Bishampton (Worcs.)	7 h.	Æthelflæd, w. of Leofric	Bp Æthelwold	sale, see ECWM pp. 115–16	970
304	22(c)	Beeby (Lei.)	land	Bp Oscytel of Dorchester (archbp of York)	,,	will	before 972
305	(d)	,,	,,	Ely	Thurcytel, abbot of Bedford	exchange for No. 225	
306	42(a)	Harting (Sx)	40 h.	,,	King Edgar	exchange for No. 290	
307	47(a)	Marsworth (Bu)	estate	King Edgar and his w. Ælfthryth	Bp Æthelwold	gift	after No. 308
308	(b)	,,	,,	Ælfgifu	King Edgar	will	
309	49a	Kensworth (Bed)	2 h.	Leofsige	Bp Æthelwold	sale for 4 pds (subsequently lost)	966×975

CHAPTER XI

LAND TRANSACTIONS IN THE RAMSEY CHRONICLE

T OWARDS the close of the thirteenth century a monk at Ramsey put together in the form of a chronicle all the surviving evidences for the early history of his house. For the most part he used original materials, but occasionally, on his own admission,[1] he had resort to the oral traditions of the house. Although in many cases his sources were contemporary with the transactions they described, it is possible that for his account of some of the donations he drew upon later lists of benefactors and similar material. The land transactions described below comprise all those entries in the Chronicle for which evidence is lacking as to the exact source of the information which lay before the compiler. Whatever the origins of this material, the information supplied tallies with what we know from other sources far too often to admit of any doubt that the facts recorded are authentic.

HUNTINGDONSHIRE

310. c.958 King EDGAR to Ælfwen, the wife of Ealdorman Æthelstan of East Anglia. 10 hides at *Westona* (Old Weston).

> Chron Rams pp. 11–12, 52. Ælfwen had been King Edgar's foster-mother, evidently during the reign of Eadwig.

311. 969 × 983 ÆTHELWINE, ealdorman of East Anglia, to his foundation at Ramsey. Grant of the Isle there, with the surrounding marshes and pools; the land at *Upwode* (Upwood), with its fisheries, which he had received from King Edgar, and where he had his hall and kept his court; the berewick of *Raflean* (Raveley), which he had also re-

[1] E.g. Chron Rams p. 157.

ceived from King Edgar; all that he held at *Saltretha* (Sawtry), which had been given to Ramsey by his wife Æthelflæd, by inheritance from her father, who had obtained it in exchange for part of his patrimony from Ealdorman Æthelstan; land at *Brinintuna* (Brington), which he had inherited from his father; 10 hides at *Westona* (Old Weston), which King Edgar had given Æthelwine's mother Ælfwen, for acting as his foster-mother; 10 hides at *Giddinge* (Gidding) and *Weletona* (Wood Walton), which he had bought from Othengar; 7 hides at *Stivecle* (Stukeley), for the soul of his wife Æthelflæd; pasture and a mill at *Hocton* (Houghton), which he had bought from a relative named Siric; and 30 hides at *Hemingforde* (Hemingford) which he had obtained from Bishop Æthelwold in exchange for 40 hides at *Hathfelde* (Hatfield, Herts.).

Chron Rams pp. 52–5. These gifts were not all made at the same time. Ramsey itself must have been given in 969, but Hemingford did not come into Æthelwine's possession until at least 975 (Nos. 18, 272, and 318).

312. 969 King EDGAR to Ramsey Abbey, on the occasion of its foundation, at the request of Archbishop Oswald [of York]. The church and 3 hides of land at *Guthmuncestria* (Godmanchester).

Chron Rams pp. 47–8. Subsequently alienated, see No. 313. The importance of this reference for the early history of Godmanchester has recently been commented upon by H. J. M. Green, CAS LIV, 1960, p. 94.

313. 969 × 974 King EDGAR to Oswald, archbishop of York, in exchange for the vill of *Nidingworthe* (Needingworth) which Oswald had previously bought from Edgar, and also the church and 3 hides at *Guthmuncestria* (Godmanchester), which the king had previously given to Ramsey Abbey. The vill of *Wystowe* (Wistow).

Chron Rams pp. 48–9. Oswald had purchased Needingworth with the intention of endowing Ramsey, but he exchanged it for Wistow because the latter estate was nearer to the abbey. For Godmanchester, see No. 312. The church there was attached to the royal manor by the time of the Confessor, and there is no record in DB of a separate endowment of 3 hides (VCH *Hunts.*, I, p. 340b). By 1284 its endowment was only 61 acres (*ibid.*, II, p. 294).

314. 969 × 974 DUNSTAN, archbishop of Canterbury, to Ramsey Abbey. Warboys.

Although this gift is not separately recorded in the Ramsey Chronicle, there is no reason to doubt the statement in Edgar's confirmation charter (No. 18).

315. 969 × 975 King EDGAR to Ramsey Abbey. One hide at *Stivecle* (Little Stukeley), which formerly belonged to one Turkemer.

Chron Rams p. 48. The personal name *Turkemer* appears to be unique, and if it does not arise from a scribal error, it probably represents a hybrid, the first element being Scandinavian and the second OE.

316. 975 × 979 King EDWARD [the Martyr] to Ramsey Abbey. 2 hides in *Broctuna* (Broughton).

Chron Rams p. 74; see Nos. 16, 20, 42, 317, and 322. Broughton became the head of the barony or honour of Ramsey; cf. VCH *Hunts.*, II, p. 159.

317. 975 × 979 EADNOTH, prior of Ramsey, to Æthelwold, bishop of Winchester, patron of the church of Ely, in exchange for 1 hide at *Broctona* (Broughton). The church and 40 acres at *Wilburgeham* (Wilbraham, Cambs.), which had been given to Ramsey by one Wulfhun, on the occasion of his profession as a monk.

Chron Rams pp. 74–5. This, together with another transaction by which a hide at *Bottintonia* (Boughton, Northants.) was given by Abbot Brihtnoth and the brothers of Ely to Ramsey, was completed by the presentation of four turves of green grass, cut from the said land, on the altar of St Gregory in the crypt of Ramsey church, before many witnesses, including Æthelsige the uncle of Ealdorman Æthelwine, and Ælfgyth. The exchange was probably made soon after No. 316. The one hide at Broughton had been given to Bishop Æthelwold by King Edgar; see No. 16. For Wilbraham, see No. 24.

H*

318. 975 × 983   The monks of ELY to Æthelwine, ealdorman of East Anglia, in exchange for 40 hides at Hatfield (Herts.). 6 hides in *Winningetune* (Wennington in Abbots Ripton), 30 hides in *Hemmingeford* (Hemingford Abbots) which Wulfstan of Dalham had left to Ely in his will, and 5 hides at *Gyllinges* (Yelling), which Wulfwine *cocus* and his wife Ælfswyth had forfeited by their many misdeeds. This agreement was made in the place called *Sloththere* (Slaughter, Glos.), in the presence of Ealdorman Ælfhere (of Mercia), Æthelwine (presumably the ealdorman), Ælfric Cild (son of Ealdorman Ælfhere), and many others. The sureties (*fidejussores*) were Æthelmær Cild, and Alfwold (probably the brother of Ealdorman Æthelwine).

> Chron Rams pp. 54–5; LE pp. 79–81; cf. VCH *Hunts.*, II, p. 305, and *Cambridge Historical Journal*, X, 1952, pp. 263, 267.

319. c.1007.   Will of the priest GODE. The church and land which he holds at *Haliwelle* (Holywell) to descend to Ramsey after his death.

> Chron Rams p. 85. Presumably this followed Ælfwaru's gift of Holywell to Ramsey (No. 28).

320. 1016 × 1034   ÆTHELRIC, bishop of Dorchester, to Ramsey Abbey, for the support of the monks. The estate at *Athelin*[*tone*] (Elton), and 3 hides at *Brouctone* (Broughton).

> Chron Rams pp. 135–40, 144; cf. VCH *Hunts.*, III, p. 158. Cart Rams I, p. 267, calls Æthelric the *nepos* of King Edward the Confessor, and refers to a charter of that king, confirming Æthelric's gift to the abbey—probably No. 47.

321. 1020 × 1034   ÆTHELSTAN, abbot of Ramsey, to Osgot Swegn. Lease of the estate at *Westmilne* (Westmill, Herts.), which had been left to the abbey by Æthelric, bishop of Dorchester; upon Osgot's death, the estate is to revert to the abbey, together with his own estate of *Uppefordia* (Offord Darcy).

> Chron Rams p. 145; cf. RE p. 164. Osgot appears as a witness to No. 72, dated 1043–5. His anniversary was commemorated at Ramsey on 24 August. Presumably his estate was the 4 hides

held by Ramsey at Offord Darcy at the time of DB (fo. 204*b*; VCH *Hunts.*, I, p. 344*b*).

322. 1040 × 1042   King HARTHACNUT, at the request of his mother Emma, for the soul of his father King Cnut, to the church of Ramsey. 5 hides at *Gillinge* (Yelling).

Chron Rams p. 152; in the index the estate is wrongly identified as Gidding. Cf. VCH *Hunts.*, II, p. 379.

323. c.1050 × 1065   TOSTIG, brother of Yri, being mortally ill, bequeaths 4 hides of land at *Saltretha* (Sawtry Beaumes) to Ramsey Abbey, for the salvation of his soul and the price of his burial there (i.e. his soul-scot).

Chron Rams p. 175, which goes on to say that this land was seized after the conquest by Eustace the Sheriff, who installed there his knight Walter de Beaumes, a statement supported in DB I, ff. 206, 208; cf. VCH *Hunts.*, I, pp. 351*a*, 355*b*, which shows that Tostig willed only the reversion of his estate to Ramsey. After his death it was held by his brother Yri, called "Eric" in DB, but it was to revert to the abbey after the deaths of Eric and his unnamed brother and sister.

The Ramsey account described Tostig as "unus ex baronibus regis Edwardi," and he is identified by the compiler of the index to the Hunts. DB with Earl Tostig of Huntingdon and Northumbria (VCH *Hunts.*, I, p. 408); but sufficient biographical material survives for Earl Tostig to show that this is not the case (cf. H p. 575), unless indeed the Ramsey story of his dying gift is in error. This seems unlikely, but possibly in describing Tostig of Sawtry as a "baron," the Ramsey scribe is applying to him the title of his more famous namesake and contemporary, whose Hunts. estates are described by Sir Frank Stenton in VCH *Hunts.*, I, p. 335.

324. c.1054   WACH to Ramsey Abbey, in alms for his soul. A fishery in *Witlemara*, *al. Withlismar*' (Whittlesey Mere).

Chron Rams p. 199; Cart Rams III, p. 167. The gift cannot be dated precisely, but his obit is entered under 1054. He is referred to as *Wak' frater noster*, but this does not necessarily imply that he became a monk; he may have been admitted to the confraternity of the abbey as a result of his gift; cf. Nos. 325, 344. The name is uncommon, and speaking of the early confraternity lists of Thorney, Professor Whitelock says (LVTh p.

141): "I suspect that the *Vuah* in my lists is the same as a certain *Wach* who is a donor to Ramsey in the *Historia* of this abbey. The name is OEN runic *UfagR* corresponding to ON *Ófeigr*, and it occurs in DB as *Unfac*. The Ramsey scribe has assumed that *uu* equals *w*, whereas in this case it is for *uv*." It is worth recalling, however, that a Wacher of Swaffham (Norfolk) occurs in 975 (LE pp. 127, 149).

325. c. 1055 × 1066   A matron named THURGUNT, being very old and sick of body, wills to Ramsey Abbey, for the salvation of her soul, land at *Saltretha* (Sawtry Judith), with the consent of her husband, Turkil of Harringworth. She also wills to the abbey a reliquary worth 12 mancuses of gold, an alb, chasuble, stole, chalice, and altar cloth. After her death, her husband went to Ramsey and offered the land upon the high altar there, in the presence of Abbot Ælfwine and all the brethren, by the witness of Ulf of Glatton, Leofric the son of *Dodi* (? Dodda), Leofred of Fotheringay, and many others, both laymen and clerics.

Chron Rams pp. 175–6, 199. For Ulf of Glatton, see VCH *Hunts.*, I, p. 330. Turkil held 6 hides at Fotheringay, Northants., TRE (DB I, fo. 228a; VCH *Northants.*, I, p. 350b), whence the appearance of Leofred as a witness. His Northants. estates included 5 hides at Harringworth (*ibid.*), 5 hides at Lilford, 1 virgate at East Farndon, and 2 hides (unidentified) lying in Stoke Hundred (DB I, ff. 229a, 228b, 225b; VCH *Northants.*, I, pp. 354a, 352ab, 336a). His Hunts. properties were even more extensive; besides 10 hides at Sawtry (DB I, fo. 206b; VCH *Hunts.*, I, p. 351a), they comprised 9 hides at Conington (No. 46) and 15 hides at Leighton Bromswold (DB I, fo. 203b; VCH *Hunts.*, I, p. 341b).

Turkil's name is of Scandinavian origin, as is that of his wife Thurgunt (ON *Thorgunnr*), and in the Leighton Bromswold entry in DB he is called Turkil the Dane. In the twelfth-century foundation charter of Sawtry Abbey, it is recited that King Cnut gave Sawtry to Turkil the Dane, who by the same king's orders divided the fen near Whittlesey Mere between Sawtry and the neighbouring villages (Cart Rams I, pp. 163–4). It so happens that the Ramsey Chronicle contains a long story of a Dane called Turkil, and his wife, who is unnamed (No. 70). This Turkil, who was given West Elsworth in Cambs. by Cnut, is possibly (but not very probably) to be identified with the famous Turkil the Tall, who was present with Cnut at the battle of *Assandun* in 1017, and was later awarded the earldom of East Anglia. He was banished in 1021, and died in 1039. In VCH *Hunts.*, II, p. 4, and III, pp. 146, 207, he is confused with Turkil of Harringworth, but it is to be noted that nowhere in the Ramsey Chronicle or the Ramsey Cartulary does this confusion occur. The reapportionment of the fen south and east of Whittlesey Mere[1] —an important event in fenland history—is to be regarded, therefore, as the work of Turkil of Harringworth, and not of Turkil the Tall; and it appears probable that it was effected towards the end of Cnut's reign, rather than at its beginning.

No. 46 shows that Turkil of Harringworth had dealings with Thorney Abbey as well as Ramsey, and Professor Whitelock has shown (LVTh p. 140) that both he and his wife Thurgunt appear in the early list of those admitted to the confraternity of Thorney. It is from an entry in the Red Book of Thorney (Dugdale II, p. 604) that we learn that after the Norman Conquest Turkil left his lands and went over to "the Danes who were his kinsmen." Professor Whitelock (*op. cit.*) suggests that the occasion was the invasion by Sweyn Estrithson in September 1069. There can be little doubt of this. The entry for 1070 in the Peterborough Chronicle makes it clear that the Danes were working in close conjunction with the local forces of Hereward the Wake and it cannot be just coincidence that Turkil of Harringworth held the 15-hide manor of Leighton Bromswold; it was the forest of *Bruneswald* (Freeman, NC IV, p. 806) that provided cover for Hereward's forces. He is probably to be identified with the *Turchitellus*, *procer*, who appears in the Ely list of the leaders of the revolt (LE p. 179).

Thurkil's connection with Hereward is brought out even more clearly in the Lincolnshire Domesday, for the Turkil who had held numerous estates amounting in all to over 14 carucates in Hereward's territory—the wapentakes of Aveland, Ness, Beltisloe, Haverstoe, and Kirton[2]—is certainly our man; he even had six bovates in Bourne itself, the *caput* of Hereward's possessions. Turkil and Hereward were therefore neighbouring landowners.

The Thorney entry states that all of Turkil's lands were forfeited to the king, and given by him to Earl Waltheof, a statement borne out by DB; it is significant that in this very year Earl Waltheof, according to the Chronicle, "made his peace with the

---

[1] The initial division of the fenland long antedated the reign of Cnut—see the bounds of Nos. 8 and 9.

[2] Lincs. DB 2/32, 33; 12/90; 26/40, 41, 42; 27/15, 40, 51, 52, 53; 72/34.

king." His earldom included Huntingdonshire, and it may be surmised that some of his large holdings in that county and in Lincs. and Northants. recorded in DB in the name of his widow, the Countess Judith, were the sequestered estates of such local supporters of Hereward as Turkil, granted to Earl Waltheof by the Conqueror in return for his services in helping to suppress the revolt.[1]

326. 16 Nov. 1056   LEFGIVA (Leofgifu), a widow, to Ramsey Abbey, *Stocton(am)* (Great Staughton), *Dilinton(am)* (Dillington in Great Staughton), and *Gilling(am)* (Yelling). Land in Cambs.

> Chron Rams p. 199. In Edgar's spurious confirmation charter she is called *Livith* (No. 18), and in Cart Rams III, p. 167, she is wrongly called *Leofwina*. For her anniversary, see Dugdale II, p. 566. She is possibly a descendant of the Leofsige to whom Ælfhelm gave Staughton (No. 24). See also p. 240.

CAMBRIDGESHIRE

327. 946 × 955   EDWIN son of Othulf to Archbishop Oda. 5 hides at *Burwelle* (Burwell).

> Chron Rams p. 49. This was a reward to Oda for persuading King Eadred to consent to Edwin's marriage to the daughter of a certain Ulf.

328. 969 × 975   ÆTHELGIFU, a matron, to Ramsey Abbey. 40 acres and one virgate at *Burewelle* (Burwell), which once belonged to Guthred; and 8 hides at *Heninge* (Henny, Between Ely and Soham).

> Chron Rams pp. 49–52.

329. 969 × 975   ÆLFGAR, a friend of Ealdorman Æthelwine, to Ramsey Abbey. His estate at *Burewelle* (Burwell), comprising his houses, court, 3 hides, 40 acres, and one virgate of land, and the church of Burwell, of which he was patron.

> Chron Rams p. 51. At Burwell in the thirteenth century there were 30 acres to the virgate; cf. Cart Rams III, p. 215.

[1] Sir Frank Stenton (VCH *Hunts.*, I, pp. 330, 335) calls Turkil a thegn of Earl Waltheof, but there are good grounds for supposing that this was not the case.

330. 969 × 977   WULFHUN to Ramsey Abbey, on the occasion of his profession as a monk. The church and 40 acres at *Wilburgeham* (Great Wilbraham), and land at *Lintone* (Linton).

    Chron Rams pp. 54, 74.

331. 969 × 990   ÆLFSTAN to Eadnoth, prior of Ramsey. 2 hides at *Stapelforde* (Stapleford), for 100 silver *solidi*.

    Chron Rams p. 78.

332. c.977   Ealdorman ÆTHELWINE to Ramsey Abbey, for the soul of his wife Æthelflæd. Part of 10 hides at *Tofte(s)* (Toft).

    Chron Rams p. 54, which states that the remainder of Toft was acquired by Ramsey in exchange for land at *Lintona* (Linton), which Wulfhun had given to the abbey on becoming a monk (No. 330). According to the Ramsey obits, Æthelflæd died in 977 (Cart Rams III, p. 165).

333. 979 × 1016   LEOFMAN to the monks of Ramsey. Land at *Sneileswelle* (Snailwell), for 20 pounds.

    Chron Rams p. 76. Date: the reign of King Æthelred.

334. 1016 × 1034   ÆTHELRIC, bishop of Dorchester, to Ramsey Abbey. Estates at *Stowe* (Long Stow) and *Gretton* (Girton).

    Chron Rams p. 144.

335. 1020 × 1034   ÆTHELRIC, bishop of Dorchester, to Ramsey Abbey. 3 hides at *Bodekesham* (Bottisham).

    Chron Rams pp. 144–5, which states that Æthelstan, abbot of Ramsey, gave the estate to farm to the monk Ailric, a relative of Bishop Æthelric, but that it was seized by Walter Giffard after the Conquest. This is borne out by DB I, fo. 126, where the estate is rated at 2 hides. See, further, RE pp. 158–9.

336. 1043 × 1066   ÆLFSIGE of *Langwathe* (Langworth, Lincs.) and his wife Leva to Ramsey Abbey. The reversion of land at *Borewelle* (Burwell).

    Chron Rams pp. 174–5. The Ramsey account states that after

the property came into the possession of the abbey, it was let out to farm by Abbot Ælfwine to Godwine, a relative of Ælfsige, but after the Conquest it was seized by Ralph of Guader, earl of Norfolk (cf. RE p. 164). DB I, fo. 195*b*, supported by ICC fo. 77*a*, states that TRE 2 sokemen held 2½ hides at Burwell of Eddeva the Fair, and another sokeman named Eadwine held 1 hide and 1 virgate there of the same Eddeva; by 1086 these two holdings were in the hands of tenants of Earl Ralph, and they appear to represent the estate left to Ramsey by Ælfsige and his wife. It may be surmised that Leva of the Ramsey account is the Leveva who held land at Croydon (DB I, fo. 194*a*) and Arrington (fo. 194*bb*) under Eddeva; Ælfsige is possibly the sokeman of that name who held of Eddeva at Soham (fo. 195*bb*) and Exning (fo. 195*b*); and Godwine is possibly the Godwine Cild, a sokeman of Eddeva, who held at Horseheath, Fulbourn, and Weston Colville (ff. 193*bb*, 195*bb*).

337. 2 July 1044   ÆLFWEARD, bishop of London, to Ramsey Abbey. Land at *Horsete* (Horsheath), and at Hemington in Northants.

Chron Rams p. 198.

338. 1044   EADNOTH [II], bishop of Dorchester, to Ramsey Abbey. Estates at *Ouram* (Over) and *Cnapwelle* (Knapwell), and at *Bertonam* (Barton, Beds.).

Chron Rams p. 159.

(326) 16 Nov. 1056   LEFGIVA (Leofgifu) to Ramsey Abbey. *Gravele* (Graveley). Land in Hunts.

Chron Rams p. 199. See also p. 238.

DIVERS COUNTIES

339. 969 × 979   GODWINE to Ramsey Abbey. The reversion of *Hecham* (Hitcham, Suffolk) after the lifetime of the present tenants, namely his steward Æthelwold, his goldsmith Leofric, and Wulfgar; and the reversion after his wife's death of *Horningesherthe* (Horningsheath, Suffolk) which Godwine's father-in-law had left him by will.

Chron Rams pp. 83–4. Evidently the Godwine who died during the reign of Edward the Martyr, leaving Hoo to Ely (No.

78). Later, Godwine's brother Ælfmær left his share of Hitcham to Ely (No. 80). The estates did not survive as Ramsey property: Ely held the whole of Hitcham by the time of DB. An estate at Horningsheath had already descended to Bury St Edmunds (No. 49).

340. 969 × 983   Ealdorman ÆTHELWINE to Ramsey Abbey. 6 hides at *Wammaforde* (Wangford near Thetford, Suffolk).

Chron Rams p. 54. See also No. 276.

341. 969 × 983   Ealdorman ÆTHELWINE to his foundation at Ramsey. *Helingeye* (Hilgay, Norfolk), which is surrounded by marsh and water, and its berewick *Snores* (Snore Hall) which lies outside the island (of Hilgay), and a mill nearby; half the fishery there to Ramsey and half to his sons; 5 hides at *Walsokne* (Walsoken, Norfolk), and half of his fishery at *Wella* (Upwell and Outwell, Norfolk and Cambs.), with the reversion of the other half, together with the houses and tofts of the fishermen.

Chron Rams pp. 52–5.

342. 972 × 992   ÆLFWINE, son of Brihtsige, to Ramsey Abbey, on the occasion of his becoming a monk there. *Laushella*, *Halistede*, and *Ryseby* (Lawshall, Hawstead, and Risby, all in Suffolk).

Chron Rams p. 81. Subsequently, at the request of Archbishop Oswald, Ælfwine granted a lease of Risby to Wulfric for life. According to the Ramsey obits, Ælfwine died in 1022 (Cart Rams III, p. 167). By the time of DB, Lawshall was the only property owned by Ramsey in Suffolk (VCH *Suffolk*, I, p. 515).

343. 1042 × 1060   LEOFSIGE the nephew of Leofsige the deacon, to Ramsey Abbey. Land at *Moeringe* (Mareham on the Hill, Lincs.).

Recited in No. 47; subsequent charters entered in the Ramsey Cartulary make it clear that the land was in Horncastle wapentake. For the identification, see Ekwall p. 299. There is no record of Ramsey Abbey holding land at Mareham in DB, but a late record (Cart Rams I, p. 281) claims that Threckingham, Lincs., was also given to the abbey by this Leofsige, and DB shows that Ramsey held Threckingham TRE (Lincs. DB p. 59, no. 4).

344. 1051   JOL to Ramsey Abbey. *Querenton(am)* (Quarrington), *Cranewell(am)* (Cranwell), and *Sleiford(am)* (Sleaford), all in Lincs.

Chron Rams p. 199; Cart Rams III, p. 167. Confirmed in No. 47, where the donor is described as "Jool de Lincolnia." He was admitted to the fraternity of the abbey for his gift, which survived as Ramsey property (Lincs. DB p. 59, nos. 1, 2, 3, and 5).

J. H. Round, in FE p. 328, suggests that Jol was a Breton. However, Professor Whitelock, in LVTh pp. 141–2, draws attention to a lady bearing the uncommon name *Scheldwara*, who appears as a benefactor to Ramsey (Chron Rams p. 199), and compares the entry with one in the *Liber Vitae* of Thorney: *Iol 7 his wif Scelduuere*. Her name comes from ON *Skialdvor* and Professor Whitelock identifies her tentatively with the person of that name who was the mother of *Rolf*, a thegn who figures prominently in the Lincolnshire DB; she concludes that Iol could be a strong variant of ON *Ióli*. On the face of it, it would appear more likely that two persons bearing ON names should marry, than one with a Breton name and one with an ON name. One might recall that Yawthorpe in Lincs. is DB *Iolethorp* from *Ióli's* thorpe, where the personal name is almost certainly ON.

CHAPTER XII

GRANTS TO PETERBOROUGH RECORDED
BY HUGH CANDIDUS

HUGH CANDIDUS was a monk of Peterborough who wrote a Chronicle of his house some time in the mid-twelfth century. In the course of this he made use of some material which has not survived elsewhere, and which he introduced with the following passage:[1] "And now our pen is busy writing of lands, I will tell you briefly what I know about them, the names and titles of their donors, and the names also of the abbots in whose times the grants were made, for I would not have them forgotten. But my words shall be few, because our knowledge of them is not great, and we cannot describe them all, since by the carelessness of those whose duty it was to record them, they have not come to our notice. Moreover we omit both those lands which are inscribed in the ancient charters, and also those which were acquired by St Æthelwold or Adulph [the abbot during Æthelwold's time], which we have mentioned elsewhere; and write only of those which were acquired in later times."

In the following summary all the grants appearing in Hugh's Chronicle are recorded, whether the lands lie within the seven counties with which we are chiefly concerned in this book, or not.[2] It is not known whether written records of title were drawn up contemporaneously with the transactions. Hugh's sources appear to have been original documents rather than a list of benefactors, for his account of the donations made to Peterborough in the period 984 to 1066 is shown by DB to be far from complete.[3]

---

[1] HC pp. 67–8.   [2] The transactions appear in HC pp. 40, 67–71.

[3] For example, Lincs. DB p. 16, no. 8 records the gift to Peterborough by a nun named Elswith of a messuage and land at Grantham, with sake and soke, which must have been made c. 1060. At the time of DB, the thegn Colegrim held this property, which was the only holding in Grantham outside the soke

345. c.985 FRANE *æt Rogingeham* (Rockingham, Northants.) gave *Langtun* (Langton, Leics.).

Presumably the Fræna who acted as a surety for the purchase by Bishop Æthelwold of a number of estates near Rockingham for the endowment of Peterborough (R pp. 78, 80, 82). He sold an estate to Earl Ælfric of Mercia at Northampton in 983–5 (R p. 76).

346. c.990 FREDGIST son of Cate gave *Turlebi* (Thurlby, Lincs.) and *Guedhafring in Holandia* (Quadring in Holland, Lincs.).

Presumably the Frithegist whose sons Osferth and Æthelwold act as sureties for the purchase of estates for Peterborough in the time of Bishop Æthelwold (R pp. 74, 78, 80, 82). He may be the Frithegist who together with Fræna (cf. No. 345) deserted the English cause in an encounter with the Vikings at the mouth of the Humber.—ASC E *s.a.* 993.

347. 993 × 1006 Ealdorman ÆLFHELM gave to St Peter *Cotingham* (Cottingham), *Middletune* (Middleton), and *Benefeild* (Benefield), all in Northants., with all their appurtenances.

Ælfhelm first witnesses as ealdorman in 993; his earldom was of southern Northumbria. He was murdered in 1006 (see D. Whitelock, in Clemoes pp. 80–1). His brother, Wulfric Spott, owned land in Lincs. (No. 152), and his daughter Ælfgifu, later King Cnut's concubine and mother of his sons Swegn and Harold, is described as "of Northampton."

348. 1017 × 1023 Ealdorman LEOFWINE, son of Ælfwine, gave to God and St Peter *Adeluuoltune* (Alwalton, Hunts.).

Presumably the earl of the Hwicce of that name, who became earl of Mercia in 1017, and probably died in 1023; see R p. 396,

---

of Queen Edith, the Confessor's widow. Although it is not stated in DB, it appears probable that Colegrim, a large landholder in Lincolnshire, held this Grantham property on lease from Peterborough, for HC pp. 109–16 reproduces a charter of Pope Eugenius III, dated 1146, in which the estates of Peterborough Abbey are confirmed, including "*in Graham, mansuram et terram quam Colegrim dedit ecclesie de Burch.*" A second charter of the same date (pp. 116–18) confirmed to the sacrist of Peterborough a rent of one mark for the land there.

W p. 150, and Freeman, NC I (3rd edn), pp. 418, 737 f. His gift to Peterborough probably dates from after the time when he acquired the Mercian earldom. This record is the only one to name his father.

349. c.1020 ÆLFSIGE CILD, son of Outi, gave *Osgotebi* (Osgodby in Lavington, Lincs.).

Possibly the Ælfsige Cild who witnesses a Kentish marriage agreement c.1013 × 1020 (R LXXV). A man of the same name held 2 hides at Bluntisham (Hunts.)—LE p. 99. For the Lincolnshire holding, see Lincs. DB p. 55, no. 8.

350. c.1020 HALFDENE, son of Brenting, gave to St Peter *Walecote apud Trikingham* (Walcote-on-Humber, near Threckingham, Lincs.), *Brerchesthorp* (Birthorpe in Sempringham, Lincs.), *Ryale* (Ryhall, Rutland), and *Belemesthorpe* (Belmesthorpe, Rutland).

VCH *Rutland*, II, p. 269, dates the gift *ante* 992, but gives no reasons for this dating. More probably it should be assigned to the abbacy of Ælfsige (1006 × 1041), for Hugh Candidus assigns to that period the translation of the relics of St Tibba from Ryhall to Peterborough (HC p. 51). Brenting is probably to be identified with the man of that name who acted as a surety when Maxey (about 5 miles from Belmesthorpe) was bought for Peterborough c.984 (No. 164). For the later history of Belmesthorpe, see No. 160; for the Lincolnshire holdings, see Lincs. DB p. 55, no. 9.

351. c.1024 THURKIL HOCHE gave to St Peter *Colingeham* (Collingham, Notts.), a moneyer at *Stanford* (Stamford, Lincs.), and land there "on this side of the water" (i.e. on the south bank of the River Welland at Stamford).

The donor is to be identified with the *Turkyl Hoʒe* who appears in the Thorney *Liber Vitae* (LVTh p. 140), and the *Thurkyl hoga* who witnesses a charter of Cnut in 1024 (K 741). The land given is that part of Stamford known as Stamford Baron, represented by the parish of St Martin, lying on the Soke side of the Welland; cf. HC pp. 110, 128–9, 171. It is not clear how Thurkil was in a position to "give" a moneyer (which amounts to a mint) to Peterborough Abbey, but there is known to have been a mint at Stamford at this time. See, further, *The Making of Stamford*, ed. Alan Rogers, Leicester University Press, 1965, p. 24.

352. 1041 × 1057   Earl RAULF the nephew of King Edward [the Confessor] gave to St Peter *Estun* (Easton), *Brinninghurst* (Bringhurst), *Prestegraue* (Prestgrave), and *Dreitun* (Drayton), all in Northants., and *Glathestun* (Glaston, Rutland).

Although Earl Raulf of Hereford was buried at Peterborough (ASC *s.a.* 1057), his gift of Glaston did not remain for long in the abbey's possession, for DB says that TRE it was held by one Edward, and at the time of the Survey, by Countess Judith (VCH *Rutland*, 1, p. 142; VCH *Northants.*, 1, p. 353).

353. 1042 × 1055   The lady GODGIT gave to St Peter *Hah* (Haugh, Lincs.), *Langeledenham* (Leadenham, Lincs.), *Wassingburche* (Washingborough, Lincs.), *Binitun* (Binington, ER Yorks.), *Cunninggesburch* (Conisbrough, WR Yorks.), land in *Bernuele* (Barnwell, Northants.), and a chasuble.

Conisbrough had been given to Ealdorman Ælfhelm of Northumbria by his brother Wulfric Spott (W xvii). Presumably, therefore, the lady Godgit is to be identified with Godgifu, the wife of Earl Siward of Northumbria and Huntingdon, from whom she may have obtained Conisbrough; she also gave Ryhall and Belmesthorpe to Peterborough (No. 160). It is interesting that alone of all the versions of the OE Martyrology, the one given by Hugh Candidus mentions that the relics of St Rumwald were kept at Haugh (HC p. 62).

354. c. 1050   ÆLFGAR of *Dunesbi* gave to St Peter *Dunesbi* (Dunsby, Lincs.).

For its subsequent history, see W p. 211.

355. 1051 × 1060   Archbishop CYNESIGE [of York] gave *Tineuuell* (Tinwell, Rutland), of his patrimony.

Hugh Candidus gives a long list of associations between the archbishops of York and Peterborough Abbey in the late Anglo-Saxon period (see further D. Whitelock, in Clemoes p. 76). Together with Tinwell, Cynesige is said to have given a text of the Gospels beautifully worked in gold, and ornaments worth three hundred pounds. He is said to have died at Peterborough, and to have been buried to the north of the high altar. Queen Edith is said to have stolen Cynesige's gifts (she held part of

Rutland as her dower), but Peterborough was still holding Tinwell at the time of DB (VCH *Rutland*, I, p. 141).

356. c.1060 BURRED and his parents gave to God and St
Peter *Bartune iuxta Ketteringe* (Barton near Kettering,
Northants.).

This sounds like a gift accompanying the presentation of
Burred as a novice at the abbey. There is no means of dating it
precisely, but it seems to belong to the end of the period.

357. c.1060 Earl HAROLD gave *Cliftune* (Clifton, Warwicks.),
and land beside the monastery of St Paul in London, next
to the landing place called *Etheredeshythe*.

There is no means of dating this gift precisely.

358. 1060 Restoration by King EDWARD to Leofric, abbot
of Peterborough, of *Fiskertune* (Fiskerton, Lincs.), *Osgoteby*
(Osgodby, Lincs.), *Fletuna* (Fletton, Hunts.), *Ouertuna*
(Orton, Hunts.), *Aluuoltuna* (Alwalton, Hunts.), *Burchle*
(Burghley in the Soke of Peterborough), and *Astuna* (Ashton in Bainton, Northants.), which had come into the
hands of Queen Edith.

Queen Edith held part of Rutland as her dowry, and it looks
as if these estates had been assigned to augment her holding.

359. c.1066 ULF son of Tope gave St Peter *Mannetorpe*
(Manthorpe, Lincs.) and *Carletun* (Carlton-le-Moorland,
Lincs.).

See W xxxix.

CHAPTER XIII

LISTS OF BENEFACTORS TO
BURY ST EDMUNDS

Lists of benefactors to Bury St Edmunds Abbey are recorded
in several of the unpublished cartularies of the house,
namely nos. 105, 117, 118, and 123 in Davis. These have
all been consulted, together with the published lists in Dugdale
III, pp. 138–40, and Lord Francis Hervey, *The Pinchbeck Register*,
Brighton, 1925, II, pp. 283–91. The lists differ only in minor
details. The benefactions summarized below are those for which
there is no evidence that contemporary records of the grants
once existed. Approximate dates have been supplied.

360. c.951.   GODRIC CHARKE and his son gave part of Nowton
    and Horningsheath (Suffolk).

> Presumably soon after Bishop Theodred had willed land in
> these two places to Bury (No. 49).

361. 955 × 957   King EADWIG gave Beccles and Elmswell
    (Suffolk).

> These estates remained in the possession of Bury at the time
> of DB.

362. 1039 × 1043   ÆLFRIC [III], bishop of Elmham, gave South
    Runcton in Norfolk, and Soham, *Thorpe* (Westhorpe),
    Southwold, Westley, Saxham, parts of Brockford and
    Bradfield, and the third part of Palgrave (all in Suffolk).

> In the lists he is termed "*cognomento bonus.*"

363. 1042 × 1065   ALNOTH, *prepositus* of King Edward, gave
    Great Fornham (Suffolk).

364. 1044 × 1065   LEOFSTAN, the steward of Abbot Leofstan,
    and his relative Stannard gave Whelneatham and Hawsted

(Suffolk), and Greenfield, and land in Roding (Essex).

Stannard is probably the *Stanhand* mentioned in the will of Wulfsige (ECEss I, No. 45), and as the name is uncommon, one may assume that he is the *Stanart* or *Stanhard* who figures prominently in the Little Domesday (DB II, ff. 19*b*, 20, 98*b*, 174, 174*b*, 179, 183, 185, 320*b*, 330*b*, 419, 441*b*, 445*b*). Some of these entries name him as the son of Æthelwig of Thetford (Norfolk), a thegn whose importance is shown in many DB entries. Æthelwig survived the Conquest, but was dispossessed early in William's reign, his estates being forfeited to Roger Bigot; several of these estates were then held of Roger by Stannard; cf. Freeman, NC, v, pp. 815–17. See, further, H p. 555.

365. 1044 × 1065   SIWARD gave Tivetshall (Suffolk).

A monk of Bury, he was made dean by Abbot Leofstan. He obtained Tivetshall from his parents.

366. 1044 × 1065   A monk of Westminster gave Hengrave (Suffolk).

He inherited Hengrave from his parents and went to live there; Eadred (some versions have Eadric) the *prepositus* of Bury was very angry, and told the monk that it was a scandal that he should try to live as a layman; he would neither be allowed to live there, nor to sell the estate "within the hundreds of St Edmund." The monk therefore surrendered the estate to Bury St Edmunds.

367. c.1044 × 1065   WULFRIC "*vir dives*" gave Herringswell (Suffolk).

The date is uncertain, but the gift is included in the lists with those of the time of Abbot Leofstan.

368. c.1044 × 1065   MANNING Swartingsone gave Chepenhall in Fressingfield (Suffolk).

Cf. VCH *Suffolk*, I, p. 504. After Manning's gift, his son Ulf stole the estate, but being bitten by a snake and in fear of death, he went to the monks and offered them the choice of Chepenhall or Syleham (Suffolk). The monks chose Chepenhall "because it abounded in woods," a statement borne out by DB.

ADDENDA AND CORRIGENDA

THE EARLY CHARTERS OF ESSEX (SAXON PERIOD)

p. 11, Nos. 2, 3, and 4; p. 12, No. 5. These are re-edited on pp. 122–45.

p. 14, No. 13. It is not necessary to assume from the entry of this charter in the Codex Wintoniensis that Æthelstan left this estate to Winchester. The process by which the charter came to be entered into the Codex is similar to that described in ECWM pp. 21–2. On fo. 81b is entered a charter concerning an estate at *Hamme* which has been identified as Ham in Wiltshire (CS 677), an identification supported by the bounds. On fo. 82 is entered another form of the bounds of the same estate (CS 679), and on fo. 83 is entered the will of the thegn Wulfgar (CS 678), by which the reversion of the estate was given to Winchester. The charter concerning East and West Ham in Essex follows this on the same folio.

p. 17, No. 22. *For* Milton Ernest, Beds., *read* Milton, Cambs.; cf. LE p. 105 n. 2. This transaction should be dated 971 × 984, as Dr E. Blake has established fresh dates for the abbacy of Brihtnoth (LE p. 411).

p. 17, Nos. 23 and 24. These transactions relate to Wennington in Abbots Ripton, Hunts. (Nos. 17, 26, and 311 above), and not to Wennington, Essex.

p. 18, No. 25. Now dated 989; see No. 24 in the present hand-list.

p. 18, between Nos. 25 and 26. *Insert:*

N.D.   (991)   Will of Ealdorman BRIHTNOTH. *Ratendune* (Rettendon) to Ely Abbey. Lands in Cambs. and Northants.

Lost.

LE II, c. 62; Chron Rams pp. 116–17.

p. 18, No. 26. Now dated 996 × 1029, after the death of Abbot Brihtnoth.

p. 19, No. 29. The MS. is described in Ker p. 112.

p. 19, No. 31. *For* East Mersea *read* West Mersea.

p. 20, No. 33. *Hæðfelda* is Hatfield, Herts. The MS. is a detached leaf from a gospel-book, almost certainly from Ely, which owned Hatfield; cf. Ker pp. 35–6.

p. 20, No. 35. Now dated 1002 × c. 1016, owing to revised dates for the abbacy of Ælfsige of Ely (LE p. 413).

p. 21, No. 36. The diplomatic is the same as that of King Edgar's charter granting Linden End, Cambs. (No. 56 above). See LE p. 417.

p. 22, No. 43. This transaction is recorded in several Bury cartularies, e.g. Dugdale II, p. 139. The entry in the *Pinchbeck Register* has
the note "sed sine carta" appended.

p. 23, No. 45. W xxvII. In the OE version the name appears as
Wyken. Professor Whitelock says "This might represent Wyken near
Ixworth, Suffolk, Ash Wicken, or Wick in Garboldisham, Norfolk."
In BBL Wulfsige is described as a *procer*, and it is stated that he gave
also the wood belonging to the estate to the abbey. He gave other
property to *Standhand*, no doubt the *Stanhard* of No. 364 above.

p. 25, No. 50. The Latin version of this OE will (W xxx) is here
printed from MS. Lambeth 1212, fo. 331.—

Ego Thurstanus concedente et consentiente domino meo
Rege Eadwardo concessi ecclesie christi in dorobernia
terram partimonii mei nomine Winebisc ad opus et victum
monachorum pro salute anime mee et leofuuare. Primo
autem anno quo ista terra ad dominium iam prefate ecclesie
christi peruenerit, monachi eiusdem ecclesie x[ti] dent ecclesie sancti augustini que sita est extra ciuitatem Doro-
bernie[ ]¹ pro salute anime mee et leofuuare et æthelgyue.
Hec igitur donatio facta est presente eodem rege.

p. 26, No. 53. Dugdale I, p. 97, dates this 1046, and calls Wulfgyth
the relict of Ælfwine.

p. 26, No. 54. Printed here from MS. Lambeth 1212, fo. 331.—

Ego Godwinus concedente et consentiente domino meo
rege Eaduuardo dedi ecclesie christi villam patrimonii mei
nomine Cice, ad victum monachorum in eadem ecclesia
christi in dorobernia pro salute anime mee, liberam ab
omni seruitute seculari, sicut dominus meus rex Cnut illam
michi dedit.

p. 26, No. 55. Edited here on p. 73.

p. 27, No. 56. The authenticity of this charter is defended by Dr E.
Blake, LE pp. 417–18, who limits the date to 1042 × 1057. Dr Blake
(personal communication) points out that this is the earliest reference
to Hadstock by that name; it is called *Cadenho* both in earlier Ely
sources (Nos. 33 and 66 above), and in DB and IE. It does not appear
again as *Hadestoc* until the Pipe Roll of 1167.

p. 27, No. 58. *For* Ralph *read* Ranulph; *for* Dawncing *read* dansinge;
for Stuart *read* our steward.

p. 29, No. 63. Edited by D. Matthew, *The Norman Monasteries and*

¹ The OE text shows that there must be a lacuna here.

their English Possessions, Oxford, 1962, Appendix 1A, pp. 143–9, from a much more accurate text which he discovered at Rouen.

The diplomatic of this charter deserves further study. Down to "Date et dabitur uobis," the formula repeats K 537, a charter of King Edgar dated 967. The quotation from Solomon is paralleled in R cxxx, a charter of King Edward dated 1061, which copies one of King Æthelbert of Wessex dated 864 (R IX). The anathema expands that of K 687, dated 994.

The version of the bounds in Morant's edition (re-edited in ECEss II, pp. 23–5) results from an attempt to translate the OE bounds into Latin by one well versed in Latin but ignorant of OE. The name *Deramy* arises from misreading OE ð as Medieval Latin d, and mistakenly extending it to *der*. Thus *ðam→deram*, further extended to *Deramy*! In the bounds, *ðam stane* became Deramy's Stone, *ðam dican* became Deramy's Ditch, *ðære stræte* became Deramy's Street, and only Dr Matthew's discovery of the Rouen text has saved us from permanent disaster.

Morant's version is however most useful for supplying passages illegible in the Rouen text. Thus, in the bounds, after ". . . to ð a(m) dican betwyx east meresege" we can supply, conjecturally, "and west meresege." More important still, in the body of the charter, we have the phrase ". . . sicut integram hanc et possessionem habui curriculo duorum dierum post quam Dei gratia [ad apicem regiminis] perueni," with the portion between brackets supplied by Morant. I take this to imply that the charter under discussion, which is dated 1046, is in fact a confirmation drawn up later in England of a gift made by King Edward two days after his accession. His predecessor Harthacnut died on 8 June 1042, and it is known that Edward was abroad at the time; one may conjecture that he was at Rouen, that it took two days for the news to reach him, and that he immediately gave West Mersea to the monastery at St Ouen (where he was probably staying), as a parting gift in return for its hospitality to him in exile.

The present form of the witness list shows Norman influence, illustrated by spellings such as *Rotbertus* and *Harolt*; *–eo–* sometimes appears as *–y–* or *–i–*, giving *Lyfrac* for Leofric, *Lyfnoð* for Leofnoð, and *Birn* for Beorn; OE "thorn" sign is misread as *B*, and the insular "r" is misread as *f*, giving *Befkytel* for Thurkytel (and incidentally demonstrating that an eleventh-century document lay before the transcriber of the surviving text at Rouen).

p. 30, No. 68. On the date, see LT p. 102.

p. 30, No. 69. *For* The Third *read* A.

THE EARLY CHARTERS OF THE WEST MIDLANDS

p. 117, Powick, Leigh. *Add to note*: See also Brian S. Smith, *A History of Malvern*, Leicester, 1964, pp. 16–19.

THE EARLY CHARTERS OF WESSEX

p. 188 n. 1. *For* CS 398 *read* CS 395 *(twice)*.

p. 188 n. 3. ,,　　,,　　,,　　,,

p. 89, No. 268. *For* Cf. (75), p. 45 *read* Cf. (75), p. 90.

p. 87, No. 260. The three hides at Frustfield in this charter and of No. (108), p. 97, are identified by Mr Christopher C. Taylor with the now lost Abbotstone, the site of which lay probably at Titchborne Farm, 2 miles s.w. of Whiteparish (Grid reference SU 220219). Four pieces of land must be added: Privett Wood, now Cheyney's Wood, in Downton (210237); Newhouse Park; the land between A36 and the western boundary of the parish; and 54 acres in Redlynch called Black Down (214227).

p. 170, No. 593. *Add to note*: Mr Christopher C. Taylor, however, identifies the land of this charter with Lynch Farm, Corfe Common, and the site of Corfe village. He believes that the same area is covered by No. 596, q.v., with the addition of Blashenwell and Encombe.

p. 175, between Nos. 615 and 616. *Insert*:

> 1000　King ETHELRED to Cranborne Abbey. Confirmation of grants made to the abbey by Ælfgifu, widow of Ailward Meaw, the founder, with the consent of her son Ælfgar, viz., 10 "mansae" in Cranborne, 5 in *Wynburnia* (Wimborne), 15 in *Deuelisa* (Dewlish), and 25 in *Acston* (Higher Ashton).　　　　　　　　　　　　*Lost.*

Bodleian MS. Top. Glouc. d. 2. I am indebted for this reference to Mr C. Hohler.

p. 183, No. 654. Dr C. R. Hart has identified this Winterbourne with Winterbourne Bassett. He contributes the following commentary.

The charter describes a ten-hide estate split into two halves by a brook called the *Winterburna*, running in a N.–S. direction. The boundary clause is confined to the five hides to the west of the brook; the five hides to the east of the brook do not have any bounds, being part of a stretch of common land.

Winterbourne Bassett, a ten-hide estate in DB (fo. 71; VCH *Wilts.*, II, p. 145, no. 274), is divided by the upper part of the River Kennet (formerly the Winterbourne) into two halves. The charter boundary follows the western half of the modern parish boundary, commencing near the church and proceeding in a clockwise direction. It can easily be followed on the 2½-inch OS sheets SU07 and SU17. *Stan mere* occurs at the right place in the charter bounds for Stanmore Copse, between Winterbourne Bassett and Clyffe Pypard. *hwæt hylle* later in the bounds is evidently the high ground towards Broad Hinton. This is now known as "Whettles"; it was "Whetehill" in a survey of 1570 (PN *Wilts.* p. 500).

The interest of the charter lies in its revelation that Hackpen Hill was common land. Evidently the whole stretch of the Marlborough Downs between the Winterbourne and the Ridgeway was a sheep-grazing area; each adjacent estate must have had a share of the common grazing rights, for which a hidage assessment was imposed. The suggestion in VCH *Wilts.*, II, p. 13 that the common land of this charter was cultivated in strips does not take into account the topography; this was downland, thin chalky soil evidently under grass at the time of the charter.

THE EARLY CHARTERS OF DEVON AND CORNWALL

p. 11, No. 27. The boundaries of CS 728 are those of Lyme Regis, not Uplyme.

p. 14, between Nos. 51 and 52. *Insert*:

> ? c.1010   Ælfgar, son of Ailward Meaw, the founder, to Cranborne Abbey. *Losberge* (Loosebeare in Zeal Monachorum), with 1 "cassatum" at *Midland*.   *Lost.*

Bodleian MS. Top. Glouc. d. 2 (I am indebted for this reference to Mr C. Hohler). DB shows the church of Cranborne still in possession of a half-hide at Loosebeare, but one hide at Medland in Cheriton Bishop (probably the *Midland* of Ælfgar's charter) had passed into other hands.

The references are to the numbers in the hand-list.

Charter	No.	Charter	No.	Charter	No.
Bury St Edmunds		CS 843	145	H 62	45
(BM MS. Harl. 1005)		871	163	79	73
fo. 195	133	875	5	80	113A
		893	6, V	94	162
Cart Rams		940	8, VI		
I, p. 188 }	44	1003	9	K 715	84
III, pp. 38–9 }		1043	10	719	30
		1059	122	725	66
Christ Church,		1060	59	726	165
Canterbury		1061	26	733	32
(MS. Lambeth 1212)		1062	60	734	71
fo. 326	79	1082	76	735	86
fo. 331	117	1084	75	740	125
		1258	15	784	161
Chron Rams		1266	55	785	134
pp. 59–60	21	1268	56	806	157
pp. 60–1	22	1269	77	808	158
pp. 76–8	23	1270	150	809	47
pp. 78–80	54	1280–1	15	818	156
pp. 129–34	70	1297	16, VII	819	159
		1305	57	895	102
Crawf v	52	1310–11	18	907	35
		1346	51	910	102
CS 22, 22a	1			919	39
28	2	H 8	95	927	160
32	3	9	106	1308	X
48–9	146	14	111		
81	II	15	114	LE II, c. 83	87
82	III	16	137	c. 88	68
87	I	17	139		
271	147	20	115	R VII	149
383	148	22	138	XXX	7
571	48	25	119	XXXVII	12
712	4, IV	56	126	XXXIX	13
774	120A	57	34	XL	164
808	74	58	38	XLVIII	55
809	85, XI	59	42	LXXIII	83
840	143	60	140	XCII	91
842	144	61	135	XCIII	93

INDEX OF PLACES

N.B. References are given in the normal form, to pages. A small raised figure after the page-number, e.g. Ailsworth 110², signifies that the place occurs in more than one item of the hand-list on that page. County abbreviations are those used in the English Place-Name Society's publications.

INDEX OF PERSONS
AND CORPORATE BODIES

N.B. References are given in the normal form, to pages. A small raised figure after the page-number, e.g. Ælfgar of Moulton 227², signifies that the name occurs in more than one item of the hand-list on that page.